TRIUMPH OF THE YUPPIES

TRIUMPH OF THE YUPPIES

America, the Eighties, and the Creation of an Unequal Nation

TOM McGRATH

GRAND
CENTRAL

NEW YORK   BOSTON

Grand Central Publishing
Hachette Book Group
1290 Avenue of the Americas, New York, NY 10104
grandcentralpublishing.com
@grandcentralpub

First Edition: June 2024

Grand Central Publishing is a division of Hachette Book Group, Inc. The Grand Central Publishing name and logo is a registered trademark of Hachette Book Group, Inc.

The publisher is not responsible for websites (or their content) that are not owned by the publisher.

The Hachette Speakers Bureau provides a wide range of authors for speaking events. To find out more, go to hachettespeakersbureau.com or email HachetteSpeakers@hbgusa.com.

Grand Central Publishing books may be purchased in bulk for business, educational, or promotional use. For information, please contact your local bookseller or the Hachette Book Group Special Markets Department at special.markets@hbgusa.com.

Library of Congress Cataloging-in-Publication Data
Names: McGrath, Tom, author.
Title: Triumph of the yuppies : America, the eighties, and the creation of an unequal nation / Tom McGrath.
Description: New York : GCP, [2024] | Includes index. |
Identifiers: LCCN 2023052691 | ISBN 9781538725993 (hardcover) | ISBN 9781538726013 (ebook)
Subjects: LCSH: Young adults—United States. | Yuppies—United States | Lifestyles—United States. | Equality—United States.
Classification: LCC HQ799.7 .M285 2024 | DDC 305.2420973/09048—dc23/eng/20240131
LC record available at https://lccn.loc.gov/2023052691

ISBNs: 9781538725993 (hardcover); 9781538726013 (ebook)

Printed in Canada

MRQ

Printing 1, 2024

For the Twizzlers—Kate, Hannah, and Sarah

Introduction

It arrived just after Christmas in 1984, landing on newsstands and in mailboxes across America. The new issue of *Newsweek* magazine, the final one of a consequential year, featured two characters from the iconic comic strip *Doonesbury* on its cover—except Mike and Joanie looked a little different than they had before. Gone were the casual, counter-cultural togs they'd sported since the strip's inception in 1970, replaced by power suits and other signals of hard-charging 1980s status: Leather briefcase. Walkman. New Balance running shoes. "The Year of the Yuppie," the cover proclaimed in large white type. The story on the inside wasn't about *Doonesbury* at all, but something much broader—a new clan with whom Americans had become obsessed.

Inside, *Newsweek*'s editors had produced a sprawling fifteen-page feature detailing how Yuppies—a.k.a. young urban professionals, that elite, highly educated segment of the Baby Boomer generation—had altered the culture over the previous twelve months. The story examined Yuppies from an array of angles, delving into their preoccupation with money and career success; their colonization of previously working-class neighborhoods in cities across the country, where trendy boutiques and dessert shops were fast replacing laundromats and shoe-repair stands; their self-evident self-absorption; and their seeming obsession with having just the right status-signifying stuff—from BMWs, VCRs, and designer water to American Express cards, Cuisinarts, and health club memberships.

"Money means a lot to my happiness," one Yuppie, a twenty-eight-year-old Los Angeles attorney, told the magazine. "I want to be able to go to Europe when I want to, to buy clothes if I want to." She confessed that she'd be comfortable earning $200,000 a year (the equivalent of more than a half million dollars four decades later) as long as she and her husband didn't have kids. If they did reproduce, clearly she'd need more.

A Boston-based marketing executive, age twenty-five, who'd seen the value of her condo skyrocket in a year, said, "I'm totally infatuated with the world of real estate. It makes me feel smart and gives me more control over my life."

A twenty-nine-year-old TV executive from Atlanta offered the following: "I want to be rich. I want to have more money than I can spend. I want a Jaguar and maybe a quarter-of-a-million-dollar house. That's not unrealistic to me, whereas my mother's generation would say, 'Ha-ha.'"

Precisely how many of these Yuppies there were was tough to say—*Newsweek* estimated somewhere between two million and twenty million, depending on where exactly one put the income threshold—but even if the Yuppies' numbers were on the smaller side, their impact was mighty. "Even those who don't meet the statistical criteria may find their lives and spending habits to a large degree falling into patterns set by the Yuppies," the magazine said. What Yuppies did, ate, bought, thought, and aspired to impacted everyone. Yuppies mattered.

Less than three years later, in the wicked wake of the 1987 stock market crash, *Newsweek* and many other media outlets reversed course. They didn't just proclaim Yuppieness passé; they somewhat gleefully pronounced it dead altogether. America's sudden financial reckoning, prognosticators predicted, would bring on an abrupt cultural and moral reckoning as well, and Yuppies—in all their red-suspendered smugness and I've-got-mine-good-luck-getting-yours self-absorption—would go the way of flappers, hippies, and other ghosts of twentieth century past.

But here's the question: Did Yuppies disappear? Did that reckoning actually come about? No less important: Where had Yuppies come from in the first place? What confluence of social and economic forces had created them? Why had their obsessions become their obsessions, their pretensions their pretensions? Why were they so different from the generation before them? And how much impact did Yuppies really have on business, politics, cities, food, fashion—the overall direction of the country?

This book is an attempt to answer those questions. It's a tale about how Yuppies became a phenomenon, but even more it's about the world that made and sustained them, one marked by revolutions on Wall Street and in corporate America as well as a lurch rightward politically, a growing fixation on money, status, and materialism, and a widening cultural divide. Perhaps more than anything, it's an attempt to chronicle and understand the choices a country made during a turbulent decade—and how those choices helped form, in a way that can't be overstated, the unequal and unsettled America we live in today.

PART I
1980

CHAPTER 1

The Reinvention of Jerry Rubin

In the last week of July 1980—with fifty-two American hostages in their ninth month of captivity inside the US embassy in Iran; with the Soviet Union dominating the Summer Olympics in Moscow thanks to an unpopular and ineffectual American boycott; with the inflation rate at home at a banana republic–esque 14.4 percent—one of the most high-profile revolutionaries of the 1960s shared some surprising news about himself with anyone who cared to listen.

He had decided to become, of all things, a capitalist.

In an attention-grabbing op-ed that appeared in the *New York Times* on July 30, Jerry Rubin explained that he had accepted a job on Wall Street working for the financial firm of John Muir & Co. His new daily focus, Rubin noted proudly, would be to "find, analyze, and develop financing and marketing plans" for the entrepreneurs he believed would lead America into the future—"socially aware risk takers who will become tomorrow's titans."

If anyone reading the op-ed thought, at least initially, that it might be a high-profile prank Rubin had somehow carried off in cahoots with the nation's most prestigious newspaper, that was understandable. For starters, there was the photo accompanying the piece. It had been taken in 1967, and it showed Rubin dressed in what he had called at the time his "revolutionary of the future" outfit: a Che Guevara–esque beret atop his head; a bandolier across his chest; and Vietcong-style black pajama bottoms covering his legs. No human being had ever looked *less* like a Wall Street broker.

Even more incongruous, though, was Rubin's own history and modus operandi. He'd made a name for himself during the '60s not only with his politics—he called for a "youth revolution" and urged America's young people to "kill your parents!"—but also for drawing attention to himself and his causes with high-profile stunts. Once in the mid-'60s, Rubin and his friend Abbie Hoffman—with whom he'd go on to cofound the radical Youth International Party, a.k.a. the Yippies—stormed the New York Stock Exchange alongside a small group of fellow activists, throwing hundreds of dollar bills from the balcony onto the trading floor and watching with delight as the traders literally dove all over one another to grab the cash. Was there any greater image of capitalistic greed? A few months later, to publicize a massive anti-war rally they were leading in Washington, DC, Hoffman and Rubin announced plans to make the Pentagon levitate—and actually received a government permit to do so. As for the "revolutionary of the future" outfit: Rubin had worn it in his second appearance before the House Un-American Activities Committee, which was holding hearings on the anti-war protests taking place on college campuses across the country. In his first appearance, Rubin had dressed as a Revolutionary War soldier. In his third, he came dressed as Santa Claus.

All of that, however, was many years—and at least a couple of different Jerry Rubins—ago. Rubin was forty-two now, entering middle age, and the bearded, long-haired, peace-and-love look he'd cultivated in the late '60s had been replaced by conservative suits and a neatly trimmed hairstyle that revealed his receding hairline. He no longer looked like someone who was trying to overthrow the system, but like someone who was part of it. Which was exactly what—for real, no put-ons—he was trying to become.

What had sparked this reinvention? In part it was one of necessity. For the first time in his adult life, Rubin needed a job. For all the fame and status he'd achieved in the '60s, the '70s hadn't been an easy time. After the counterculture began to fizzle and his dreams of revolution ended in the early part of the decade, he'd turned inward, trying to "find himself," as the saying went, through yoga and est and various other New Age endeavors. He seemed to achieve some measure of personal happiness in the second half of the decade—he married a young woman named Mimi Leonard—but by then the fame he'd garnered had faded, and the various projects he'd concocted to keep himself relevant—books, speaking tours, events—mostly hadn't panned out as he'd hoped. When Mimi took a job working for a commodities firm in 1979, Jerry's eyes opened—he saw a potential new chapter for himself. He put together a résumé and sent it to hundreds of people connected to Wall Street, most of whom either ignored him or told him he was unemployable. But one—Ray Dirks, who ran John Muir & Co. and shared Rubin's taste for big gestures—saw the PR potential in hiring Rubin and made him an offer. The former radical was coming to Wall Street.

But Rubin's interest was deeper than just a steady paycheck. He had always prided himself on being attuned to cultural trends, and he sensed something shifting now—not only among fellow members of the '60s generation, but within America itself. Indeed, if the '70s had been tough on Rubin, it hadn't exactly been a banner decade for the country, either. After a quarter century of unparalleled prosperity, the once-powerful US economy had veered into a ditch, derailed by soaring energy prices, stiff competition from Europe and Japan, and unemployment not seen in a generation. Trying to get inflation under control, the Federal Reserve had jacked up interest rates, which only seemed to make things worse. That summer mortgage rates were at 13 percent; new car loans at 14 percent. There was a foreboding feeling that America's best days might be behind it.

For a growing number of people, particularly on the right but increasingly in the center, the solution to what ailed America, to restoring that period of unmatched prosperity and power, was clear: Capitalism needed to be unshackled. Taxes had gotten too high. Regulations too onerous. In early 1980, the conservative economist Milton Friedman, who'd won a Nobel Prize a few years earlier for his research on monetary policy, hosted a multipart series on PBS called *Free to Choose*, which presented free markets and limited government as the solution to practically everything. The series generated a lot of chatter, and an accompanying book Friedman wrote with his wife, Rose, had been on the bestseller list for months.

Even more telling was the traction former California governor Ronald Reagan was getting with Republican voters. For years, the conservative policies that Reagan had championed—lower taxes, fewer regulations, less government overall—had been considered by many people, including a majority of Reagan's fellow Republicans, to be too far outside the mainstream for Reagan to be a viable national candidate. But in the winter and spring of 1980, the Gipper buzzed through the GOP presidential primaries, easily capturing enough delegates to secure the nomination for that fall's general election. George H. W. Bush, Reagan's main rival in the primaries, might have called Reagan's ideas "voodoo economics," but voters were fed up enough with gas lines and double-digit inflation and other countries sticking it to America to put their faith in something magical.

And so, in his own way, was Jerry Rubin. He wasn't a Reaganite—he was leaning toward third-party candidate John Anderson over Reagan and incumbent Democrat Jimmy Carter in the fall—but as the '70s passed, he'd come to appreciate, he wrote in the *Times* that summer, the beauty of money. "Raising money for projects in the last few years, I have learned that the individual who signs the check has the ultimate power," he said. "Money is power."

So what better place to be than Wall Street? Rubin insisted that his ideals hadn't changed—he still believed in a fairer, more just society, the very things that had animated him and his fellow activists in the '60s, and he was proud of the things his generation had marched in support of. The end of the war in Vietnam. Civil rights. The women's movement. But he sensed a new era dawning, and he now believed that capitalism, not radical activism, was the best way to empower people; that entrepreneurs, not radical activists, would be the ones to bring about change. "I know that I can be more effective today wearing a suit and tie and working on Wall Street than I can dancing outside the walls of power," he wrote. "Politics and rebellion distinguished the '60s. The search for the self characterized the spirit of the '70s. Money and financial interest will capture the passion of the '80s."

The op-ed did exactly what Rubin hoped: It brought attention to Jerry Rubin. News outlets across the country picked up on what was an undeniably great story: One of the most radical voices of the '60s enters the most establishment-led sector of American life, the financial markets. Which wasn't to say that all the attention was positive. Hardly. The *Times,* for instance, was so besieged by mail that two weeks after the op-ed ran, it published a half page of letters to the editor, almost all of them critical.

"The 'old' Jerry Rubin, as Mr. Rubin himself would surely agree, was hardly a model of intellectual rigor," one letter writer said. "The new one, however, simply sounds pathetic as he tries to convince us (and himself) that the ideals of a radical activist can be easily maintained while doing financial analysis for a firm of stockbrokers."

"The only thing about Rubin that has not changed," said another commenter, "is his ability for self-promotion and the media's treatment of him as a spokesman for ideas rather than the huckster he is."

Said a third: "I follow Jerry Rubin's varied career with interest. Perhaps Mr. Rubin could found a new society: 'The Weather Vanes.'"

The backlash was so harsh that Rubin's young wife, Mimi, was deeply thrown by it. While her husband had spent much of his adult life in the spotlight, she was unprepared for this level of attention and criticism. Concerned about her—and mindful that, in the fall, he and Mimi were due to promote a new book they'd cowritten about sexuality called *The*

War Between the Sheets—Rubin sent a quick note to her father, George Leonard, the onetime editor of *Look* magazine.

"If you would talk to her about fame, whatever, I would really appreciate it," Rubin wrote to his father-in-law. "Am I wrong for becoming famous again and bringing all this negativity down on me and Mimi?"

In Rubin's own mind, of course, the answer was no. He was back in the spotlight he craved so much—in exactly the right place, he hoped, at exactly the right time.

* * *

Rubin had a knack—perhaps a need—not just for understanding the zeitgeist, but for being as close as possible to the center of it. The protest and radicalism of the '60s. The inward turn of the '70s. And now, as the '80s began, the belief that money and capitalism would take center stage for his generation.

How sincere he was in any of these things always seemed to be an open question. One day in 1978, when he and Mimi were promoting a large self-help conference they were producing in Manhattan called The Event, a photographer Rubin had known for years came to their East Side apartment to take pictures. "What's your scam now, Jerry?" the photographer asked.

Rubin had grown up in Cincinnati in the 1940s and 1950s, the older son of a middle-class Jewish couple whose lives were typical of the era (his father was a truck-driver-turned-labor-leader; his mother a homemaker). It was a time when America was ascendant. In the wake of the war, the country was the unquestioned leader of the world, with enormous influence on the international stage and an economy—powered by a massive manufacturing sector that had helped defeat the Nazis and the Japanese—that was booming as never before. Living standards rose year after year after year. Between the late 1940s and the early 1970s, the income of the average American family no less than doubled. Suddenly, people who'd only been able to rent were buying homes of their own. Households went from having zero cars to one and then two. Families gobbled up TV sets and dishwashers and embarked on two-week vacations. America had transformed itself, as journalist David Halberstam would later put it, into the first truly middle-class society.

The country remained deeply flawed, of course. Black people and many others were systematically discriminated against and denied opportunity. Women's roles were limited. But from a cultural perspective, there was a tremendous amount of unity. As a general rule, Americans consumed the same news and entertainment. They bought the same products. They believed in God and went to church regularly. People even seemed to share the same vision of what the good life looked like: owning your own home in the rapidly expanding suburbs.

Most significantly, the country seemed to have an enormous sense of confidence, a belief in its own virtue, and an abiding faith in progress. All of it translated into a hunger to take on big challenges. Defending freedom and democracy around the world was tops on the list (which would eventually lead to the tragedy in Vietnam), but there were other examples of boldness, too. Putting a human on the moon. Passing legislation to fight racial discrimination. Ending poverty. Each issue came with its share of disagreements, but they were mostly about whether the United States *should* do something, not whether it *could*.

Ironically, it was this America—the America of what *Time* magazine founder Henry Luce had called the American Century—that Jerry Rubin spent much of the '60s and early '70s protesting, transforming himself into a professional radical. Early on the issue was America's involvement in Vietnam, but before long the goal became bigger—changing American society itself. Not only was "Amerika," as Rubin always referred to it, an imperialist warmonger, but its capitalistic system made it corrupt, soulless. All those cars and dishwashers and suburban tract homes simply anesthetized people to how empty their lives really were. When the youth revolution came, he and others in the counterculture preached, the synthetic-ness of American life would disappear, everyone would be free to be exactly who they were, and everything anyone needed would be provided to them.

9

Rubin's notoriety peaked not long after the 1968 Democratic Convention in Chicago, where he, Hoffman, and several other leading radicals led a series of demonstrations that devolved into clashes with the Chicago police. The following year they were indicted by the Justice Department for inciting a riot (Rubin mockingly called the charges "the Academy Awards of Protest"), and in September 1969 the trial of the Chicago 8—renamed the Chicago 7 when a mistrial was declared for defendant Bobby Seale—commenced. Well aware that the eyes of the country would be on them, that this would be the biggest stage they ever had, Rubin and Hoffman did everything they could to turn the trial into a circus. Hoffman blew kisses to the judge, Julius Hoffman, and called him Julie. He and Rubin arrived in court one day wearing judicial robes. When the judge ordered the pair to take them off, they did so—revealing blue police uniforms underneath.

In the wake of the trial (the defendants were found guilty of several charges, but their convictions were eventually overturned by an appeals court), Rubin became increasingly in demand as a speaker on college campuses. But even he was aware of the odd situation he was in, calling for the overthrow of a money-driven, capitalistic system while pulling in thousand-dollar speaking fees and banking tens of thousands of dollars in royalties from a memoir-slash-manifesto he'd written called *Do It!*. Within a couple of years, it all caught up with him, as younger members of the movement began looking at him—already past age thirty—as, at best, a relic; at worst, a hypocrite. The low point came at the 1972 Democratic Convention in Miami Beach. Rubin showed up, hoping it would be another Chicago, but he was called out by some younger activists for sleeping in a hotel rather than outside in the park. They eventually marched to his room and threw a cake in his face.

Depressed, written off as a has-been, Rubin moved to California and threw himself into what was dubbed the human potential movement, eventually producing a book about his experiences there. By the end of 1976, though, he'd broken up with his longtime girlfriend, moved to New York full-time, and seemed lost. The dreams of the '60s were over.

The self-help movement had turned into a dead end. But what was next wasn't clear. In his journal, under the heading "I Want," Rubin scrawled a list of ten things he longed for, none of which sounded like those of a man particularly intent on self-enlightenment or social change.

- I want to do [a] networking salon the right EXCLUSIVE way, one night every week followed by a meal in a restaurant.
- I want to do an invitation-only brunch or dinner with and for 20–30 people every week at a great place.
- I want a restaurant called "Jerry Rubin's," which can be my Elaine's, and where I can make money, have a base, do my networking, and make money.
- I need a lot of money—a strong flow of money so that I can do what I want to do.
- I want a blonde society beautiful wife.
- I want a high executive lifestyle made up of high-level decision-making.
- I want to go to every important party in the city.
- I want to meet as many interesting people as I can. On every level.
- I want to marry a 25-year-old Jewish American Princess who has money and beauty.
- I love (sexual) romance.

*   *   *

As it happened, Jerry Rubin's funk coincided with the beginnings of a downturn in America itself. The unrest of the '60s, the lost war in Vietnam, and the corruption of Watergate had all undercut the country's confidence. But perhaps even more difficult were the economic challenges the nation was facing.

The first big blow had come in the fall of 1973, when Arab nations that were members of OPEC, angry at US support of Israel in the Yom Kippur War, cut off oil sales to the United States. The dark side of America's growth and prosperity during the postwar years had been an

11

increasing dependence on foreign oil, and the embargo immediately disrupted not only the economy, but also America's way of life. The price of oil quickly quadrupled, and people suddenly faced unheard-of gasoline prices, gasoline shortages, long lines at the pump, and rationing, not to mention something the country hadn't really felt in decades: a sense of vulnerability; a feeling that it was no longer completely in control of its own fate. The embargo was lifted in March 1974, but by that point the entire economy—sideswiped by inflation that exceeded 10 percent and unemployment that kept rising—was already in a recession that would last more than a year and a half.

But the energy crisis wasn't the only challenge. As the '70s wore on, once-dominant US corporations were beginning to battle ever-stronger foreign competitors. In the steel and auto industries, for instance, Japanese companies—many of which had newer, more advanced equipment and more efficient processes—were steadily taking market share from American companies that had long seen themselves as invincible. Meanwhile, productivity across the entire economy was slowing down, and there was an increasing belief that US companies in general had gotten fat, bloated, and lazy.

For American families, none of the challenges—especially high and persistent inflation, which quickly swallowed up any raises people were getting—were academic. In the 1960s, family income in America grew by an average of $6,000. Between 1970 and 1980, it *fell* by $723.

Adding to the frustration was the sense that America's standing in the world was slipping. In January 1979, Iranian militants overthrew the US-backed Shah of Iran, installing an Islamic government and cutting off oil sales to the United States. Gas prices spiked again. Lines at the pump came back and inflation zoomed ever higher. In November, revolutionaries attacked the US embassy in Tehran, taking fifty-two Americans hostage. Six weeks later, the Soviet Union invaded Afghanistan. All of it was destabilizing to the international order, but even worse was the feeling that the US seemed incapable of doing anything about it. A mission to free the hostages ended in a debacle—eight American servicemen died—and when Jimmy Carter announced the US would boycott the Olympics being held in Moscow in response to the Afghanistan invasion, it seemed more like a snit than the act of a superpower.

All of this had contributed to the feeling, at least in some quarters, that the country's best days might have passed, that Henry Luce's American Century had turned out to be more like a quarter century.

The belief that the country was headed in the wrong direction was best summed up by the plight of a young woman from the South Side of Chicago named Cathy Saban. During the early '70s, after she'd earned her driver's license, Saban had received a brand-new Chevy from her parents. Her father was no corporate titan; on the contrary, he was a steelworker. But such was the economy then: Even a regular guy could afford to give his daughter a lavish birthday gift.

Less than a decade later, Cathy Saban was feeling far less optimistic about where she—and the country—was headed. She hadn't gone to college, and was managing a jewelry store and living with her mother because she couldn't afford her own apartment. She and her boyfriend, a construction worker, were trying to save money before they got married, but she worried about the future. "I think our parents gave more to their kids than we'll be able to give to ours," she said. It was a dark thought that, for the first time in their lives, many in her generation shared.

*　　*　　*

If, in the summer of 1980, Jerry Rubin was reinventing himself, the same seemed to be true of the '60s generation—the children of the postwar Baby Boom—more broadly. By 1980 the oldest Boomers—those who'd been born between 1946 and 1950—were on the far side of thirty. Meanwhile, the most populous part of the generation—the forty million babies born in the 1950s—were beginning their adult lives. The Baby Boomers, in short, were growing up.

There had never really been anything like the Boomer generation in all of US history. In 1946, after a couple of decades in which the birth rate in the US had gotten perilously low, the number of babies born to

American women began to spike. That year—the year after World War II had come to an end and thousands of American GIs returned home—more than 3.2 million babies were born, and for more than a decade the number of annual births just kept going up. In 1950—3.6 million new babies. In 1954—4.0 million babies. In 1957—4.3 million babies. New births stayed above 4 million all the way until 1965, when demographers officially proclaimed that the boom was over. But what a run it had been: Over the course of eighteen years, 75 million children had been born. By the mid-1960s, more than *half* of all Americans were under the age of twenty-five.

What had caused all the procreation? Sociologists would credit it, in part, to a deep desire for normalcy after more than fifteen years of economic depression and world war. What a relief it was—a true joy—simply to be able to focus on working a steady job and creating a home and building a family.

At the same time, it was clearly no accident that America's postwar Baby Boom had coincided with its postwar economic boom. Powered by the juggernaut of US industry, millions of Americans found themselves with not only the money necessary to raise kids, but an unshakable optimism that the good economic times were here to stay. It was another expression of the country's self-confidence, its belief in the future. What's more, parents passed that optimism on to their kids. *You've been born in the best possible place at the best possible time, and you can become anything you want to be.*

The Baby Boom generation was so vast that it would transform American society simply by being part of it. In cities and towns all across the country, new schools had to be built in order to accommodate all the kids. The Boomers' embrace of television and rock and roll was so widespread and powerful that it turned those phenomena into unparalleled cultural forces. And the prosperous times in which they were being raised not only made them a potent consumer class—the "Pepsi Generation," a marketer had dubbed them in 1963—but shaped how they viewed the world. By and large they were free from the worries their parents had when they were young—economic scarcity, world war—and their minds could focus on higher things. "Never have the young been so assertive or so articulate, so well-educated or so worldly," *Time* magazine wrote as it named "The Under 25 Generation" the Man of the Year for 1966. "Predictably, they are a highly independent breed, and—to adult eyes—their independence has made them highly unpredictable. This is not just a new generation, but a new kind of generation."

It was right around that moment, though, in the mid-'60s, that a divide began to appear in the largest generation in US history. A central tenet of the postwar American Dream was that as many young people as possible should go to college; it would be good for them as individuals, and it would be good for the country as a whole. The Boomers were the first generation to make it a reality en masse. In 1950, 15 percent of Americans had a bachelor's degree. By 1970, it was 30 percent.

Still, the spike came with unintended consequences. While those whose educational careers ended after high school—still the majority of the generation—would embark on lives that were likely to look fairly similar to those of their own parents (blue-collar job, marriage, family, home), the Boomers who were fortunate enough to go off to college, particularly the most elite colleges, were heading down a different path, exposed to new ideas, experiences, and points of view.

The first big sign of the divide was, of course, the war in Vietnam. While campuses erupted in protest against the war, the fighting in Southeast Asia was actually being done by young men who weren't in school and hadn't been eligible for the draft deferment afforded to those pursuing a degree. Indeed, 90 percent of American soldiers who saw combat in Vietnam had a high school degree or less. In Harvard's graduating class of 1970, only two members took part in combat.

For at least some of the young students on America's most elite campuses who were already questioning the morality of the country's involvement in Vietnam, it created a tension. Jim Kunen, who'd grown up in an upper-middle-class family in Massachusetts, had enrolled at Columbia in 1966. "All of my college years were totally about the war," he'd say later. "Every single day you woke up in an intolerable situation. Every single day somebody my age was dying in Vietnam while I was safe in college just because I had more money than them. And so this is an intolerable situation you can somehow do nothing about, or you find something to do about it."

Kunen, and tens of thousands of other students who were enrolled in some of America's best universities, chose to do something about it. At first it was simply marching and protesting against the war, but before long—as had been true for Jerry Rubin—it became broader and deeper than that: questioning nearly everything about the America their parents and grandparents had built. Its materialism. Its economic system. Its foreign policy. Its injustices. And the more they talked to one another and marched and protested, the more they began to believe they had the power to change all of it.

"Upper-middle-class guy, Columbia University, Ivy League school— I'm thinking we're going to change the world," remembered Kunen, who in 1969 published a well-regarded book called *The Strawberry Statement* about his experiences as a student radical. "We, the young of America, are not going to put up with this capitalist imperialism anymore. We were like a force of nature, this tidal wave that would just wash away all kinds of antiquated evils in front of us. And we're all hearing the same music, we're all smoking the same dope, we're all growing our hair long. It felt like the generation was an actual powerful entity."

It was only later that Kunen would recognize what a bubble he and his contemporaries had been in. Not only were college students overall a minority of the generation, but those who wanted radical change were a minority on their own campuses. "Little did I realize that there were a whole lot of people, perhaps between the two coasts, perhaps of lower socioeconomic status, who weren't in that 'we' at all—and didn't want to be," he said. It was, Kunen came to believe, a permanent schism in his generation.

The dream of a youth revolution was over by the early '70s, but the values that had animated students in the '60s—distrust of authority and conformity, a focus on personal liberation, a desire not to live as their parents had—didn't disappear. Daniel Yankelovich, the well-respected researcher and social scientist, spent much of the 1970s trying to understand the shifts that were taking place in American life. His conclusion: The immediate postwar years—those years of unchallenged American power and prosperity—had been dominated by what he called a "giving/getting compact," in which Americans suppressed many of their own personal needs and desires in exchange for a stability they considered even more important: a rewarding family life, an ever-growing standard of living, a strong country. But the well-educated elite of a new generation were turning that compact on its head, putting personal happiness first. They wanted their lives to have meaning, pleasure, enjoyment. Their quest, Yankelovich said, was for "self-fulfillment."

In the first half of the '70s, that quest was defined by concepts like getting in touch with yourself and figuring out who you were. But by now, 1980, with millions of Baby Boomers entering the workforce each year and with economic anxiety in America rising, "self-fulfillment" was taking on a different form: It was becoming more and more about performance, achievement, outward success. This younger generation still had no desire to be exactly like their parents, but rather than seeing the previous generation's lives as hollow and conformist, they were now more likely to see them as something else: banal.

"A lot of us had these misspent youths," writer Cathy Crimmins, who'd spent a chunk of the '70s in an English grad program at the University of Pennsylvania, would later remember. "Personally, I felt like I was in graduate school for a million years. But as we got into our late 20s, we suddenly realized we were grownups. We started to professionalize ourselves. But we didn't want to be as corny as our parents. We didn't want it to be *Leave It to Beaver*. We wanted to become grownups with a twist. We wanted an upgraded version of adulthood compared to what our parents had."

That instinct was displaying itself in a variety of ways—where they lived, what they wore, ate, and purchased—but one of the clearest signs of it was in the vast number of Baby Boomers who were enrolling in graduate school, not for PhDs in English, but for law degrees and medical degrees and, most especially, MBAs. In 1960, forty-five hundred students per year were earning MBAs in the United States. By 1976, it was nearly fifty thousand—and growing fast. And who could blame someone? Starting salaries for MBA graduates were 50 percent higher than for those with just a bachelor's degree.

What was fascinating, too, was that this focus on the self was no longer coming just from the cultural left, but from the cultural right as well. In 1977, a California real estate broker named Robert J. Ringer—who'd hit the bestseller list a few years earlier with a book called *Winning Through Intimidation*—self-published a new tome called *Looking Out for #1*. Its premise: that the key to happiness was in making rational decisions aimed at giving *yourself* the greatest amount of pleasure and least amount of pain over the long term. It was, in essence, the precise opposite of Daniel Yankelovich's giving/getting compact.

"It's only when you pervert the laws of nature and make everyone else's happiness your first responsibility that you run into trouble," wrote Ringer. "The idea that self-sacrifice is virtuous is, in fact, a fiction created by those who aspire to control the lives of others. (Think politicians.)"

By 1980, *Looking Out for #1* had sold more than two million copies, which, not surprisingly, pleased Ringer immensely. As he put it in the introduction to a subsequent edition of the book, "Anyone familiar with my philosophy would be disappointed if I didn't say my sole reason for writing it was to make as much money as possible."

*   *   *

Though the polls had shown a tight race up until the early fall, in November 1980 Americans overwhelmingly elected Ronald Reagan as president. His ideas were different, but to a majority of Americans frustrated by the status quo—the struggling economy, Jimmy Carter's perceived weakness—different was what was called for.

Six weeks after the election, Jerry Rubin passed the exam to become a stockbroker. While it allowed him to buy and sell stocks on behalf of clients, just as important to Rubin was that it offered him another bite of the publicity apple. In January, he persuaded the *New York Times* to write a piece about his new accomplishment. "I've really been an entrepreneur my whole life," he told the paper.

As it happened, Rubin would never actually buy or sell a stock on behalf of a client. But that hardly mattered. He was back in the public consciousness—a born-again capitalist who, like thousands of others shaped by the '60s, was hoping he'd figured out a new way forward.

CHAPTER 2

Urban Elite

In the summer of 1980, as Ronald Reagan readied himself to accept the Republican nomination for president and Jerry Rubin readied himself for a new job in the epicenter of American capitalism, a new restaurant was opening in Center City Philadelphia, right on the edge of the city's prime business district. Actually, Frog, as it was called, wasn't really *new* new. The original version of the restaurant had opened seven years earlier in a tiny storefront space around the corner, the creation of an affable young University of Pennsylvania grad named Steve Poses. That Frog was a funky, offbeat place with mismatched furniture, lots of potted ferns, and an overabundance of frog decorations—the kind of relaxed space where Poses had imagined his friends from college might hang out and discuss the issues of the day.

But something extraordinary happened at the original Frog: It had become, very quickly, a mini sensation. Poses's friends did come, and so did a lot of people just like them—socially aware college grads who'd opted to settle in the city—and then so did a lot of other curious Philadelphians. They were attracted by the buzz, but also by Frog's vibe—so different from the fine dining restaurants in Philadelphia—and by its food: a mix of dishes that took traditional French cuisine, lightened it, then mixed in Asian and American influences. Poses himself wrote the menu on a blackboard twice a day—once for lunch, then again for dinner. Eventually, he decided he could afford two blackboards.

The original Frog was such a hit that Poses was emboldened to expand his operation. In 1977, he launched what was essentially a modern gourmet cafeteria a few blocks away—a place called the Commissary that opened early in the morning and didn't close until late and was unlike anything Philly had ever seen. It featured a wine bar and a piano bar, plus a special counter serving fresh pasta and omelets, as well as an array of salads and soups and charcuterie and amazing pastries. The Commissary was an even bigger hit than Frog—Philly's cadre of young professionals and office workers loved it—and Poses kept going. He launched a catering operation, then a gourmet market attached to the Commissary, then another upscale cafeteria across town called Eden. Now, finally, he'd decided it was time to redo his original creation, Frog. His customers weren't grad students anymore, and they were ready for something grown-up. And so he was moving Frog into an elegant town house on Locust Street, confident loyal Frogsters would be happy to move with him.

Poses, a soft-spoken, humble guy who turned thirty-four in 1980, hadn't really planned any of this. He'd grown up in Yonkers, New York, a middle-class kid who was president of his high school class and an editor of the yearbook before enrolling at Penn in the fall of 1964, the first year that Baby Boomers began showing up on college campuses across the country. His original plan was to study architecture, but by the time he graduated, in 1968, the world had changed completely, and Poses had changed with it. He'd gotten deeply interested in social issues, opposing the war in Vietnam, and ending up with a degree in sociology. Afterward, anxious to stay out of a war he detested, he landed a draft-deferring job working at a school for kids with learning disabilities and pondered what he might do with his life. That's when he hit on restaurants. He'd developed an interest in cooking during college, and so he quit the school after a couple of years and started working as a busboy at one of Philadelphia's most proper French restaurants. His job was hardly glamorous, but it taught him the business, and in 1973 he opened the original Frog, putting an emphasis, as he'd later say, on "food and community—those two things meshing."

Now, seven years later, Poses was unexpectedly running an operation with several hundred employees and millions in revenue. Perhaps even more importantly: He and the young professionals who frequented his restaurants were injecting a small but much-needed dose of modern energy into Philadelphia's struggling downtown. As one observer put it, thanks to Poses, "suddenly, there were places to eat in Philadelphia other than Arthur's Steak House and Bookbinders."

Steve Poses was focused on Philadelphia, but by 1980 similar pockets of energy were popping up all around the country. Boston. San Francisco. Chicago. Washington, DC. New York. Over the previous half dozen years, a small influx of young professionals had been quietly settling in working-class, sometimes struggling neighborhoods in all those cities. Compared to the enormity of the Baby Boom generation writ large, their numbers were tiny, but the presence of the new group—the vast majority of them white and well-educated—had become increasingly noticeable. Restaurants were opening that catered to their palates and general vibe. Small, upscale boutiques were popping up right next to the hardware stores and laundromats and bodegas that had previously served the neighborhoods.

The arrival of this young professional class cut against the grain of what had been happening in American cities over the previous quarter century. Indeed, among the few losers in America's great postwar period of power and prosperity had been the country's urban areas. With incomes rising and the middle class expanding, millions of Americans had left cities behind for the utopia of the suburbs. In just twenty years, between 1950 and 1970, the country's suburban population more than doubled to nearly seventy-five million people. In the wake of their exodus, cities looked to be trapped in a death spiral: People left, businesses disinvested, and poverty and crime grew, causing more people to leave, more businesses to disinvest, and poverty and crime to grow even more. The population numbers told the sad tale. Between 1950 and 1980, Philadelphia's population dropped from 2.0 million to 1.7 million; Chicago's from 3.6 million to 3.0 million; Boston's from 800,000 to 600,000. The prevailing narrative about urban areas was grim: They were increasingly poor. They were increasingly dangerous. They were failing.

So why, now, was a small, elite slice of a new generation—many of whom had themselves grown up in the suburbs—reversing the migration and moving *back* into cities? Cost was part of the answer. As inflation spiked following the Arab oil embargo and then continued to run hot through the end of the decade, the prices of places in the burbs were becoming out of reach for a lot of young people. In contrast you could get a deal in the city—once-stately old homes with great bones were selling for $30,000, sometimes even less.

Even more powerful, though, for a group of Baby Boomers still determined to set themselves apart from those who'd come before them, was what living in the city said about your identity: You were cosmopolitan. You were sophisticated. You were not, above all, your conformist, suburban-dwelling parents.

Robin Palley set down roots in the city during the 1970s, and in many ways her story was typical of the Boomers embracing urban life. Palley had grown up in a middle-class family in the small Jersey Shore town of Margate in the '50s and '60s, a period, as she'd later put it, "where your shoes and your bag had to match. Everything was about measuring yourself with a financial yardstick and how well you fit in."

As with others of her generation, Palley's worldview had begun to change when she went off to college—in her case, to the University of Pennsylvania in the fall of 1968. (Steve Poses had finished several months earlier.) Early in her time at Penn, Palley walked onto the campus's main quad and saw it filled with small white crosses, each representing a life lost in Vietnam, and it had spurred her to protest alongside her classmates and friends. But as with Poses, as with Jim Kunen, as with Jerry Rubin, opposing the war was only the beginning of her political awakening. The mood on campus was about breaking free from conformity and embracing your individuality—although, as Palley would later come to note wryly, she and her friends all expressed that individuality in precisely the same way: with long hair and blue jeans.

Palley graduated in 1972 and left Philadelphia for Paris, where she ran a bookstore for a couple of years. When she returned to the US, she and her young husband—a medical resident—were certain of one thing: They would *not* live in the suburbs. "I came back and did not want to go back to that suburban life and fitting into that straitjacket of being," she said later. "I wanted to live my ideals, which had to do with equality and being around all kinds of people."

The couple ended up buying a house in the Fairmount section of Philadelphia, close to the impressive Philadelphia Museum of Art and only about a mile from the Center City neighborhood, where Steve Poses had opened Frog. Actually, it was really more of a shell of a house—most of the innards had been stripped away; opportunistic vandals had even stolen the crossbeams. But the young couple loved the working-class, mostly Puerto Rican neighborhood they'd be moving into, and they were excited about the vitality of city life. They bought the place for $9,000 and got to work fixing it up.

The ethnic and racial diversity of city neighborhoods was one draw for Robin Palley and other Baby Boomers like her, but there were other lures as well. The ability to walk places or take public transportation. The easy access to the array of interesting things—museums, parks, funky restaurants—that city life offered. And then there were the homes themselves: Magnificent brownstones. Century-old Victorians. Cool loft spaces. They might be run down—they might be missing their crossbeams—but they had character. Middle-class America of the 1960s had prized things that signaled a certain kind of societal progress in living and comfort. New construction. Wall-to-wall carpeting. Drop ceilings. Formica countertops. Fluorescent lighting. These new city dwellers, eager for their own identity, rejected all of it. They prized the "original features" unearthed in the homes they were moving into: Hardwood floors. High ceilings. Bare brick walls. Butcher-block countertops. Their parents' lives were plastic and phony. This group wanted authenticity.

By the late '70s, the phenomenon of young professionals situating themselves in cities was widespread enough that it had earned a name: the "Back to the City" movement. Reporters started writing occasional pieces about what was happening—perhaps cities weren't dead, after all?—and curious academics decided the phenomenon, while still nascent, was worthy of study.

In 1977, the Parkman Center for Urban Affairs in Boston hosted a conference that brought policy wonks together with a group of young Boston professionals. (The Parkman folks also fanned out around the country to interview even more city-loving young professionals.) They discussed the array of things that were drawing the new generation: the eclectic nature of city life; the proximity to restaurants and museums and shows; the extraordinary craftsmanship of the homes they were buying and rehabbing. Mostly, though, the organizers of the conference came to understand that the decision to live in the city was about identity—the fact that the new city residents were rejecting the conventional norms and styles of middle-class living in the 1970s. As a subsequent Parkman report noted, the new urbanites were "asserting status by denying it."

Indeed, what was perhaps most interesting about the group of young city dwellers was their own view of themselves. "I'd say we were more concerned about intellectual things," a conference attendee who lived in Boston's Back Bay said. "We want to have seen the latest films. We want to know what people are reading."

Said a New Yorker: "I want a racially and socially mixed neighborhood. It's the way I think this country has to go. To put it another way, I don't want to live with a collection of people who are just like I am professionally and socially. The friends I have tend to share those feelings."

Perhaps the most telling comment came from a young St. Louis woman, who said simply, "We're more interesting."

The comments were, in many ways, understandable. Most of the Back to the City–ers had been to college—they *were* more intellectual than the average person. What's more, they were part of a generation that had always bent the world to its will. They rarely lacked for self-assurance.

The remarks certainly caught the attention of the Parkman team. "Whether the young professional emphasizes intellect ('the latest films'), or living style (bare brick, butcher block and hanging plants, for instance), or a Thoreauesque standing apart from convention, there are very often feelings of superiority toward his or her suburban counterparts," they noted in their report. "In this sense, at least for the duration of their time in the core city, young professionals identify themselves as part of an elite within the middle class elite."

What also stood out to conference organizers was the power and status of this new group, and their potential to help reinvigorate cities more broadly. Yes, their numbers were small, but they were young, they were educated, they were increasingly affluent, and they were on the leading edge of the culture, all of which made them influential.

And in fact, by the summer of 1980, their influence was already spreading, their numbers already expanding. As Robin Palley would note, once again wryly, about her own decision to live in the city, "Just like with blue jeans, I got the idea at the same time tens of thousands of other people did."

* * *

The Back to the City phenomenon was happening in select urban neighborhoods all across the country. In Boston's Back Bay and South End. In Chicago's Wicker Park and downtown Loop. On Capitol Hill in Washington. But nowhere was the trend more vibrant than in New York.

The city, of course, had suffered its own spectacular fall in the preceding decades, with things hitting their low point in the mid-'70s. Between 1970 and 1976 alone, New York lost nearly 600,000 residents and nearly 600,000 manufacturing jobs. The disappearing tax revenue, combined with the liberal benefits New York had given its workforce, quickly brought about a financial catastrophe, and the city had famously reached the brink of bankruptcy in 1975.

But even amid that trouble, even amid America's broader economic struggles, there were signs of things…happening. One place you could see it was the Upper West Side. Once an affluent and vital neighborhood filled with beautiful brownstones and ornate apartment buildings, it had suffered through an economic downturn in the '30s and '40s, and by the '60s was home to an increasing number of low-income Black and Latino residents, many of whom lived in what had been converted into single-room occupancy (SRO) buildings. In the early '70s—thanks in part to a city-led push for urban renewal that had begun a decade earlier—a handful of middle-class residents had begun to buy some of those brownstones on the cheap, and a growing number of young professionals, most of them white, had started to move into the neighborhood.

One of them was a young woman named Betsy West, who in 1975 leased an apartment on the Upper West Side. West had grown up in New England—her father was an educator—and she'd spent her undergraduate years at Brown, arriving in 1969, just in time to catch the height of the anti-war movement. But by the time she graduated four years later, the vibe had changed. "It just felt like the excitement of the '60s—the air had gone out of the balloon a little bit," she recalled later. "Everyone seemed to have a sense of, 'Now what?'"

Following graduate school at Syracuse, West landed a job with ABC Radio, and eventually moved—excitedly—to Manhattan, where she found herself surrounded by an emerging demographic that looked just like her: young, well-educated Baby Boomers. New York might have been at a low point, but to most of them it didn't matter. "There were so many things about cities that I think appealed to us in that generation," she said. "We'd read Jane Jacobs, and it was like this celebration of urban life. Many of us had been brought up in the suburbs, which now we thought were milquetoast and boring—*get me out of here, I want something gritty and real and cultural and with history.*"

If gritty and real was what she and other Boomers were looking for, the Upper West Side—like many of the neighborhoods young people were moving into in cities across the country—certainly had it. Used needles were abundant on the sidewalks, and West would go from block to block, trying to assess the differences in crime levels. Was this street safe? What about that one? But her own concern about crime was nothing compared to that of her poor suburban mother, who not long after West moved to New York bought her daughter a present: karate lessons.

Still, things were starting to change. One of the key people on the West Side was a developer named Bob Quinlan. Quinlan wasn't a Boomer—he was born in 1934, a generation earlier—but it was young Boomer professionals who were on his radar as he put his focus on a shabby stretch of Columbus Avenue near Seventy-Second Street. Beginning in 1972, Quinlan had purchased and renovated several apartment buildings along that corridor, attempting to turn them into attractive residences for the middle class. Early on it was a challenge—to savvy New Yorkers, Columbus Avenue was a tough sell—and so Quinlan and his team had gotten creative. A favorite tactic: One of Quinlan's rental agents would make a trip to LaGuardia or JFK Airport, trying to entice flight attendants who were moving to New York from other cities to lease an apartment on Columbus Avenue. It was, Quinlan's agent told them, New York's next hot neighborhood.

By the second half of the '70s, that was what Columbus Avenue—indeed, the entire Upper West Side—really was becoming. By that point, the working-class shops that typified the street were quickly being joined by restaurants with trendy cuisines, quirky boutiques, and other outlets geared toward the young professionals moving into the neighborhood. And that population was growing quickly. By 1980, the number of people between the ages of twenty-five and thirty-four who were living within a handful of blocks on New York's Upper West Side had risen by more than five thousand over the period of a decade. "It was all about energy," Bob Quinlan said. "There was just an energy in the city you couldn't get in Pleasantville."

Similar things were happening in other parts of New York that had, in the previous decades, been abandoned by residents and industry—SoHo, the Seaport, Tribeca, the Lower East Side. With a record number of young people graduating from college each spring, all these neighborhoods now attracted young professionals, and all began to change because of it. Suddenly, the New York real estate market, just a couple of years after the city's fiscal crisis, started to take off. Upper West Side brownstones that people had bought for next to nothing in the late 1960s were, a decade later, fetching six figures.

For New York itself, the budding rebound was double-edged. The influx of people and money was helpful for a city that had spent a decade on its ass, but as neighborhoods changed, low-income New Yorkers were being displaced. And while diversity was part of the draw for some new city residents, it wasn't necessarily true for all of them. "Who wants to live in a building that's 100 percent Black and Hispanic? It's unhealthy and dangerous," a white Upper West Sider complained to a reporter in 1978, not even attempting to hide his racism. Said another New Yorker, a self-described "liberal" who was bullish on building a new middle class in the city: "Blacks just aren't needed anymore. What's the logic for their existence here now?"

*   *   *

In 1966, while the US was in the midst of an economic boom and Western Europe was also beginning to prosper, a thirty-four-year-old British urbanist and city planner named Peter Hall published a book titled *The World Cities*, a study of some of the globe's largest metropolises, including London, New York, Moscow, Paris, and Tokyo. Hall's thesis: that societal changes and shifts in the economy were only going to make such cities even more important, and more interconnected, as time went on.

"At the very center of each world city there is found a small nucleus of highly skilled professionals who live, in one way or another, by creating, processing or exchanging ideas," Hall wrote. He mentioned stockbrokers. Lawyers. Consultants. Editors. TV producers. Advertising copywriters. Professors.

"All these people live only on their ideas," Hall continued. "The central business district therefore can be seen as a specialized machine for producing, processing and trading specialized intelligence. And the ideas industry is growing many times faster than industry as a whole."

Nearly a decade and a half later, Hall's insight was proving to be spot-on—perhaps even more than he had predicted. While the rising interest in city living reflected, in part, the tastes and values of a new generation—their desire to avoid suburbia, their interest in the city's authenticity—the energy was also the by-product of something else: a fundamental shift in the economy. A place like New York might have lost hundreds of thousands of manufacturing jobs, but it was quickly replacing those jobs, even as the broader American economy strained, with other kinds of positions. And as it happened, those were the occupations—law, finance, media, business—that the Baby Boomers emerging from America's top universities in the 1970s actually wanted. American parents might have sent their kids off to college with an idea that one day they'd return to whatever community they'd come from, but real life was playing out differently. The big opportunities were in the big city.

In January 1979—the same month that Iranian militants overthrew the Shah of Iran, setting off a second energy crisis and driving inflation in America to even higher levels—the *New York Times Magazine* published what amounted to its own version of a "Back to the City" story. Except this piece, written by reporter Blake Fleetwood, went beyond merely noting that young professionals were moving into urban areas that were otherwise fading and broken down. Instead, it offered a provocative premise about the near future: These educated, affluent people would soon dominate cities—and New York was a shining example of what was coming.

"The evidence of the late '70s suggests that New York of the '80s and '90s will no longer be a magnet for the poor and homeless, but a city primarily for the affluent and educated—an urban elite," Fleetwood wrote in a piece titled "The New Elite and an Urban Renaissance." He pointed out that a similar phenomenon was already happening in

Europe, where well-off residents had moved to city centers, driving out the poor—"a gradual process known by the curious name 'gentrification,' a term coined by the displaced English poor and subsequently adopted by urban experts to describe the movements of social classes in areas around London."

In writing about this new gentry in New York, Fleetwood chronicled how much the city—actually, Manhattan—reflected the vision Peter Hall had laid out fifteen years earlier: It was the headquarters of dozens of billion-dollar organizations, including a plurality of the Fortune 500. It had a robust network of professional services outfits—law firms, accounting firms, advertising agencies. It was the headquarters of the media industry. And it was fast replacing London as the home of international finance, drawing innumerable financial jobs to the city. Meanwhile, just four years after the low-water mark of New York's fiscal crisis, private enterprise had committed nearly a billion dollars for construction in Midtown Manhattan (including office towers and high-rise apartments). Office vacancies were near zero.

Given all that energy, given the way the economy was shifting, and given their own ambition, it was little wonder that a still-small but undeniably growing number of ambitious young Boomers were eyeing the Big Apple. In 1975, Harvard Law School had sent seventy-six young lawyers (out of roughly 550 in its graduating class that year) to New York–based firms. Two years later, in the class of '77, the number of new attorneys who were New York–bound had shot up to 117. As one of the school's placement officers put it, observing the abrupt and aggressive mood shift among graduates in the second half of the '70s, "making it in Milwaukee just isn't the same."

"The New Elite and an Urban Renaissance"—widely read, widely talked about—made a compelling argument, but there remained much to be skeptical about. To begin with, even as Peter Hall's "ideas industry" prospered in Manhattan, poverty was spreading in the rest of the metropolis. The notion that New York would become a place dominated by an elite seemed to ignore well more than half the city.

31

What's more, the influx of a relatively small number of educated young professionals in cities across the country hardly qualified as "an urban renaissance"—a point that a writer named Dan Rottenberg made in May 1980 in *Chicago* magazine. Rottenberg's story, titled "About That Urban Renaissance…," took issue with the widely spreading notion that cities like New York and Chicago were making a comeback after decades of decline. That wouldn't really be true, Rottenberg argued, until middle-class families (white and Black) were choosing city living over suburbia, and so far there was little evidence that was happening. No, the new energy in cities was really being driven by only one small group—young professionals. Except that's not what Rottenberg called them.

"Some 20,000 new dwelling units have been built within a mile of the Loop over the last 10 years to accommodate the rising tide of 'Yuppies'—young urban professionals rebelling against the stodgy suburban lifestyles of their parents," Rottenberg wrote. "The Yuppies seek neither comfort nor security, but stimulation, and they can find that only in the densest sections of the city."

He went on to use the term "Yuppie" a dozen times in the story as he made the case that just because a young elite was choosing the city at a particular moment in their lives did not mean cities had been saved.

Rottenberg would always insist that he hadn't coined the term "Yuppie"; it was in the air, he said, a term he'd heard people using around Chicago. Was it marketing jargon? A real estate expression? Was it a deliberate play on Jerry Rubin's "Yippies," who'd so disrupted Chicago a dozen years earlier? Rottenberg—no one—seemed to know.

Of course, the bigger issue was the deeper meaning of what was now happening in cities—of Yuppies in the Loop, of Ivy League lawyers moving to New York, of young professionals (and flight attendants) colonizing the Upper West Side, of all those Penn grads flocking to Steve Poses's eateries in Philadelphia. Was it a sign that cities were on the rise? Or was it all just a phase, driven by the educated, original-features-loving elite of the largest generation in American history?

CHAPTER 3

Milken

J erry Rubin's attention-getting decision in the summer of 1980 to take a job on Wall Street highlighted the growing energy, among Baby Boomers and within the country at large, around free enterprise and free markets. But it signaled something else, too: the changes that were starting to happen in that most clubby of American milieus, the world of finance.

Wall Street, of course, had been vital in helping to create America's postwar dominance and prosperity—in driving up living standards and helping middle-class families afford all those houses and cars and appliances and vacations. When corporate America needed capital—for new factories, new products, new markets, all the things that helped the broader economy grow—it was Wall Street's investment banks that helped them raise it by underwriting and selling new issues of stocks and bonds. The firms, the most prestigious of which had their roots in the nineteenth century, essentially served as middlemen between the companies that wanted to raise capital and the institutions and individuals who had cash to invest. They made their money in large part by taking small pieces of the action—a commission when they underwrote new stocks and bonds on behalf of a company, additional commissions when the firm's trading arms bought and sold securities on behalf of investors.

Even as the American economy had boomed during the '50s and '60s, Wall Street had remained a traditional place. One summer morning in the 1950s, for instance, a young Goldman Sachs associate named John Whitehead (who'd go on to become cohead of the firm) arrived at the office proudly wearing a brand-new white-and-blue seersucker suit. Whitehead got on the elevator, and after him came Walter Sachs, one of the firm's senior partners and the grandson of the cofounder. "Good morning, young man. Do you work at Goldman Sachs?" Sachs asked.

Whitehead stuck out his chest and said brightly, "Yes, sir, I do."

"Well," said Sachs, "in that case go home now and change out of your pajamas."

It was a place, too, where networks and long-standing relationships mattered most. One person who'd seen how Wall Street operated, and who, by 1980, was watching it change, was Hardwick Simmons. Simmons—known as Wick—was the great-grandson of the cofounder of the investment banking firm Hayden Stone. He'd first gone to work in the financial world in the mid-'60s, when the culture wasn't vastly different from what his great-grandfather had known. "It was a real family business in those days—the whole New York Stock Exchange family," recalled Simmons, a graduate of Groton and Harvard and Harvard Business School (with a stint in the Marine Corps included). Twice a year most of the industry would get together—at the Greenbrier resort in the mountains of West Virginia in the spring, in Boca Raton every December—while in between people saw one another at the various lunch clubs on Wall Street. The closeness was in part out of necessity; most of the firms didn't have enough capital on their own to finance a really big deal, and so they regularly brought in other firms to help out with big underwritings. But the friendly atmosphere was also because there wasn't really any competition—the commissions the firms charged were standardized across the industry. Sure, a corporation could try to shop its business around among various investment banks, but why bother? The cost was always the same—the deal you got was the deal you got.

For the firms, all of this was lucrative. With the economy roaring for much of the '60s, people working on Wall Street—as analysts, as traders, as brokers—could do well. Even run-of-the-mill talents could make $40,000 or $50,000 per year in those days, while real hustlers could do even better.

Then came the '70s, and everything went to hell. Over the course of five years—from late 1969 to late 1974—the market lost more than 20 percent of its value. There were a variety of reasons for the decline: The escalating cost of the war in Vietnam spooked investors, as did Richard Nixon's shift in US monetary policy, moving the country off the gold standard. Then came the Arab oil embargo and the energy crisis, which set inflation spiraling and plunged the country into recession. On Wall Street, things were grim. More than 150 investment firms merged or closed altogether, and many Wall Streeters who'd made nice livings in the '60s started looking for other lines of work, convinced that the good times were over for good. A fellow named Bagley Reid walked away and got into the landscape architecture business. An analyst named Gerald Supple quit and opened his own bike shop in suburban New Jersey. A young guy named Michael Phillips, who'd made and lost a bundle in the market, decided to try his luck in Hollywood. The first film he invested in, *Steelyard Blues* starring Jane Fonda and Donald Sutherland, had been a flop, but he did better on his next one. *The Sting* won the Academy Award for Best Picture, and Phillips, who put in $1,500, came away with between $3 million and $4 million.

Still, even as the Street struggled—the Dow essentially finished flat for the entire decade of the 1970s—below the surface things were starting to change; the old order was being shaken loose. In 1975, the Securities and Exchange Commission put an end to fixed commissions, forcing the Wall Street firms to start competing with one another in earnest. Trades started being done via computer, which sped up what had been a slow, manual process and greatly increased the number of daily transactions. And many of the firms reorganized, transforming themselves from chummy partnerships into corporations, which limited their liability if anything went wrong, while allowing them to raise money from outside investors. As Wick Simmons, who'd seen Hayden Stone go through a series of mergers in the 1970s, put it, "suddenly, other people's money came into the business, and the ability to take risks was huge."

All of it coincided with a rush of new blood. With transactions growing, Wall Street firms began hiring a new crop of young employees, including some of those tens of thousands of Baby Boomers emerging from MBA programs every year. Even more significantly, there were new leaders—men who didn't necessarily hail from the old-guard families, but who'd grown up in the swelling American middle class and gotten to the top thanks to their smarts and aggressiveness. Felix Rohatyn was turning the investment firm Lazard Frères into a powerhouse, mostly on the strength of the strategic advice he was able to give corporate CEOs. At other firms, leaders were starting to come not from the more genteel corporate finance side of the investment houses (the groups involved in underwriting new issues of stocks and bonds), but from the rougher, gruffer trading side of the organizations, which made money for clients and themselves through savvy swapping of securities. Sandy Weill at Shearson was one member of the new guard. John Gutfreund, a longtime trader who'd risen to the top at Salomon Brothers, was another.

Of course, as much influence as those men were having on how Wall Street was run, their impact was nothing compared to that of a young Californian named Mike Milken.

*   *   *

Milken was just thirty-four years old in late 1980, but he was already something of a legend at the Wall Street investment bank Drexel Burnham Lambert. He arrived at his office, located not in New York but in the Century City section of Los Angeles, by four thirty every morning, and he often worked late into the evening and on weekends. Milken—who went bald at an early age and typically wore a curly-haired toupee—had a wife and small kids he was dedicated to, but the vast majority of his waking hours were devoted to doing research on companies, making phone calls to clients, and doing deals. And he expected no less from the traders and other staffers around him. No one left the office for meals—food was brought in; help was hired to handle small errands. Once, the story went, a colleague was departing the office early after learning that his mother had been diagnosed with cancer. Milken asked him where he was going, and the colleague explained that he was worried—other close family members had died of cancer. Milken, the colleague would recall, simply said, "When are you going to be back?" (Milken would dispute the details of this story, but not the notion that he was demanding.)

As for Milken's power within Drexel, it was so great that, in 1978, when he told his bosses he wanted to move the department he oversaw from Manhattan to Southern California, where Milken had grown up (and where Milken's own father was ailing), they had little choice but to say yes: Milken was essentially responsible for *all* of Drexel's profits.

It was not something that had happened by chance, but a feat Milken accomplished through his mastery of a relatively obscure financial instrument called a "high-yield bond" (if you were being nice) or a "junk bond" (if you were being snarky). Milken hadn't invented junk bonds, but by 1980 no one knew more about them—or believed in the potential they held for Wall Street and corporate America.

Milken was born in 1946, the first year of the Baby Boom, and he grew up in perhaps the most vital place in postwar America, Southern California. In high school he was head cheerleader and homecoming king, and he never showed a great deal of interest in the political or cultural upheaval of the '60s—even though he did his undergrad years at Berkeley. But *Time* magazine's description of Baby Boomers from 1966—"they are a highly independent breed... and their independence has made them highly unpredictable"—absolutely applied to the way his mind worked. Even as a teenager he was fascinated by the financial markets, and while he was in high school, he'd actually managed the portfolios of a handful of people that his father, an accountant, had referred to him. The arrangement: Mike would reimburse a client for 100 percent of any losses his trades might incur, but in exchange he got to keep 50 percent of any profits. He made a bundle.

After graduating from Berkeley in 1969, Milken and his wife, Lori (whom he'd known since grade school), moved east, where he enrolled in the MBA program at Wharton. He landed a summer gig working in the Philadelphia office of what was then called Drexel Firestone, and in 1970 was hired full-time at the firm's New York office, eventually going to work in the bond-trading department. Early on he rode the bus every day from Cherry Hill, New Jersey, a Philly suburb, to Drexel's office in Manhattan. It was a two-hour slog each way, often in darkness, but he didn't seem to mind. As he sat in his bus seat, he strapped on a miner's headlamp and got lost in the reports and spreadsheets and research he lugged with him.

The object of Milken's obsession, corporate bonds—instruments that allowed companies to borrow money from investors in the open market, paying the money back over a period of years, with interest—had long been divided into two main types. "Investment-grade" bonds were ones that the ratings agencies, such as Standard & Poor's and Dun & Bradstreet, deemed safe: The companies issuing them had good financial track records and were a solid bet to pay back investors, with interest, in a timely manner. "High-yield" bonds, in contrast, were considered risky: The companies issuing them weren't a safe bet to pay back investors. Why would anyone ever buy such a bond? To compensate for the higher risk, investors were paid a higher interest rate, or yield. The bigger upside theoretically balanced out the lower downside—if you had the stomach for it.

At the time Michael Milken was immersing himself in the bond world, high-yield bonds were overwhelmingly looked down upon by most traditional Wall Street investment firms. For starters, there weren't that many of the bonds; most of those that existed were "fallen angels"— bonds that had been considered a safe bet when issued but were downgraded by the rating agencies after the issuing corporations had fallen on hard times. But an even bigger turnoff was that perceived high risk of default. Why would the firms want to get their clients involved with companies that might not be able to pay the borrowed money back? Such "junk bonds" cast a shady sheen over an investment firm, the kind of thing that might drive top-tier clients away.

But Milken was fascinated with junk bonds, in part because of research done decades earlier by an academic named W. Braddock Hickman. Hickman examined their performance in the first half of the twentieth century—how often the bond issuers defaulted, what kind of returns investors received—and came to a startling conclusion: If an investor held a large enough number of high-yield bonds for a long enough period of time and from a diverse enough group of companies, they actually *outperformed* the higher-rated investment-grade bonds. Yes, individual issuers of junk bonds were more likely to default, but taken all together the higher interest rates that junk bond holders earned more than made up for those losses. In short, an investor could make *more* money buying junk bonds than good bonds.

Armed with this knowledge, a subsequent academic study that confirmed everything W. Braddock Hickman had said, and his own research, Mike Milken began, in the early 1970s, singing the praises of high-yield bonds to anyone who'd listen, trying to get investor clients Drexel worked with to acquire them. He met with plenty of skepticism— more established colleagues at Drexel who worked with investment-grade bonds looked at him like a leper—but on his own Milken found a handful of renegade investors willing to take a chance. A big part of his pitch was that the system Wall Street had used for decades was basically flawed. When it came to assessing companies and their credit-worthiness, ratings agencies only looked backward, at what a company had done in the past. Thanks to his prodigious research, Milken looked at how a company was performing *now* and what it would likely do in the future. That, he believed, hedged much of the risk.

Milken's approach was stunningly successful: He started bringing in big returns for the handful of clients who'd trusted him. What's more, he did equally well with the relatively small amount of money that Drexel had given him to invest on the firm's behalf. In 1973, Milken was allocated $2 million of firm money to invest—money he doubled in the junk bond market. The following year he was given $4 million—and he doubled it again. By 1976, thanks in part to a deal Milken had struck with Drexel that let him and his small team keep 35 percent of their profits, Milken was said to be *personally* making $5 million per year.

At Drexel, which had long been considered a second-tier firm on Wall Street, Milken's bosses started to see the potential in what he was doing, and they doubled down. The firm launched a high-yield-bond fund to attract even more investors, and then, for the first time ever, underwrote a new issue of high-yield bonds on behalf of a client, raising $30 million for a corporation called Texas International. For Drexel, the math was simple: The commission the firm received when it issued investment-grade bonds on behalf of a client was seven-eighths of 1 percent of the value of the bond; when it issued junk bonds for a client, it got 3 to 4 percent of the value of the bond.

By 1980, the junk bond market, while still relatively small and still looked down upon by most leading Wall Street firms, was growing briskly, and Drexel, thanks to Milken's mastery and passion, began transforming itself into a powerhouse in the space. In 1979, $1 billion in new high-yield bonds were issued, with Drexel underwriting $408 million of that. Within a couple of years, $1.4 billion of new high-yield bonds had been issued, with Drexel underwriting more than $1 billion. The establishment crowd on Wall Street might still be skeptical, but it couldn't help but notice.

*　　*　　*

For Drexel's status as a firm, junk bonds were starting to be a game changer. For Milken himself, they were personally lucrative. But it wasn't necessarily the money that seemed to be driving him. Sure, making millions was great, but he and Lori and their kids didn't live lavishly. They had a nice house in the modest LA suburb of Encino. What appeared to compel him even more was something that seemed generational: proving how wrong the old system was.

Under Wall Street's clubby old way of doing business—with the ratings agencies dictating what was risky and what wasn't—the only corporations that truly had access to the bond market were large, and already well-funded. New or smaller companies that needed capital to expand had to rely on loans from banks or insurance companies, which typically either required significant collateral or had restrictive covenants. Who knew how many great young companies never really got off the ground because of that? Why was capital reserved for only a privileged few?

The ability for a smaller company to raise money through high-yield bonds opened a world of possibility. Milken never talked to the press, but to the people who worked with him every day, his drive to create a new way of doing things was palpable. "Mike was on a mission," Gary Winnick, a member of Drexel's high-yield bond team, would later say. "I've never seen anybody in my career who has unbridled brilliance and unbridled ambition and total conviction."

There was no better illustration of how impactful Milken's approach could be than Steve Wynn. Wynn, then thirty-six years old and the owner of a single casino in Las Vegas, the Golden Nugget, had been introduced to Milken in 1978, not long after the Drexel trader had moved back to California. Wynn had been spending time in Atlantic City, where gaming was legalized a couple of years earlier, and he was dazzled by the possibility of opening a second Golden Nugget there. The problem? Constructing a new hotel casino tower would cost at least $100 million, and Wynn's company was far too small to arrange that kind of financing through a traditional source. But after meeting with Wynn, Milken understood the opportunity—and he was convinced that his stable of clients would be willing to buy enough bonds to finance his new casino.

Wynn crisscrossed the country, schmoozing potential investors that Milken connected him with. It was grueling, but Milken encouraged Wynn that the effort would be worth it, and he was right: In the end they were able to sell $160 million worth of high-yield bonds. In December 1980, just fifteen months after the project broke ground, Golden Nugget Atlantic City opened its doors. Within three years, it would be the most successful casino in town.

Wynn understood the role Milken played in his career. "He made me," he'd say years later. As for Milken, his confidence in what junk bonds could do was only growing. By the end of 1980, with Wall Street changing, with America's mood shifting, and with a new generation passionate about, as Jerry Rubin put it, "money and financial interest," Milken started wondering how junk bonds could transform not just Wall Street, but all of American capitalism.

CHAPTER 4

Cuisinarts and Perrier

Precisely how many Yuppies—to use the word Dan Rottenberg introduced in *Chicago* magazine—there were in places like Chicago and New York and Boston and Philadelphia and DC by the end of 1980 was impossible to say with any great degree of accuracy. The cadre of people Rottenberg had been writing about weren't part of an official organization, after all; you couldn't simply count all the dues-paying members. Rottenberg had defined Yuppies as "young urban professionals," but even that was vague. Did young mean under thirty? Under forty? Did being a professional require a particular degree? A certain level of income? In fact, what Rottenberg was describing—or at least what was emerging in cities—was less a strict demographic group than a collection of people with a shared set of attributes, attitudes, and tastes.

At the top of the list of those traits, above all else, was a keen focus on achievement and success, particularly career success. It was a quality seemingly embodied in the growing number of Harvard Law School grads who were eschewing nice-enough lives in Milwaukee for shots at really big success in New York, as well as in the thousands of Baby Boomers now coming out of America's MBA programs.

What was driving this newfound seriousness, this hard-core focus on identifying as a professional and presenting yourself to the world as such? To an extent it was an outgrowth of the national mood, the particular moment the country found itself in. In the '50s and '60s, with a confident America so clearly dominating the world, a rising standard of living was more or less taken for granted by nearly everyone. You didn't really need to sweat it so much. But now, after a half dozen years of economic stagnation, of flailing productivity, of inflation eating away at paychecks, and of international events derailing American life, prosperity no longer felt like a sure thing. Yes, there would still be winners in America, but it was becoming clearer that there might be plenty of people who didn't win, too. People like Cathy Saban, the young woman from Chicago who'd gotten a new Chevy when she learned to drive but was now afraid that she and her fiancé would lose ground compared to their parents. Or like Dennis Greenwood, who was making $6,000 per year selling lumber in a town near Boston while his wife made $12,000 a year as a secretary. Or like Dennis's coworker Ron Levasseur, who at age twenty-four was trying to support his wife and baby on $12,500 per year. He couldn't remember, he told a reporter, the last time he'd been out to dinner. His only dream was to keep the bills paid.

The economic burden fell particularly hard on the Baby Boom generation, who were twice as likely to be unemployed as their parents had been in the '50s and who, even if they had jobs, hardly felt like they were getting ahead: Adjusted for inflation, the average salary of people ages twenty-five to twenty-nine had actually decreased by $300 between 1970 and 1980. And people at higher income levels—those with college or even graduate degrees—weren't stress-free, either. In 1980, a law industry placement firm calculated that the odds of a new law school graduate one day becoming a partner at a New York firm were about one in fifteen—just half what they were only five years earlier.

All of this produced an economic anxiety—and a consequent need to really prove yourself—even in the most elite places. William Zinsser, the writer and editor who for years taught at Yale, reported seeing a distinct difference in the students he dealt with in the late '70s compared with those of an earlier era. Once, students had been somewhat carefree, eager to explore the various intellectual opportunities that college presented to them until they found the right professional path for themselves. Now, Zinsser said, they were focused on picking a career as quickly as possible so that they didn't fall behind and land on the wrong side of the winner/ loser divide. Students were coming to him in the middle of their sophomore years, unhappy with the career path they'd picked out all of a year before, but frightened to change it. "If I don't make all the right choices now," one student told Zinsser, "it will be too late." The kid was eighteen.

But economic angst was only part of what was driving this focus on success. It also had a generational quality to it, something particularly Baby-Boomerish. Theirs was a generation, after all, that had not only been told from the beginning that it was special, that it could become whatever it wanted, but that had bent the country to its own needs and desires and beliefs. Now that Boomers were focused on work and career, well, of course they would be special at that as well.

"This generation was in many ways educated for success," journalist Mary Alice Kellogg wrote in her book *Fast Track*, which came out in 1978 and explored how a particularly ambitious set of people under the age of forty were rapidly rising to the top in their professions. "It came to expect success, but on its own terms. 'See, we were right about the war, and we can be right about what's wrong with this society, too,' they seem to trumpet."

Fast Track—whose title was a term that had originated in the railroad industry but had slowly been co-opted by business in the late '60s and the '70s—profiled a couple of dozen young superachievers. There were Alan Dershowitz, who at age twenty-eight was named the youngest tenured professor in the history of Harvard Law School; Dick Ebersol, who at age twenty-eight had become the youngest vice president in the history of NBC; Patricia de Blank, a thirty-one-year-old Wall Street executive; and Lee Eisenberg, the editor of *Esquire* at age twenty-nine. Part of the secret of their success was impatience. They weren't content to sit back and wait until something was handed to them—they went after it. But there was something equally important: They'd all delivered. They'd all achieved.

Kellogg, *Fast Track*'s author, represented yet a third reason for the heightening focus on success: the arrival of tens of millions of women in the workforce. For all of America's prosperity and dominance during the postwar boom, women had largely been left out, their roles often relegated to raising kids and taking care of the home. But with the emergence of the women's movement, all of that was changing quickly. In 1960, only about 30 percent of American women worked outside the home; by 1980 it was 50 percent—and among Boomers, it was closer to 70 percent. Many women had gone to work out of necessity; as the country's economic picture grew bleaker in the '70s, more families needed two incomes just to get by. But equally important was the growing insistence, particularly among younger women, that they be given equal opportunity and equal treatment. Now.

Kellogg, who turned thirty-two in 1980, was in the first wave of those making a push. She'd been raised in Tucson, Arizona, by a single mother. At the University of Arizona, she was sympathetic to the antiwar movement, but the campus wasn't particularly radical, and Kellogg had instead thrown herself into other activities, a classic overachiever. She wrote for the student newspaper, was president of four different honor societies, and earned the school's best female graduate award. All her efforts were geared toward doing something more fulfilling than what her own mother had done.

"If you grew up in the postwar years, that was a booming time," she said. "You could make a living wage, and your parents did better than their parents had. And there was this emphasis on, well, what do I *want*? I don't need to go to work in the widget factory. Perhaps I could do something that's more satisfying."

For Kellogg, that was journalism. After graduation in 1970, she landed a job as a researcher at *Newsweek* and moved to New York, leasing a small apartment in Greenwich Village. Women at *Newsweek* had long been relegated to purely supporting roles—they weren't allowed to write or report—but the week Kellogg arrived, a group of female staffers won a discrimination case they'd filed against the magazine, and doors began opening. Within a year, Kellogg was promoted to correspondent, the youngest in the history of *Newsweek*, and she moved to Chicago. She came back to New York in 1975 after a promotion, then moved into TV, working for a local New York station. Her ambition was palpable. "Achievers are going to want everything," she said of her mindset. "I wanted a book, I wanted to do TV. It was great. I loved it."

Fast Track didn't sell well. The book came out during a long newspaper strike in New York, which made getting reviews or publicity an enormous challenge. But it effectively captured the mentality of a certain segment of the generation.

The presence of smart, accomplished women like Kellogg (and so many others) in the workforce was changing not only the workplace, but also the broader world, particularly for women of the Baby Boom generation. The very real possibility of a career—combined with the ability to control their reproductive lives thanks to birth control and legal access to abortion—had many women, particularly those who went to college, delaying both marriage and childbirth. In 1960, the average woman in America got married at age twenty-one and had her first child at age twenty-three. By 1980, both those numbers were marching steadily higher.

Which brought other changes. One was an increasing number of childless, two-career couples, where both partners worked good jobs and found themselves with lots of disposable income. "It was very important for me to marry a professional person," a twenty-eight-year-old named Robert Drumheller told an interviewer writing about the state of the Baby Boom generation in early 1981. "One of my goals was to have a high standard of living, and with two incomes you get to the easy life much faster." Drumheller and his wife, who each had MBAs from the University of Chicago and now lived in a loft in Greenwich Village, were hardly the only high-achieving couple. Agents said a major factor in the real estate market in New York, which had picked up substantially in the second half of the '70s, was the presence of two-income couples who had the resources to bid up prices.

A second ripple effect was even more widespread—the creation of what amounted to a new stage of life for a young, highly educated elite, a period in which you were out of school and earning a good income but didn't yet carry the responsibility and expense of a family. It was a period in which you could focus, more than ever, on yourself.

* * *

In 1978, just a few months before Mary Alice Kellogg published *Fast Track*, Jane Fonda broke her foot while shooting the movie *The China Syndrome*. Fonda, who'd recently turned forty, was wearing platform heels, and she fell as she ran across the set. For *The China Syndrome*'s producers, the mishap created a logistical challenge—for several weeks, they were forced to shoot around the Oscar recipient (Fonda won Best Actress in 1971 for her role in *Klute*), going back to fill in her scenes later. Of course, the broken bone was an even bigger hassle for Fonda. Not only did she need to let her foot heal, but she needed to figure out a way to stay fit while she did so. When *The China Syndrome* wrapped, she was due to shoot another movie, *California Suite*, in which she was slated to wear a bikini.

For years Fonda had relied on ballet to stay in shape—whenever she was shooting on location, one of the first things she did was see if there was a ballet school nearby—but now that kind of stress on her foot was out of the question. And so on the recommendation of her stepmother, Fonda instead joined an exercise studio in Century City, California (coincidentally, not far from where Michael Milken would open the West Coast office of Drexel Burnham Lambert that same year). It was part of a small Southern California chain started by a woman named Gilda Marx. Fonda began taking classes with instructor Leni Cazden, and she quickly found Cazden's routines—up to ninety minutes of movement, all set to an upbeat music soundtrack—to be "a revelation." She not only felt fantastic physically; she felt empowered being in the presence of other women.

Fonda hired Cazden to give her private classes, and within a few months, by the time she was shooting another movie, *The Electric Horseman*, Fonda herself was leading the cast and crew through Cazden's routine. An idea arose: What if the two of them, Fonda and Cazden, opened their own studio? With Cazden's workouts and Fonda's name recognition, it was sure to be a success. Even more importantly, it would be, for Fonda, the solution to a problem. Two years earlier she and her second husband, Tom Hayden—the longtime activist and one of Jerry Rubin's codefendants in the Chicago 7 trial—had formed an organization called the Campaign for Economic Democracy (CED), which advocated for an array of liberal causes while giving Hayden a platform for his burgeoning political career. The challenge was how to keep CED afloat financially. The pair had considered launching a business to fund the organization—Lyndon LaRouche had done something similar—but no venture felt right. Until the workout studio idea came along.

Fonda and Cazden began making plans for the business, though as the months passed, Cazden seemed to grow ambivalent, in part because Fonda insisted that the studio be owned by CED. Finally, one day over lunch, Fonda told Cazden she was moving forward—with or without her. Cazden was crushed; while the two would eventually make amends, she felt like Fonda had taken everything from her. In any event, in September 1979, with Leni Cazden nowhere in sight, a studio called Jane Fonda's Workout opened in Beverly Hills. Within months, just as Jane Fonda had predicted, it was a smash success.

Like Jerry Rubin, Fonda had long seemed to march in lockstep with the zeitgeist. In the '50s, as part of a family that was Hollywood royalty, she'd received the finest upper-crust education at an East Coast boarding school, followed by four years at Vassar. In the '60s, thanks in large part to her role in the movie *Barbarella*, she'd become a symbol of the country's emerging sexuality (she was featured on the cover of *Newsweek* under the headline "The New Permissiveness"). And by the early '70s, she'd become a full-blown, and controversial, activist, embracing feminism, speaking out in support of groups like the Black Panthers, and famously traveling to North Vietnam to protest America's involvement in the war (a trip that earned her the name "Hanoi Jane" among vets and detractors).

Now she was connected to another growing phenomenon. Indeed, by the time Fonda's studio opened in Beverly Hills, working out was becoming part of the daily routine of many of the young professionals who were infiltrating cities. New fitness clubs—modern upscale places, totally different from some of the grimy gyms that had been around for years—were launching in New York, Boston, Philly, and other cities, with fitness-conscious young professionals as their target market.

It was a phenomenon that had its roots in a couple of different places. One was the self-help, self-improvement ethic that had emerged out of the late '60s counterculture. Within the human potential movement that Jerry Rubin had so immersed himself in, for example, there was a major focus on health food, meditation, and yoga. (Rubin admitted once to drinking so much carrot juice that his legs turned orange.) But as with the overall focus on the self, it was not just driven by the cultural left; in the mid-1970s, corporate America also began to embrace health and fitness, understanding that the martini-swilling, steak-eating, sedentary lifestyles of many of its executives were costing firms money. (*Fortune* magazine estimated the annual health toll on corporations to be $500 million in 1975.) Hundreds of companies opened corporate fitness centers and started nudging managers to take care of themselves.

Meanwhile, there were individuals who were creating the trend at the grassroots level: Arthur Jones invented the Nautilus machine, which was growing in popularity. Jacki Sorensen, a military wife, pioneered "aerobic dancing" in 1969 and was, by 1980, overseeing a business with four thousand locations nationwide. Jim Fixx published the best-selling *Complete Book of Running* in 1977, helping to set off a nationwide jogging craze.

For an emerging cadre of young professionals, this newfound focus on fitness aligned beautifully with their equally newfound focus on success. Exercise made you look good. It made you feel good. Most significantly, it marked you as a go-getter, an achiever, someone who took competition and performance seriously. Indeed, it was extraordinary just how much participation in the fitness movement broke down along educational and income lines. In 1978, when the number of Americans who exercised daily had reached 50 percent, twice what it was in 1960, the Gallup Organization noted that the exercising set was overwhelmingly "upscale" and educated. Of America's fifteen million runners, roughly 50 percent had gone to college—almost twice the percentage of college grads in the population at large.

"These people are almost a race apart," journalist John Van Doorn wrote in a *New York* magazine cover story in 1978 titled "An Intimidating New Class: The Physical Elite," which chronicled this new cohort. "Their behavior doesn't seem to conform to the urges that govern the rest of us. They stop smoking and drinking without hitch or pain or plaint. They become vegetarian and give up all that dangerous dairy stuff, not because they believe it's right but because they prefer it that way.

"What's more, it's not just the observations of you, me, or laboratory psychologists looking on like young Darwins at quaint behavioral tics that set these people apart," Van Doorn continued. "The Physical Elite adorn themselves with satin, terry toweling, tennis shoes, running shoes, skates, skis, or shiny leather cases handcrafted to carry their squash racquets. With these emblems, they signal their presence to one another and their exclusivity to all of us."

Within a couple of years, yet another emblem, one that linked physical fitness with career success, also emerged. In April 1980, New York City's transit workers went on strike, shutting down subways and buses across the five boroughs. Determined to get to work, resourceful young professional women in Manhattan took the sneakers they'd been wearing to the gym and put them on with their business attire every morning, stuffing their heels into their bags as they headed out the door for the extra-long walk to the office. The transit strike lasted eleven days. The new look, the one marking you as a certified traveler on the fast track? Even after the strike was resolved, it showed no signs of going anywhere.

*   *   *

Fitness was just one element in what amounted to a lifestyle revolution that had begun in the late '60s and early '70s, another by-product of America's economic domination, overall affluence, and rising education levels. Freed from merely having to provide, to cover the basic necessities of life, consumers were growing more sophisticated in everything from food and fashion to home design. It was, too, a reflection of the shift toward focusing on the self that had taken place in the '70s.

A telling indicator was a series of changes the *New York Times* editors instituted in 1976, remaking the paper's format such that, in addition to covering international, national, and business news, each day's paper also contained a section dedicated to a different element of lifestyle. The "Weekend" section, published on Fridays, had come first, providing readers expanded movie reviews and arts reporting, as well as more in-depth restaurant coverage. "Living" came next, focused heavily on home design and food; in time, those topics would be given weekly sections of their own, as would health.

The *Times* hadn't created the sections out of high-minded journalistic purpose, of course. It essentially did it for money—or, more accurately, survival. In the early and mid-'70s, the paper's circulation had been declining, and as it searched for solutions, the powers that be brought in researcher Daniel Yankelovich (who'd observed and articulated the idea of "self-fulfillment" among younger generations). The recommendation from Yankelovich and his firm: The paper could no longer just tell readers what it, the *New York Times*, deemed to be "important"; it also needed to give readers information about topics the readers were already interested in, things they enjoyed and that improved their lives. The upping of lifestyle coverage—which, to the paper's credit, it did in a very *Times*-ian way, treating each subject seriously and with depth—paid off handsomely. Within the first year, daily circulation went up substantially, and suddenly lifestyle brands were clamoring to advertise in the sections. Over the next several years, the "sectional revolution," as some wag had dubbed it, would be imitated in big-city papers across the country.

For the cadre of young professionals colonizing New York and other cities in the late 1970s, the lifestyle subjects the *Times* and other papers were covering were both things to be enjoyed and things that demonstrated status. A knowingness about food, fashion, and art—it was an opportunity to show that you had grown beyond your middle-class, middlebrow suburban upbringing and were now part of that emerging urban elite, a person who was educated, sophisticated, and high-achieving. You were neither your parents nor the Cleavers, but someone living an upgraded version of adulthood. Committing yourself to working out was one important step. Another: becoming sophisticated about food.

America had never been a gourmet nation, and in the '50s and '60s, in keeping with the forward-thinking, can-do mindset of the country, the focus of the masses was less on quality and creativity than on efficiency and convenience. It was the era of TV dinners and Tang, of the birth of fast food, and all of it fit an energetic country that was moving the world forward.

But beneath the surface, other things were happening. Julia Child helped to popularize classic French cooking in America in the early 1960s, and a decade later a burgeoning gourmet class was embracing the lighter nouvelle cuisine. This was the opposite of a burger, fries, and a shake. It was food that was meant to be savored, appreciated. Meanwhile, in California's Bay Area, in a section of North Berkeley that would become known as the Gourmet Ghetto, a generation that had come of age in the counterculture was putting *its* imprint on food. The Berkeley Food Co-op offered a wide variety of natural foods and ingredients. The Cheese Board Collective not only sold fine cheeses, but introduced patrons to the sourdough baguette. Peet's Coffee imported coffee beans from around the world. Restaurateur Alice Waters opened the influential Chez Panisse, famous for its emphasis on fresh, local ingredients as well as an open kitchen. In the same block was Chocolat, a dessert shop that specialized in chocolate truffles.

The result of all this: By 1980, for a small but growing number of people, food was no longer just something to eat, but something to talk about, argue about, and obsess over, the way people talked about and argued about and obsessed over sports, politics, books, and movies. And city-dwelling Boomers, with time to spare and money to spend and identities to create, were crucial in helping the new, more sophisticated food culture take shape.

For starters, there were the trendy products they were helping to popularize. In 1976, Gustave Leven, chairman of Perrier, France's leading brand of sparkling water, set his sights on the American market, where the company had previously had only a minimal presence. There was plenty of skepticism—what American in their right mind would pay for water, when you could get it for free out of the tap?—but Leven forged ahead, and in 1977 Perrier launched a $5 million ad campaign that targeted young professionals in the US, zeroing in on their desire for two things: health and status. Or maybe those were the same thing. Ads—including a series of TV spots voiced by Orson Welles—played up the fact that Perrier was all-natural, "from the center of the earth," while the French name and small green bottles and barely there taste simply oozed sophistication.

"If people are looking for the kind of flavor blast they've been conditioned to from age one—in baby foods, presweetened cereals, and soft drinks—they're not going to find it in Perrier," Leven said, brilliantly taking what might have been Perrier's biggest drawback—the fact that it didn't taste like much—and turning it into its greatest asset. *Really, you're such a rube that you want flavor? Maybe it's time for you to grow up.* Perrier's marketing, which also included sponsorship of the nascent New York City Marathon and other fitness events, couldn't have been more effective. In 1975, Americans purchased 2.5 million bottles of Perrier. Three years later, they were buying seventy-five million bottles.

Perrier wasn't the only French import that was catching the attention of an educated segment of Baby Boomers. In 1971, a retired American electrical engineer named Carl Sontheimer—an MIT graduate who'd invented an array of devices, including a microwave detection finder that was used in NASA moon shots—came across a blender-like appliance at a Paris food show. Sontheimer, who'd grown up in France and was a lifelong fan of French cuisine, was bored in retirement and looking for a product he might import and sell in the US. The contraption he stumbled upon, which had been sold in France since the '60s, intrigued him, since it didn't just blend; it also cut, chopped, kneaded, diced, and grated. He struck a deal with the French manufacturer to distribute a modified version of the machine in the US, gave it a new name (a blend of "cuisine" and "art"—Cuisinart), and introduced it in America. He sold very few—until 1975, when *Gourmet* magazine gave the product a rave review. Two years later, Cuisinart sales in the US had risen to $4.5 million, and Cuisinart was on its way to becoming a staple in trendy kitchens.

Finally, there was Häagen-Dazs, another import from Europe—or at least that was what the name was designed to make you think. In fact, the ice cream was made in New Jersey, and it had been created in 1960 by a Manhattan entrepreneur named Reuben Mattus (who had emigrated from Poland forty years earlier, when he was eight). The ice cream business the Mattus family opened after their arrival in the US was muscled out of existence by larger operators in the late 1950s, and Reuben had been forced to look for another niche. He landed on the idea of an ice cream that was supremely high in butter fat, in direct contrast to the aerated ice creams the middle-class masses were buying in supermarkets. He gave it the Danish-sounding, but completely made up, name of Häagen-Dazs, and it slowly started becoming popular, first in neighborhood delis in New York, then in college towns in the Northeast. By the late '70s, what had turned Häagen-Dazs into a must-have among young professionals was its premium price—75 percent more than other ice creams. But that was no accident. Mattus had done research indicating that people increasingly associated a higher price with a better product, and so with his more expensive, premium ice cream he'd found the perfect niche. As he frequently put it: Not everyone could afford a Rolls-Royce or a Louis Vuitton handbag, but for $1.65 anyone could have "the best" ice cream.

Individual products were only part of the food revolution, though. Also significant in this budding upscaling of food was where people were shopping. The supermarket had symbolized the postwar suburban era, but now, in certain big-city neighborhoods across the country, a spate of higher-end markets and gourmet to-go operations were opening, putting a focus on quality over quantity, on exotic over mass appeal.

In 1977, Bob Quinlan, the developer who was responsible for transforming Columbus Avenue in New York, got a call from one of his neighbors at the Dakota, the apartment building on Central Park West where Quinlan lived with his wife. Sheila Lukins wondered if she and her friend Julee could pop by to get Bob's opinion on something. A few moments later Lukins and Julee Rosso, both in their thirties, arrived and were standing in his kitchen.

The pair loved to cook, and they'd launched a catering business in Sheila's kitchen in the Dakota. They now felt that they were ready to open a retail shop, and they'd found a place over on Madison Avenue, in the 60s. What did Bob think? Quinlan considered it for a moment. Getting the food from Lukins's kitchen all the way over to the East Side was going to be an ordeal every day, he told them. Why not find a place closer to home? In fact, he said, he had a space he could lease them at the corner of Seventy-Second and Columbus Avenue. Within a few months, the pair had opened the Silver Palate, which quickly caught on with the growing population of hard-working young professionals on the Upper West Side who were too exhausted to cook but still craving a wonderful "homemade" meal. (Among their early customers was another Dakota neighbor, John Lennon.)

The Silver Palate was a hit, but hardly unique. In New York, E.A.T., on Madison Avenue, had opened several years earlier, and by 1980, Pasta and Cheese on the Upper East Side and Dean & DeLuca in SoHo were also in business. In Washington, DC, in 1980, a thirty-year-old entrepreneur named Jeffrey Cohen opened Sutton Place Gourmet, a seventeen-thousand-square-foot food department store in the city's Northwest section. That same year, Steve Poses opened the Market at the Commissary in Philadelphia, while in Austin, Texas, young business partners John Mackey and Renee Lawson merged the natural foods store they'd opened a couple of years earlier, SaferWay, with a competitor named Clarksville Natural Grocery. They called the new endeavor Whole Foods.

For a certain type of customer, the appeal of such stores was undeniable. They offered not only high-quality take-out meals, but also an array of foods and ingredients that had never been seen in the freezer section of your mother's A&P. At Sutton Place in DC, for instance, the shelves included hundreds of different cheeses, eleven varieties of mushrooms, seven kinds of foie gras, butter from France, and estate-bottled olive oil from Tuscany. Yes, it all cost more than what you found at your mother's A&P, but didn't a higher price just mean better quality?

To paraphrase Reuben Mattus: Not everyone could afford a Rolls-Royce, but for just a few dollars, anyone could have wild rice grown by a Native American tribe in Wisconsin.

*   *   *

A fast-track career. A commitment to fitness. Sophistication about food. What tied them together was the idea of optimizing your life—excelling, being your best, experiencing the best. Certainly not every young professional in every major city in the country was approaching their life that way, but for a certain few, that was the culture, the ethos, now forming.

And, increasingly, it was the attitude that was shaping their consumer decisions. In the 1960s and early 1970s, Sears had been the dominant retailer in America, largely because it offered solid merchandise at a price most middle-class families could afford. But a new generation of young professionals wanted something more, something less common. The buzzword that people started using was "quality." They didn't necessarily need a *lot* of things, but the things they purchased would be, like the lives they were trying to create for themselves, excellent.

And how could one recognize quality in an object? One sign was the materials used to make it. In the '60s, Americans had marveled at all the synthetic stuff that had made modern life easier and cheaper and better. (As the line had gone in *The Graduate*: "I want to say just one word to you, just one word...plastics.") But by the late '70s, among the group of young city dwellers anxious to demonstrate their sophistication, the pendulum had swung hard the other way. The true sign of quality now was natural materials—not just hardwood floors in the Capitol Hill town house you were rehabbing, but cotton and wool and silk in the very professional clothes you were now wearing.

Another sign of quality: an exclusive brand. Couture clothing had long been a symbol of wealth, but in the late '70s America experienced its first truly mass taste of label consciousness with the designer jeans boom. In putting their names on their products, designers like Calvin Klein and Gloria Vanderbilt had taken what had been a commodity—casual, comfortable, everyday blue jeans—and elevated them, passing along a certain status (not to mention a higher price) to the consumer. The designer jeans fad was cresting by 1980, but the template was set: Buying the right brand—a Cross pen, a Rolex watch—said something significant about who you were. And if you discovered an exotic new brand that made you the envy of other people? Even better. "Your first taste of caviar wasn't what you expected, either," read an ad in 1980 for Aalborg Akvavit, a Danish liquor that was trying to make inroads among the young professional crowd in New York. "Like so many of life's rare pleasures, Aalborg Akvavit may take a little getting used to." But, of course, it was worth it. "Aalborg Akvavit. Acquire some soon."

It marked, in a way, the beginning of a significant shift in consumer culture. The decades after World War II—what observers had deemed a quintessential "keeping up with the Joneses" period—had certainly had its conspicuous consumption, but the historian Daniel Boorstin, for one, had seen it as an inclusive kind of materialism. In a highly mobile society like the US, said Boorstin (who was named librarian of Congress in 1975), people found community not just in their neighborhoods, but, thanks to advertising, in the products they bought. The owner of a Chevrolet felt a bond with other Chevrolet owners. What's more, membership in such communities was open to the masses. Anyone could walk into a big-city department store like Macy's or Marshall Field's. Lots of people were part of the tribe of Chevy owners. You consumed to be part of something larger.

But with their focus on quality and exclusivity, a new generation of consumer was flipping that concept on its head: In buying a product, the idea wasn't to show that you were part of the group, but that you were somehow superior to the group. As the columnist George Will would later write of the new mindset, "the point of owning Henckels cutlery is that so many people do not."

*   *   *

The new lifestyle that was emerging—one filled with sessions at the health club and trips to the gourmet market and shopping for just the right products—certainly wasn't cheap, even if you were part of a two-income couple. Parents of the new breed of young professionals, shaped by the values of a different era, were concerned. Shouldn't you be saving your money? But the economic reality of the time—the double-digit inflation of the Carter years—actually suggested the opposite, the kids would respond. Spend your paycheck now because in six months it will only be worth less. It was tough to argue with.

What's more, a money-fueled life was becoming the thing. In 1980, the journalist Andrew Tobias published a collection of his magazine pieces called *Getting By on $100,000 a Year (and Other Sad Tales)* ($100,000 being the equivalent of $350,000 four decades later). Tobias, a Boomer who'd graduated from Harvard in 1971 and lived in New York, had made a name for himself with his smart, funny writing about money and business. The title of the book came from a piece he'd written in 1978, showing that everyone, even successful young professionals in Manhattan, was feeling a little stretched by the rough economic times. Tobias wrote of a friend he called Stanley, a single investment banker in his early thirties who lived on the Upper East Side; Stanley pulled in great money, but boy, it went fast.

"You know, it's incredible," Tobias quoted Stanley as saying, "but you just can't live in this city on a hundred thousand dollars a year." Stanley realized how absurd it sounded, but he went on to break down his list of annual expenses: $40,000 in taxes; $5,000 for rent (a bargain, actually—he had a rent-controlled apartment); $10,000 for a summer rental on Long Island; $2,000 for various club memberships; roughly $15,000 on nights out in Manhattan; $3,000 for cocaine ("a business expense," Stanley cracked); and thousands more for various incidentals, including weekend trips to St. Croix, maid service, and his monthly cable TV bill. When you got to the end of the year, Stanley sighed, there just wasn't that much left over.

"Stanley is probably one of the million most privileged human beings on Earth," Tobias wrote. "And yet, whatever it says about social justice or human nature—or simply, the human comedy—to this very special, extraordinarily fortunate group of people, the problems *are* real."

Was it all a little over the top? No doubt. But it struck a chord. *Getting By on $100,000 a Year* was a bestseller, and Stanley's ledger of expenses only added to the perception of what "success" looked like, what it really meant to make it as a young professional in the big city.

CHAPTER 5

Triumph of the Preps

Five years after buying and renovating a home in Philadelphia's Fairmount neighborhood, Robin Palley was willing to admit to just about anyone who asked that she was feeling a little ambivalent about the whole thing. On one hand, she was still excited by many of the aspects of urban living that had first enticed her and her husband—and thousands of other young professionals across the country—to reject suburbia and embrace the city. The adventure of it. The proximity to restaurants and museums and other cultural attractions. The different races and ethnicities and types of people you encountered on a daily basis. All of it was stimulating, exactly what they wanted.

But Palley was clearer eyed now about the challenges. She was aware, for instance, that the more young professionals like her bought houses in city neighborhoods, the more longtime residents seemed to resent it. She was conscious, too, of the hassles of city life—trash, noise, crime. On her block someone had planted a tree, but the local kids literally took it down limb by limb. A replacement tree was now encircled in rings of barbed wire, and it had become for Palley a symbol of the contradictions and complications of urban life.

Most challenging of all was the school system. As a good liberal, she believed deeply in public education, and in a perfect world, she and her husband would have happily sent their daughter to the neighborhood public school for kindergarten. Except that the world and the neighborhood and the school weren't perfect. Classrooms were overcrowded, there were discipline problems, and for many of the kids at the school, English wasn't even their first language. As idealistic as she was, Palley was concerned about how her daughter would do in such an environment.

Near the end of 1979, Palley penned an essay about how difficult it was for a liberal like her, a member of the '60s generation, to hold on to—and live out—the beliefs that had long felt like so much a part of who she was.

"It was easy to be a liberal when you grew up in a nice safe suburb in the lovely, optimistic 1950s," she wrote. "Those were the years when the *Weekly Reader* and National Scholastic joined forces with the rest of the world to persuade us that our future incomes would be directly proportional to our levels of education.... They were the years when it was easier to believe in God, America and apple pie. God hadn't been declared dead yet, America wasn't dropping napalm on Vietnam, and apple pie wasn't pumped full of BHA and BHT.

"If you'll forgive the cliché, times have changed. And nothing is harder on a young idealist than a few years in what we used to call the real world. I'm speaking from experience. After growing up in those fine, committed hippie days, I've joined that living cliché: the Young Professional. That's the Young Professional who renovates an old shell in the inner city and makes peace with the various 'ethnics' who were living there first and who are furious that said Young Professionals have arrived. That's the Young Professionals (hereafter YPs) who...drive Volkswagens...who waited until they were older to have their kids or get married at all...maybe they're still 'just living together after eight years.'"

The specific challenge, Palley continued, was that her life and the lives of other Young Professionals she knew were becoming contradictions.

They simultaneously loved the city and felt repelled by it. Every year it seemed harder to live up to their ideals.

She was, of course, hardly alone in this internal conflict. The previous half century of American life—the decades in which the country had achieved unprecedented power and prosperity—had been dominated not just by faith in the American system, but by a trust in the American government. And that government—whether it was the president or Congress or the Supreme Court—had done much to move the country forward, from the economic fairness of the New Deal to the building of an interstate highway system to the expansion of civil rights to sending astronauts to the moon. But in the wake of Vietnam and Watergate and most especially an economic malaise, that trust was harder to come by. There was a sense that liberalism had gone too far—that permissiveness had led to a spike in crime; that a too-generous safety net had sapped people's will to work; that unions and regulations were dragging down the economy.

During the first week of November 1979, Ted Kennedy, the last surviving Kennedy brother, had announced he was taking on Jimmy Carter for the Democratic presidential nomination. Challenging a sitting president of your own party was never done lightly, but Kennedy had strong reason to believe he could win. Given the difficult state of the economy, Carter's approval rating that fall was at a historic low, under 30 percent, and when pollsters asked people whom they favored in a Carter-Kennedy matchup, the Massachusetts senator led by a three-to-one margin.

But from the outset, nothing seemed to go right for Kennedy's campaign. In early November, when asked by CBS News anchor Roger Mudd why he wanted to be president, Kennedy had no real answer. It was the most fundamental question any candidate faced, but Kennedy seemed unprepared, giving a rambling response that didn't say much of anything. Worse for his fortunes, that was the very day the Iranian revolutionaries who'd driven the shah out of power stormed the US embassy in Tehran and took fifty-two Americans hostage. Outraged, the American public began rallying around Carter in a show of patriotism, and his approval numbers climbed. By January, he was leading Kennedy in the polls, and he easily captured early state contests in Iowa, New Hampshire, and Maine.

Still, Kennedy's biggest problem was less his timing than his message, which reflected his old-school liberalism: He called for national health insurance, advocated strongly for support of unions, and spoke out on behalf of the poor and other people who lived on the margins. It was the type of message that Americans—Democrats especially—had long been supportive of, particularly when the country was doing well. But that was no longer the case.

By spring, Carter had all but wrapped up the nomination. Kennedy mounted a late surge near the end, but it came too late and Carter was the nominee.

During a prime-time speaking spot at the Democrats' 1980 convention in San Francisco, Kennedy voiced what amounted to a defense of liberalism and the entire liberal, postwar era. He acknowledged the frustration people were feeling with government, but said it was important to persevere and continue the policies that had helped so many.

"It is surely correct that we cannot solve problems by throwing money at them, but it is also correct that we dare not throw out our national problems onto a scrap heap of inattention and indifference," he said. "The poor may be out of political fashion, but they are not without human needs. The middle class may be angry, but they have not lost the dream that all Americans can advance together."

Kennedy mentioned, by name, real Americans who were facing struggles and whom the country needed to find a way to help. A West Virginia glassblower who'd lost his job after thirty-five years. A farm family in Iowa who wondered if their children would be able to sustain a farming life. A grandmother in East Oakland who could no longer call her grandchildren—she'd disconnected her phone in order to pay the rent.

As the speech came to a close, Kennedy harked back to the idealism both of his brothers had summoned in the country and let it be known that those values should endure.

"May it be said of our campaign that we kept the faith," he declared. "For me, a few hours ago, this campaign came to an end. For all those whose cares have been our concern, the work goes on, the cause endures, the hope still lives, and the dream shall never die."

It was a rousing address, the best Kennedy had ever given, but of course it wasn't a victory speech laying out where the country was going; it was a speech from a candidate who couldn't even win the nomination of his own party. For all the applause and cheers, it wasn't what voters—even longtime liberals—wanted to hear.

As for Robin Palley? Well, she and her husband finally made up their mind about kindergarten. They'd send their daughter to private school.

*　　*　　*

Given the frustration and economic anxiety people felt, the high infla-tion and loss of purchasing power, it was perhaps not surprising that by 1980, Americans were showing a newfound interest in wealth—and the wealthy. When people at every economic level were seeing their incomes rise, there was less temptation to gawk at the well-to-do. But now that the economy had stalled, there was a growing fascination with those whose lives were free of economic anxiety. For some voyeurs, the moti-vation might have been envy, even scorn. For others, it was something else: aspiration.

In the late spring of 1978, CBS had aired a five-part miniseries called *Dallas*, focusing on the lives of two rich, powerful Texas oil families whose worlds and interests collide when their offspring elope. The series had been created by a thirty-nine-year-old screenwriter from Baltimore named David Jacobs, who originally pitched a story about four families living on a cul-de-sac in Southern California, inspired by the Ingmar Bergman film *Scenes from a Marriage*. The production company liked the families angle but told Jacobs his idea needed to be glitzier, more of a saga. For some reason Jacobs's mind went to Texas ranches—even though he'd been to Texas only once in his life.

Neither the producers nor the network had outsized hopes for *Dallas*, but the miniseries performed well enough that CBS opted to make it a regular prime-time series in the fall of 1978. Viewer reaction in that first season was middling—it ranked a not-terrible fortieth in the Nielsen ratings—but in the second season something seemed to click, and America found itself hooked on the millionaire travails of J. R., Bobby, and the rest of the Ewing and the Barnes clans. By the spring of 1980, when season 2 ended with conniving J. R. being shot by an unknown assailant—Jacobs, the show's creator, had certainly come a long way from Ingmar Bergman—*Dallas* was morphing from TV hit into cultural phenomenon. All summer long people speculated about who shot J. R., and when the big reveal finally happened in late November, the show set a ratings record: Ninety million Americans—and more than half of all the households in the US—tuned in to see whodunit. (It was J. R.'s mistress and sister-in-law, Kristin—newly pregnant with his child.)

What made *Dallas* stand out—notable from a cultural standpoint—were two things. First, in contrast to nearly all other prime-time dramas, it was a full-blown soap opera, an over-the-top exercise in escapism, with arch characters, unexpected plot twists, and plenty of nasty if delicious behavior. What better way to forget, at least temporarily, that milk and car and housing prices were going up and up and up?

But equally important was its tone and subject matter. TV in the 1960s—from Dick Van Dyke to *Leave It to Beaver*—had largely been defined by middle-class families doing middle-class things. TV in the early 1970s, from *All in the Family* to *M*A*S*H*, had developed a social conscience. But *Dallas* went in a completely new direction: It was unabashedly about a rich and powerful elite who loved to spend money—their shoulder pads and designer handbags telegraphed power and wealth—and lived by their own code. It was a show about free enterprise and success, and if some of its characters were unscrupulous, that only made it more enticing to watch. Romanian president Nicolae Ceauşescu, a hard-line Communist, allowed the series to be aired in his country, believing it would show his fellow citizens the evils of capitalism. His decision backfired, as Romanians began seeking out the lavish lifestyles they were seeing on the series.

Dallas wasn't the only sign that middle-class Americans (and Romanians) wanted to escape the growing frustrations of daily life and indulge in the rarefied worlds of the rich. In the fall of 1980, the media had made a huge fuss about the America's Cup yachting competition, a blue-blooded endeavor if ever there was one, held off the coast of well-heeled Newport, Rhode Island. That fall, the young New York developer Donald Trump drew enormous press attention as he spent $100 million converting the old Commodore Hotel near Grand Central Terminal into the Grand Hyatt, a gleaming monument to glamour with seemingly gold-plated everything. And Trump promised that his next project, the Trump Tower condo building on Fifth Avenue, would be an even bigger ode to money. "There are no more middle buildings," he said at the time. "Only the rich can afford to buy."

Stories about the wealthy seemed to be everywhere. In the summer of 1980, *New York* magazine ran a piece called "Getting In," pulling back the curtain on how the *New York Times* selected the privileged young couples it featured in its well-read wedding pages. Six months later the magazine followed up with a cover story on "Social Climbing in the '80s"—a look at how striving young New Yorkers could elevate their own social standing. Among the story's tips: Buying a co-op in just the right building. Getting your new home featured in one of the high-end shelter magazines. Spending time at a luxury spa, less for your health than for the other people you'd meet there. Near the top of the list of recommendations was the magazine's simplest, most practical advice: *Achieve.* Being born into money certainly gave one a leg up in social circles, but even if you hadn't come from privilege, enough self-generated career success could help you over any hurdle. Neither the wedding story nor the social climber story was one you could imagine the magazine running when it was founded in 1968—Tom Wolfe's classic "Radical Chic: That Party at Lenny's," which *New York* magazine had published in 1970, was a send-up of such status-seeking—but the world had become a different place.

Of course, maybe the most telling signal that money and status were coming into vogue was the enormous success of a little paperback called *The Official Preppy Handbook*.

*   *   *

In the spring of 1980, a *Village Voice* writer named Lisa Birnbach received a call from a staffer at Workman Publishing, a small indie New York book publisher. At one of the company's regular brainstorming sessions, a young Brown grad named Jonathan Roberts had suggested a tongue-in-cheek book about "Preps," those old-line WASP families who spoke and dressed and lived a certain way as their money and status passed from one generation to the next. Roberts's bosses had come around to liking the idea, but Roberts couldn't tackle the project, and Workman was struggling to find someone to shepherd the book on a tight turnaround. And so they reached out to Birnbach. Would she be interested in leading a team in creating what they were calling *The Preppy Catalog*—a book, she later remembered, that seemed to be conceived as "a combination of the L.L.Bean catalog and some wry social commentary. But mostly they wanted a book about the stuff—the gear, seersucker, the madras."

Birnbach, only in her early twenties and also a recent Brown grad (she and Roberts were friends), certainly knew the turf. She wasn't a WASP—her Jewish father had escaped Nazi Germany just as Hitler was coming to power—but she grew up in Manhattan (her mother was a fourth-generation New Yorker), and she'd gone to the tony Riverdale Country School. It was a place where most of the kids, many of them from New York's elite families, adhered to a certain outlook about the world and dressed in a manner that reflected their moneyed-but-not-sweating-it lineage and upbringing—loafers, blucher moccasins, crewneck sweaters, Lacoste shirts. Workman wanted to have *The Preppy Catalog* in bookstores in the fall, which meant it needed an answer from

Birnbach in twenty-four hours. She liked her job at the *Voice* but figured this project was worth the leap. She said yes.

Over the next twelve weeks—a sprint by book publishing standards—she and a small group of writers put together what would become *The Official Preppy Handbook*, less a catalog, it turned out, than a tongue-in-cheek guide to how the average reader might emulate the preppy lifestyle.

"It is the inalienable right of every man, woman, and child to wear khaki," the authors declared in the introduction. "Looking, acting and ultimately being Prep is not restricted to an elite minority lucky enough to attend prestigious private schools, just because an ancestor or two happened to arrive here on the *Mayflower*. You don't even have to be a registered Republican. In a true democracy everyone can be upper-class and live in Connecticut. It's only fair."

From there the book—"in seven chapters as neatly arranged as a sit-down dinner for twelve," the authors noted—delved into all things prep: traditions, mannerisms, etiquette, dress codes. What made it particularly fun was that it was all done in small bite-size bits, with great illustrations. There was advice on preppy-sounding nicknames (Muffy, Missy, Buffy, and Bitsy for girls; Skip, Chip, Kip, and Trip for boys). Preppy decorating (small, worn Oriental rugs were good; wall-to-wall carpeting was not). Preppy live-in help (a nanny, a houseman, a cleaning lady were key). Picking the right prep school (boarding or day; single-sex or coed). Preppy stores (L.L.Bean, Burberry, Brooks Brothers, J. Press). Preppy catalogs (Bean, Talbots, Lilly Pulitzer). Preppy cars (VW Rabbit, BMW, Mercedes, Peugeot, Volvo). Preppy pets (golden retriever, Labrador, Old English sheepdog). There was even a short section noting that before Preps moved to Connecticut (or wherever), they spent time living in the city: "There's a real air of adventure about urban living that makes the experience exhilarating. It also has a limit in sight: most Preps know that ultimately they will move to the suburbs to spawn—in the interim, the city is home."

When the group finished writing, neither Birnbach nor Workman had extravagant hopes for the project. Workman wasn't a large publisher, the writers hadn't received a large advance, and the first printing was small. What's more, no matter what was happening in the culture that had inspired Roberts to think of the idea, the target audience seemed to be the definition of "niche"—people who knew and cared about the preppy life enough to want to read a send-up of it. As she tried to figure out her own next career step, Birnbach asked Peter Workman, the company's founder, if she should start looking for a job, or if Workman was going to need her for an extended promotional tour for the book. Peter Workman practically did a spit take. *Yeah, you probably want to get yourself a job...*

But in early October, just as the book was coming out, Workman's publicity team managed to get Birnbach a guest spot on the *Today* show, seen by millions of people every morning. In an interview with host Bryant Gumbel, Birnbach knocked it out of the park—she was funny and sassy and charming. The segment was a hit, and before anyone blinked, *The Official Preppy Handbook* was sold out in bookstores. Workman hurriedly printed more copies and threw together a book tour for Birnbach.

Over the next six months, *The Official Preppy Handbook* turned into an unexpected, and telling, phenomenon. Birnbach would fly from city to city, making appearances on local TV and radio stations, talking to local newspapers, doing readings and signings at bookstores. For her it was taxing. She was young, and by nature shy, and week after week she was in a new strange city, answering the same questions about the preppy life. The book became such a hit that readers would sometimes find out which hotel Birnbach was staying at and show up, wondering if she wanted to go out for drinks. For more than two years her life was consumed by the book, which would sell more than two million copies.

Amid all the attention, Birnbach began developing theories about why this satiric little guide struck such a nerve with the American public. The cover—type and illustrations set against an oh-so-preppy plaid background—was witty and inviting, exactly the kind of thing that was irresistible to pick up in the bookstore. The short chapters made the book easy to read. It was *funny*. Still, what was also crucial, she believed, was the fact that some portion of readers, at a moment when money and success and status were becoming more appealing than they'd been in a long time, just might have missed the joke.

"Some people read it as an insider," she said later. "But some people read it wanting to *become* an insider. What made it a bestseller were the people who read it as an actual how-to book."

*　　*　　*

By the spring of 1981, as Lisa Birnbach was traveling America, talking about Preps, Jerry Rubin's life was changing yet again. He and his wife, Mimi, had temporarily split. Part of the issue was Jerry's growing obsession, in the wake of his new job on Wall Street and reinvention as a capitalist, with power, which he was telling people he was "turned on" by. He'd met Mimi at the tail end of his "consciousness" phase, but he'd moved beyond that now and Mimi hadn't seemed to move with him. She wanted a more ordinary life, with a few close friends and quiet evenings at home watching TV.

The separation, and Jerry's growing interest in people who had what he called "leverage," had given him a chance to return to an idea that he'd once mentioned in his journal: a weekly salon for an exclusive group of people. Not only would it be a great way to market himself and his Wall Street employer, John Muir & Co., but it would also be a way for his newly single self to meet women.

Rubin began hosting the weekly parties at his apartment on the Upper East Side, and over the course of a few months he created something of a system for it, as well as a name: "business networking." (The term "networking" had been used by feminists, but not yet in the world of business.) Each week he'd send out invitations to dozens, if not hundreds, of people in his Rolodex, asking them to come to his apartment and bring someone with them. But not just anyone—it should be someone who was a player, a connector, a *someone* someone. The goal was to connect as many someones to as many other someones as possible—and to connect all of them to Jerry Rubin. Because connection was currency.

"I'm inviting the most interesting people to bring interesting people," Rubin's invitation read.

When they arrived—each week there were around a hundred people jammed into his apartment—they'd hand over their business cards to someone at the front door (Rubin wanted to build his list of influential names ever larger), then go schmooze while they sipped white wine or Perrier. The crowd varied from week to week, but Rubin was trying for a mix of businesspeople and dealmakers and entertainers and models— "high-quality people," he called them, who were "compelling, fascinating, powerful, achieving, enthusiastic, intriguing, beautiful, dynamic, unforgettable, doers, leaders." It was, he said, "a success salon for people who are into acquiring and achieving."

Naturally, once things got rolling, Rubin also invited the press. What better way to promote his new views on money and business and power? And because Rubin was somewhat irresistible as a story, the press came. In June 1981, writer Marie Brenner captured the flavor of the gathering, one eyebrow raised:

"Maybe Jerry is onto something," she wrote. "He's not afraid to go right to the heart of it, where the new romance will spring from—the resume. Rubin has never been accused of being subtle. Subtle personalities don't refer to themselves in the third person. 'People want Jerry Rubin to be the old Jerry Rubin,' he says. He's not. His days with Abbie in Chicago are over. He's finished with est training and yoga lessons. His marriage is broken up. Now he wants to be surrounded by those people who think as he does—by those who equate ego with career."

A few months later another writer, Myra MacPherson from the *Washington Post Magazine*, arrived to do another profile of Rubin. By this point, little more than a year after the splashy announcement in the *Times* that he'd become a capitalist and was taking a job on Wall Street, Rubin had actually left the world of finance to focus on his own company: the Jerry Rubin Salon Party and Catering Service. His goal: to use the salons he was hosting not just to make connections, but to make money through events and promotions.

In the *Post* story, Rubin went deeper into his new persona and the new era he saw dawning in America. He was proud of what he'd done in the '60s, he said, but he wasn't interested in that anymore. "There's things in the '60s that weren't good. There was an anti-success cult. A lot of people who were tied to the symbols of the '60s are also tied to the 'stay poor, stay ineffective, stay a rebel.' That kind of thing doesn't interest me."

He opened up about his resentments, including his inability, thanks to his activities in the '60s, to get hired by most companies, which was unfairly hindering his quest to become a mega-success. "Not to be immodest, I believe that I am a genius," he boasted. "I'm not allowed to express that genius. No corporation will hire me....I have been in many situations with people in high corporate positions where I believe I dazzled them with my ideas about what they could do. So then, a few days later they say, 'Well, look, fine, but, you know, we can't have a direct association with you.' People in business like to play it safe. The corporate mind is conservative. I'm just 'risky.'"

Rubin shared his bitterness about being called a sellout thanks to his very public embrace of money and capitalism. "Listen, the sellouts will call you a sellout. I've been called a sellout by some very wealthy people. Also, there's an identity crisis of a generation. They chose certain people to project their own feelings [onto], maybe, of being a sellout."

For Rubin, the *Post* article had exactly the desired effect—it kept him in the headlines and generated even more interest in his new company. As for the Baby Boom generation's "identity crisis," as Rubin referred to it? Well, he was certainly right that he and many others who once dreamed of building a utopian society were now focused, more than ever, on personal achievement and their own financial success.

But the Boomers weren't the only ones. It seemed to be true across *Dallas*-loving, Preppy-curious America, which, after fifty years of believing in the common good, was now ready to put its faith in something else.

PART II
1981–82

CHAPTER 6

The Supply Side

In rejecting Teddy Kennedy and Jimmy Carter and electing Ronald Reagan as president, American voters had sent a clear message: The status quo wasn't acceptable. At the time of the November election, inflation was at 12.6 percent and unemployment was above 7.0 percent. While a recession that had begun the previous January had technically come to an end, few seemed to think the country's economic problems had been resolved.

Reagan earned eight million more popular votes than Jimmy Carter and won forty-four out of fifty states in the Electoral College—an extraordinary mandate for change from the American people. For conservatives, it marked an amazing—and somewhat poetic—turnaround, given that in 1964, Democrat Lyndon Johnson had drubbed archconservative Barry Goldwater by a nearly identical electoral vote margin. In sixteen years, the country had done a 180-degree turn philosophically—in large part, no doubt, because it felt like it had done a 180-degree turn economically. Republicans also managed to take control of the Senate for the first time in a quarter century.

Particularly noteworthy about the election was that Reagan had won over segments of the electorate that had long leaned Democratic. Thanks in part to his wide, deep popularity among evangelical Christians, Reagan carried every southern state except Georgia, Carter's home turf. Nationally, Reagan won a majority of voters under the age of forty-four, and his biggest dominance in any age-group was among people in their thirties and early forties, the older chunk of the Baby Boom generation. He'd even made significant inroads among the blue-collar workers who'd been a vital part of the Democratic coalition since FDR, losing union households by only five percentage points.

The deep hunger for change could be seen in places like Youngstown, Ohio, which had long been a stronghold for Democrats. The Mahoning Valley, where Youngstown was located, had once been a perfect symbol of American might and prosperity: A thriving steel industry provided good-paying union jobs that lifted thousands of residents into the expanding middle class. It was a place of tidy houses and neatly trimmed yards, where life was centered around Wednesday night union meetings and Friday night high school football games. There, marching bands played songs like "Beer Barrel Polka" while the pom-pom girls danced and parents snuck a drink or two from a flask. It was a way of life that few thought would ever come to an end.

But by 1980, the region had become emblematic of something else: the country's economic malaise. The first blow had come on September 19, 1977—"Black Monday," locals called it—when the conglomerate that owned steel manufacturer Youngstown Sheet and Tube announced it was closing the company's Campbell Works location, eliminating five thousand jobs. The firm, the Lykes Corporation, an Arkansas-based company that had purchased Sheet and Tube from a Youngstown family eight years earlier, said it could no longer compete with Japanese steel companies. For the people of Youngstown, the shuttering was devastating. It was, one observer said, "like God had died."

One of the people impacted was a forty-eight-year-old man named Len Balluck, who'd heard news of the closure on the radio as he drove home from the golf course on his day off. Balluck told his wife, Joan, not to worry—everything would be fine—but in truth he was anxious. He'd worked inside the mill for twenty-three years; it was the job that had allowed him and Joan to buy a nice house on a quiet street near Youngstown and raise their son and daughter, now teenagers, in a certain degree of comfort and security.

But more than three years after Black Monday, Len Balluck still hadn't found a new job. Joan had started earning money as a teacher, but Len remained unemployed. No less significant, he was losing a sense of himself. His wife's job helped financially, "but it still doesn't give me anything to do as far as work goes," he said. "They say relocate. How can I do that when my roots are here all my life? So all of a sudden you pick up and go to Houston and you can get a job for $5 an hour. But yet the cost of living there is greater, and in selling your home here you're going to take a big loss because there's no demand here. It's real bad."

Balluck was hardly the only Youngstowner suffering. After Black Monday, several other mills in the area also closed, eliminating nearly seven thousand more jobs in the local steel industry alone. Without those positions, everything seemed to change. Thousands of other jobs, dependent on the steel industry, also disappeared. Local government saw its tax dollars dry up. Longtime steelworkers who, like Balluck, had mortgages and kids found their existences turned upside down. There were increases in alcohol abuse, drug abuse, child abuse.

"They're hanging around bars telling each other war stories," a resident said, "and when they get enough juice in them, to use the vernacular, they come home and beat up on the wife and the kids or find some other mechanisms to avoid their responsibilities."

Meanwhile, a younger generation of steelworkers—part of the Boomer population that hadn't gone to college—found themselves without any options at all. "If you came out of high school and had no other ambitions or didn't have the money to be a professional—doctor or lawyer or what have you—you knew the mill was there," a resident observed. "You had a livelihood....You grew up thinking there was nothing to worry about. There'd always be good work here. If you raised a family and your children chose not to go to college, they could always work in the mills." That was no longer true.

As for who was to blame for all this, well, it depended on whom you asked. To some people, it was the federal government, which had failed to protect domestic steel from foreign competitors while simultaneously imposing onerous, expensive new requirements—equipment to cut down pollution, for example—on the industry. Others blamed the Lykes Corporation for failing to invest in or upgrade the mills so that Sheet and Tube could better compete. Indeed, the company had taken the cash flow from the steel operations and used it to diversify into other businesses.

An activist priest in Youngstown named Father Ed Stanton said there was plenty of blame to be shared, but that didn't absolve anybody. "There was a moral issue that came from the fact that 5,000 men and women, and by whatever factor you want to use to multiply that, were getting hurt. Something, or someone, was hurting them. The government, the institutions, the social system, the individuals or corporate management, take your choice—but somebody's done somebody wrong.... There also arose the ethical question of the way it was being done. If there are three parties when an industry locates in a town, we feel there is a tripartite contract between the workers, the industry and the community. For one party to unilaterally break that raised some real questions about the system that allows that to happen. Not pointing a lot of fingers to a lot of bad guys, but in this instance there were corporate people, or a board, whatever you want to call it—and a board's made up of individuals—that did a job on Youngstown Sheet and Tube, and there were 5,000 casualties."

The Reagan camp was certainly aware of the distress people were experiencing in the Mahoning Valley, and despite the region's history of supporting Democrats, they sent their candidate there to campaign a month before the election. With an abandoned steel mill in the background, Ronald Reagan told scores of unemployed steelworkers that brighter days were ahead; he'd deliver economic growth and jobs for everyone. It was a message he'd repeat in other places. If elected, he said, he would "restore the great, confident roar of American progress and growth and optimism." His promise was clear: On his watch, with his policies, the prosperity and economic dominance of the postwar years, the American Century, would return.

Such messages were persuasive to people like Len Balluck, who'd voted for Jimmy Carter in 1976 but now cast his vote for Ronald Reagan. Plenty of other blue-collar workers joined him, and their support mattered. Carter had won the Mahoning Valley by forty-seven thousand votes in 1976, helping him eke out an electoral win in the state of Ohio. In 1980, then-president Carter carried the valley by only five thousand votes—and lost Ohio decisively.

Reagan's appeal—to blue-collar voters and others who pulled the lever for him in 1980—came on multiple levels. He represented strength, for one thing. He pledged to increase the defense budget and rearm the country so that enemies or potential enemies would have no choice but to respect, even fear, America again. The country would no longer be impotent in the face of threats from the Soviets or, God forbid, Iran. Reagan—the former actor, the onetime pitchman for General Electric—balanced that resolve with optimism. His great gift as a politician was a sunniness that not only made him personally likable, but made you believe him when he said everything would be okay.

Perhaps most significantly, Reagan crafted a narrative that fed into the frustration, even cynicism, that had been building throughout the struggles of the '70s, a narrative that gave people something and someone to blame for their troubles. One villain was government, which, Reagan said repeatedly, sucked up too much of Americans' hard-earned pay in taxes, placed too many regulations on businesses, and was hopelessly bloated and wasteful. It was time for government to get out of the way, let real America thrive again. The other villain? It was nothing less than a segment of the American populace. You knew who they were, Reagan said: the people who were freeloaders, always looking for a handout. When he campaigned for president in 1976, Reagan frequently talked about all the waste, abuse, and dysfunction in the welfare system. He mentioned an extravagant public housing complex with a gym and a swimming pool. He spoke of a Californian who collected food stamps while learning the art of witchcraft. He told the story of a woman in Chicago whose abuse of the system was so great it was almost hard to believe: She used eighty names, thirty addresses, and fifteen telephone numbers to collect food stamps, Social Security, veteran benefits, and welfare. She was pulling in $150,000 a year.

In fact, the woman was real. Her name was Linda Taylor, and she'd been written about by the *Chicago Tribune*: She was a con artist who was eventually convicted of bilking the government out of hundreds of thousands of dollars and sent to prison.

There was, no doubt, fraud in the welfare system. But as he campaigned, Ronald Reagan used cases like Linda Taylor's not to point out where the system needed to be fixed, but to *define* the welfare system overall. It was a system, he suggested, that was filled with either swindlers like Taylor or unwed mothers who lived permanently on the government dole while giving birth to child after child, each one fathered by a different man.

That this was a gross distortion didn't seem to bother Reagan and his team. In fact, in 1979 the average family receiving welfare in America had 2.1 children, just slightly higher than the rest of the population. What's more, while a full quarter of Americans lived in families that had received some form of government assistance between 1969 and 1978, only 2 percent—one in fifty—were persistently dependent on welfare for most of their income during that period. Most often, public assistance helped average working people through a catastrophic event like an illness, the death of a spouse, or a lost job until they could get back on their feet.

Ronald Reagan didn't share that kind of information, though. Instead, his message was that if Americans could just tame their runaway government and the people who abused it, the country—including places like Youngstown, where his sunniness and strength injected a new sense of hope—would return to the glory days of two decades before.

*   *   *

The architect of Reaganomics—the set of revolutionary policies that Reagan campaigned on and that promised to alter the trajectory of the country as fundamentally as FDR's New Deal had half a century earlier—was Ronald Reagan. His critics, and even some of his supporters, said Reagan didn't always grasp the details of what his administration was doing, and that was true. But it didn't mean he was a blank slate who simply read from a teleprompter while his aides did whatever suited them. Reagan had a clear set of beliefs, ones he'd been talking about for years, and they guided much of what he wanted to do in office.

To a large extent, those basic beliefs were based on Reagan's own experience in the world. His aversion to big government and taxes, for example, was influenced by his work in Hollywood in the 1940s, when the top marginal tax rate in the country was around 90 percent. Reagan's acting career was going well at the time—he signed a $1 million contract with a studio—but he started to see the tax code as a disincentive to work. "You could only make four pictures, and then you were in the top bracket," he'd say. "So we all quit working after four pictures and went off to the country." To him, the experience translated into a truism: From an economic standpoint, *any* tax cut was desirable.

Reagan had famously once been a Democrat, but as he moved deeper and deeper into politics—two terms as governor of California between 1967 and 1975; a run for the Republican presidential nomination in 1976—he had come to believe that liberalism in all its forms was harming the country. His basic economic outlook, he found, aligned with those of conservative thinkers. No less important, as he became more of a national political figure, he gave those right-leaning economists, whose ideas were considered outside the mainstream for several decades, an appealing and articulate champion in the public square.

The most prominent among them was Milton Friedman, who spent the bulk of his career at the University of Chicago, where he mentored a couple of generations of conservative economists. Friedman first came to national attention with the publication of his 1962 book *Capitalism and Freedom*, which argued that economic freedom and political freedom went hand in hand. Friedman believed that government's role should be extremely limited, that free markets should reign supreme. He argued, for instance, that government shouldn't even be involved with licensing physicians or regulating pharmaceuticals—the free market would, over time, root out the unqualified doctors and dangerous drugs.

Friedman also held strong views about federal monetary policy, believing that the Federal Reserve should keep the money supply constant and let the markets react accordingly. If some of his ideas seemed radical at first, by the 1970s he'd gained more mainstream acceptance. In 1976, Friedman won the Nobel Prize in economics for his work on monetary policy, and he was publicly throwing his support behind high-profile, anti-tax ballot referenda, like Michigan's Proposition C and California's Proposition 13, which attempted to strictly limit the property taxes that state legislatures could impose on citizens. (The former failed in 1976; the latter passed two years later, setting off budget chaos in California.) Friedman never held a formal role in the Reagan White House, but he was the intellectual godfather of the administration's ideas about the free market.

Also gaining Reagan's attention in the late '70s, and now as his administration got down to work, were several younger economic thinkers and politicians—including the economist Arthur Laffer and New York congressman Jack Kemp—who came to be known as the supply-siders. In their view, America's economic troubles in the '70s had been caused by the federal government, which, through high taxes, was sucking up capital that would otherwise be used for investment in private enterprise. The key to prosperity, they argued, lay in stimulating the "supply" side of the economy, the amount of capital available, by slashing taxes and letting money flow into new businesses. While even they acknowledged there was no hard economic research backing up their ideas, it hadn't stopped their proposals from getting some traction among Republicans. (In 1977, Kemp introduced a congressional bill that would have cut federal income taxes by 30 percent.)

And then there was David Stockman, the young Michigan congressman who, in early 1981, signed on to lead Reagan's Office of Management and Budget. Stockman was thirty-four, a Boomer who'd grown up on a Michigan farm before enrolling at Michigan State and becoming deeply involved in the anti-war movement. From there he headed east to Harvard, where he studied at both the divinity school and the school of government (while extending his draft deferment). By the mid-'70s, when he returned to Michigan and got himself elected to Congress, Stockman had moved rightward politically, becoming obsessed with rooting out wasteful government spending and balancing the federal budget. In his view, fiscal discipline was the key to lifting the country out of its economic malaise.

In early February 1981, just a month after he and his team took office, Reagan went on national TV to discuss where he wanted to take the country.

"Good evening," he said, looking into the camera from behind his desk in the Oval Office. "I'm speaking to you tonight to give you a report on the state of our nation's economy. I regret to say that we're in the worst economic mess since the Great Depression."

The new president went on to give the details of the situation—one he made clear he had inherited:

- The federal budget deficit was out of control, on track to be $80 billion in the coming year. The deficit alone was larger than the entire federal budget had been in 1957.
- The country had suffered through back-to-back years of double-digit inflation in 1979 and 1980—the first time since World War I.
- In 1960, mortgage rates averaged about 6.0 percent. Today, they were 15.4 percent.

- The percentage of taxpayer earnings the federal government took in had almost doubled since 1960.
- There were, at present, seven million people unemployed. "If they stood in a line, allowing three feet for each person, the line would reach from the coast of Maine to California," he said.

When he finished his recitation of grim statistics, Reagan turned to the heart of the matter, what he believed was the cause of all these very real troubles. It wasn't particularly complicated, he insisted. "[An] audit presented to me," he said, "found government policies of the last few decades responsible for our economic woes."

Now, many of those policies had been well-intentioned, Reagan allowed—government programs that were appealing, regulations that were designed to make things safer. But they all had a cost, both to individuals and to American businesses, and that was what was crushing the country.

"We invented the assembly line and mass production," he said, "but punitive tax policies and excessive and unnecessary regulations, plus government borrowing, have stifled our ability to update plants and equipment. When capital investment is made, it's too often for some unproductive alterations demanded by government to meet various of its regulations.

"We once produced about 40 percent of the world's steel," he continued, making a nod to places like Youngstown. "We now produce 19 percent. We were once the greatest producer of automobiles, producing more than all the rest of the world combined. That is no longer true, and in addition, the 'Big Three,' the major auto companies in our land, have sustained tremendous losses in the past year and have been forced to lay off thousands of workers."

That, he noted, was not the fault of workers. "I'll match the American working man or woman against anyone in the world. But we have to give them the tools and equipment that workers in other industrial nations have."

The solution wasn't complicated: The country just needed to give money back to people and companies by shrinking the size of government. In fact, it was so basic, he compared it to dealing with a child.

"Over the past decades we've talked of curtailing government spending so that we can then lower the tax burden.... But there were always those who told us that taxes couldn't be cut until spending was reduced. Well, you know, we can lecture our children about extravagance until we run out of voice and breath. Or we can cure their extravagance by simply reducing their allowance."

And that, in a manner of speaking, was exactly what he planned to do when it came to the federal budget. The economic plan he and his team were going to send to Congress for approval, he declared, would cut taxes sharply—he echoed Jack Kemp's idea of a 30 percent reduction—while also getting rid of wasteful government spending. Doing that, Reagan said, would raise productivity, create jobs, and bring prosperity back to all Americans.

"Our aim is to increase our nation's wealth so all will have more, not just redistribute what we already have, which is just sharing scarcity," Reagan said. "We can begin to reward the hard work and risk-taking by forcing this government to live within its means."

It was a forceful speech, perfectly pitched to resonate with an American public that remembered when the country was strong and prosperous. Once upon a time financial security hadn't just been the domain of a few rich characters on TV, but a dream all Americans shared. Ronald Reagan, they hoped, would bring back what was lost.

*   *   *

As overlord of the budget, it fell to David Stockman to create a plan that reflected Reagan's priorities: significantly reducing taxes, cutting government programs, and dramatically increasing spending on defense—all while balancing a federal budget that hadn't been balanced in a decade.

Despite skeptics who said reconciling those contradictory priorities was mathematically impossible, Stockman was optimistic as he got to work. But as the months passed into the summer of 1981, he, too, started to grow dubious. In part it was because members of Reagan's own team didn't agree on what was most critical. Stockman and a number of others believed fiscal discipline—a balanced federal budget—was the most significant thing they could do. It would send a positive signal to the financial markets and stop the government from borrowing more money, ultimately making capital cheaper for the private sector.

The supply-siders, in contrast, didn't much care whether the budget was balanced—to them it was all about dramatically reducing taxes in order to put money back into the hands of people who could invest it. Meanwhile, the Defense Department didn't care about balancing the budget *or* cutting taxes—it was busy drawing up a long list of ways to spend more money on America's military. And then there was Reagan himself (who'd barely survived an assassination attempt that March). Stockman knew that by far the biggest part of the federal budget—nearly 50 percent—was in Social Security, but the boss had put that off-limits. Despite a handful of conservatives who called it a Ponzi scheme, Reagan understood that the vast majority of Americans loved Social Security. Making significant cuts there would be political suicide.

As it happened, Stockman and the Reagan team ended up getting help from a source they didn't necessarily expect—the Democrats who controlled the House of Representatives. While more liberal members of the party were protective of cutting various government programs (as were some Republicans, who didn't want to lessen the amount of pork they brought back to their own districts), Democrats had seen the one-sided results of the November election as a significant ideological shift among American voters, and they believed they had no choice but to get on board. They did so by proposing their own version of significant tax cuts.

In August, after months of crunching numbers and negotiating, Congress officially passed—and Ronald Reagan signed—the Economic Recovery Tax Act of 1981. While it spared Social Security, the budget made significant cuts to an array of social programs that had been launched in the '60s and '70s, many of which were focused on helping low-income Americans: food stamps, Aid to Families with Dependent Children, Medicaid, student loans, job-training programs. Meanwhile, defense spending would grow 13 percent.

But the budget's biggest feature was tax cuts—25 percent over the next three years, with the biggest dollar savings going to wealthier households.

Indeed, while a family earning the median income in the United States in 1981—about $20,000—would save $764 on their tax bill over the next two and a half years, those making ten times the median, $200,000, would save $25,000—*thirty-three times* what the median family was going to save. People making $250,000 would do even better, saving $35,000—*forty-six times* more. The massive favoring of those on the top end of the pay scale was, it turned out, by design. As Stockman would tell journalist William Greider in a widely read, highly controversial *Atlantic* article that December, the notion of across-the-board tax cuts had merely been a "Trojan horse" to get the public at large to accept the big cuts for wealthier people.

Which is not to say Stockman, the fiscal disciplinarian, was satisfied with what was passed and signed into law. On the contrary, the administration's budget projected a deficit of more than $100 billion for the coming year, with even bigger deficits coming unless more spending was curtailed. Apparently cutting the kids' allowances was harder than Ronald Reagan had imagined.

*   *   *

Despite the budget deficit, Reagan's policies were very much in keeping with the mood that was present in the country—the skepticism about government, the rising energy around capitalism, the increased activity on Wall Street, the growing focus on financial and career success. From the outset, Reagan was clear that he believed the key to lifting America out of its 1970s economic malaise was reinvigorating free enterprise and letting the free market work its magic—and his cabinet choices reflected it. Four of his thirteen cabinet secretaries had come from the business sector, not government (more than any other president to that point).

The belief that government was too big, that decades of liberalism had softened people and made them too dependent, was a point of view that Reagan shared with his counterpart across the Atlantic, Margaret Thatcher. Thatcher had been elected prime minister of the UK in the spring of 1979, some twenty months before Reagan took office, and she faced many of the same issues Reagan did: high inflation, high unemployment, anemic productivity. Her solutions were similar: cutting taxes and reducing government spending. Thatcher also believed that Britain's trade unions had become too powerful, and much of the British public agreed with her. In fact, a series of strikes between November 1978 and February 1979, which greatly inconvenienced British residents, had destabilized the Labour Party government and helped put Thatcher and her Conservative Party in power. In office, she was taking every opportunity to stand up to unions and reduce their clout.

Eight months into office, Reagan was presented with a similar opportunity. Eight days before he signed the historic tax cuts into law in the summer of 1981, the new president fired more than eleven thousand federal air traffic controllers who'd gone out on strike. Their walkout, motivated by a desire for better wages, shorter workweeks, and better equipment, had been in direct defiance of a law prohibiting federal government workers from striking, and Reagan hadn't been shy about using his authority. "They are in violation of the law and if they do not report for work within 48 hours they have forfeited their jobs and will be terminated," Reagan said on August 3, as the thirteen thousand members of the Professional Air Traffic Controllers Organization (PATCO) walked off the job. About thirteen hundred union members did return to work; the rest Reagan not only fired but banned from federal employment for the rest of their lives.

As a political act, the firing of the air traffic controllers was savvy—in polls conducted immediately afterward, more than six in ten Americans approved of Reagan's actions. To many of them, it confirmed not only the strength of his leadership—*If you don't follow the rules, you're out*—but also the broader narrative he'd campaigned on: There were certain Americans—welfare queens, maybe some union workers—who were only out for themselves, who were always trying to bilk the system. Well, Ronald Reagan was saying, that would come to an end on his watch.

But, in fact, the situation was less cut-and-dried than it appeared. During the previous year's campaign, PATCO, which had chilly relations with the Federal Aviation Administration (FAA) under Jimmy Carter, had actually endorsed Reagan for president. Following the endorsement, Reagan sent a letter to PATCO's leader, Robert Poli.

"You can rest assured that if I am elected President, I will take whatever steps are necessary to provide our air traffic controllers with the most modern equipment available, and to adjust staff levels and workdays so they are commensurate with achieving the maximum degree of public safety," Reagan wrote. "I pledge to you that my administration will work very closely to bring about a spirit of cooperation between the President and the air traffic controllers."

Poli mistakenly interpreted the letter as a sign that Reagan—who as president of the Screen Actors Guild actually led a strike in 1960—had the union's back in its negotiations with the FAA.

The great irony, of course, was that the controllers were exactly the kind of everyday Americans whose support Reagan had asked for, and often won, during the campaign—working-class Americans, like Len Balluck, who'd achieved a middle-class life without having gone to college. In firing them, Reagan had called their strike a "peril to national safety." But he and his administration undoubtedly saw the firing as a message to labor everywhere that it was time to fall in line—a message that CEOs across the country filed away.

CHAPTER 7

Shareholders

By the fall of 1981, Paul Volcker, the chairman of the US Federal Reserve Bank and arguably the person who had the single most power when it came to the US economy, had gotten used to receiving hate mail. Most typically, it came in the form of angry, anguished letters from hardworking Americans who'd been saving diligently to buy a house, but who now—thanks to the ridiculously high interest rates the Fed's policies had brought about over the previous two years—found the ultimate symbol of the American Dream out of reach. But others had gotten more creative in their attempts to capture Volcker's attention and get the Fed to change course. Home builders in Jackson, Mississippi—whose businesses had tanked because of the high borrowing rates—had mailed Volcker a wooden two-by-four on which they'd scrawled a message: "Help! Help! We need you [to] please lower interest rates." Not to be topped, apparently, struggling car dealers, whose businesses had also cratered because of high interest rates on auto loans, had sent Volcker a batch of car keys—inside a coffin. The Fed chair wasn't unsympathetic, but he also wasn't about to change course. The policies would stay.

Volcker, a longtime Treasury Department official, had been named

Fed chair by Jimmy Carter in the summer of 1979. At six feet seven inches tall, he was hard to miss—and the approach he was leading at the Fed was equally hard to ignore. Volcker had made clear to Carter when he was interviewing for the job that finally taming inflation would be his highest priority, in part because he understood the pain it caused everyday Americans. He'd first appreciated it, Volcker told people, in 1945, when he was a freshman set to go to Princeton. His mother said the family would give him an allowance of $25 per month, but Volcker balked. He needed more, he insisted.

"That's what your sisters got," his mother said, "and that's what you're going to get."

Paul kept arguing. His sisters had gone to school during the Great Depression. There'd been inflation since then. His mother wrote to his sisters and asked for their opinions. Each agreed with their younger brother: Paul should get more. Their mother was unpersuaded. "You're going to get $25, just like your sisters got." And so it was that Paul Volcker made his way through Princeton on an allowance of $25 per month.

It was a real-world lesson in how inflation can chip away at buying power, but as he got older, Volcker saw an additional downside to rising prices: It lessened people's faith in government if officials couldn't keep inflation under control.

Throughout the '70s, the Fed had taken steps—not bold enough, in Volcker's estimation—to lower inflation, and that was now part of the problem: The public—consumers, businesses, the markets—had lost faith that anything was going to be done, that prices would begin to hold steady. In other words, Volcker believed that inflation had become as much a psychological issue as an economic one. Prices had been rising for so long that the public simply factored them into their behavior—businesses increased prices in anticipation of their own costs rising, while consumers spent money today rather than saving it for tomorrow, when it would be worth less. The problem? Both types of behavior only added to the inflationary spiral.

In order to change that phenomenon, Volcker believed, the Fed needed to do something bold—to signal to the country that it really *was* serious about ending price increases. The other thing Volcker believed necessary was for the Fed to aggressively tighten the money supply. A growing number of economists—starting with Milton Friedman— thought that too many dollars in circulation was one of the primary causes of inflation. By reducing the money supply, the Fed would increase competition for the remaining dollars, which would raise interest rates, which would ultimately slow economic activity: With higher borrowing costs, people wouldn't be able to afford new homes and new cars. As demand lessened, businesses would have no choice but to lower—or at least stop raising—prices. Stability would then return.

In October 1979, following an unplanned meeting of the Fed's governors, Volcker took the unusual step of holding a press conference to announce a change in Fed procedures: It would begin directly tightening the money supply. Not only was this the right policy, Volcker believed, but by making such a public display of the change, it would begin sending the signal of how serious the Fed was about reducing inflation.

The strategy worked as promised—the inflation rate did begin to drop—but it also helped kick off the mild recession in early 1980, and within a few months the Fed made the decision to pull back, attempting to strike a balance between lowering prices and not letting unemployment get too high. The recession came to an end. But when prices started to rise yet again at the end of 1980, the Volcker-led Fed tightened the money supply once more—this time with a determination not to let up. And it didn't, even as money got tighter and interest rates went to unheard-of heights and people sent Paul Volcker two-by-fours and coffins in the mail. By the summer of 1981, the prime rate—which banks used to set their own rates for mortgages, credit cards, and car loans—had risen to an all-time high of 21 percent, making borrowing money ridiculously expensive for consumers and businesses across the country. Meanwhile, unemployment was above 8 percent—and climbing. The economy had slipped back into another recession, just a year after the previous one had ended.

The American public weren't the only ones frustrated, sometimes outraged, by what was happening. Congress held frequent hearings, with some House members even threatening to impeach Volcker. But the chairman—perhaps occasionally thinking of his money-strapped undergrad days at Princeton—held firm, convinced he was doing what was necessary and right.

*   *   *

For the CEOs running America's biggest corporations, the back-to-back recessions were yet another challenge, coming on top of what had essentially been a decade of challenges.

In contrast to the growth that American business had seen in the 1950s and 1960s, corporate profits, overall productivity, and certainly stock prices had lagged in the 1970s. The lackluster performance had generated plenty of conversation and debate—about whether corporate bureaucracies had become bloated and inefficient; about whether American employees had fallen behind in skills and work ethic; about whether the country was going to be overtaken by ascendant economies like Japan's. (In 1980, NBC broadcast a documentary called *If Japan Can... Why Can't We?*, which looked at the extraordinary efficiency of Japanese companies.)

But the conversation about corporate America also included something more philosophical: What, precisely, was the purpose of a company in the first place? Who was it for? What ideas should guide its decisions? For much of the century, and particularly in the prosperous decades immediately after World War II, there had been a loose agreement in America that businesses existed first to serve their customers, who wanted quality products and services, and then to provide jobs to workers, who deserved decent pay, good working conditions, and job stability. Once obligations to those two constituencies had been met, a company's shareholders then deserved to make a fair profit.

But by the late 1970s, a growing number of voices—led, again, by Milton Friedman—had come to disagree with that view. In 1970, Friedman had written an influential article in the *New York Times Magazine* that took issue with the idea that business had any sort of "social responsibility" at all. On the contrary, its only obligation was to increase its own profits, Friedman argued. Not only was the view consistent with Friedman's long-held beliefs—that the markets should dictate everything—but it was also a response to the liberalism of the previous decades and to the fact that management at large corporations was starting to put a focus on things like reducing pollution and hiring more minorities.

"When I hear businessmen speak eloquently about the 'social responsibilities of business in a free-enterprise system,' I am reminded of the wonderful line about the Frenchman who discovered at the age of 70 that he had been speaking prose all his life," Friedman wrote. "The businessmen believe that they are defending free enterprise when they declaim that business is not concerned 'merely' with profit but also with promoting desirable 'social' ends; that business has a 'social conscience' and takes seriously its responsibilities for providing employment, eliminating discrimination, avoiding pollution and whatever else may be the catchwords of the contemporary crop of reformers. In fact they are—or would be if they or any one else took them seriously—preaching pure and unadulterated socialism. Businessmen who talk this way are unwitting puppets of the intellectual forces that have been undermining the basis of a free society these past decades."

Indeed, Friedman continued, the only obligation that businessmen—that is, corporate executives—had was to the owners of their businesses—that is, shareholders. And unless they flatly stated otherwise, what shareholders wanted were profits and a maximum return on their investment. When a corporate manager focused on anything other than that—providing employment, ending discrimination, reducing pollution—he was, in essence, stealing money and resources from the true and rightful owners of the company, its stockholders. Individuals were certainly free to advocate for social change in their free time, Friedman said, but not in their roles as managers or employees of a corporation. "In his capacity as a corporate executive, the manager is the agent of the individuals who own the company...and his primary responsibility is to them."

Friedman's argument was welcomed by others on the ideological right and in the world of business, who believed that free enterprise in America was under attack. And it was expanded upon six years later by two economists who had been protégés of his at the University of Chicago. In an article published in the *Journal of Financial Economics* (and which would become one of the most cited business pieces in all of academia), Michael Jensen and William Meckling agreed with Friedman that shareholder welfare should be the primary concern of corporate executives, though they noted that there were inherent conflicts in the relationship between CEOs and boards, what they called "agency costs." One way to minimize those conflicts? By making sure the CEO of a company was also a shareholder. The more stock a CEO had, Jensen and Meckling argued, the more his or her behavior would align with the goals of all shareholders.

It was a provocative theory, and the more American business struggled in the late '70s, the more it was buzzed about in corporate and legal circles. The only wrinkle was that no CEO of a major American corporation had ever put the shareholder primacy theory into practice—until Jack Welch took over the company that Ronald Reagan had once been a pitchman for.

*   *   *

Welch was forty-five years old when he officially became chairman and CEO of General Electric in April 1981. He was not only the youngest of the candidates who competed to succeed Reg Jones, the company's elegant longtime leader; he was also, by a wide mile, the most aggressive and brash. Welch, who'd grown up in a working-class family in Massachusetts, embodied the phrase once used to describe him: a "live wire." He bit his nails constantly, and he spoke with a slight stammer. (When he was a child, his mother told him that his brain just worked too fast.) He was energetic, ambitious, acerbic, impatient, relentless, frequently crass— his high school classmates had voted him the "most talkative and noisy boy"—and his working-class roots, combined with his short stature (he topped out at five feet seven inches), had seemingly given him a permanent need to prove himself.

And he had done just that, repeatedly. From the time he arrived at GE in 1960, after earning a PhD in chemical engineering at the University of Illinois, Welch distinguished himself in one endeavor after another. By his early thirties he was overseeing GE's plastics division, and within a few years he'd added the company's home appliances and financial services divisions to his portfolio as well. Using a mix of smarts, instincts, and intimidation, as well as a willingness to cut what he saw as unnecessary jobs, he got results.

The company Jack Welch was taking over, founded by Thomas Edison nearly a century earlier, had long been one of the crown jewels of business, seemingly epitomizing American ingenuity and strength. It was sprawling, with four hundred thousand employees, annual revenues of $25 billion, and a dazzling array of products and services in its thirteen divisions—from nuclear generators and jet engines to electric can openers, television sets, and, of course, light bulbs. Its massive employee base made it a vital presence in the many communities where it had plants and offices across the country—cities like Louisville, Kentucky; Erie, Pennsylvania; Schenectady, New York; and dozens more.

But it wasn't only size that gave GE its reputation: It also represented the most positive aspects of American capitalism. The imagination and resourcefulness of GE's engineers and scientists, bolstered by serious investments in research and development, had produced innovation after innovation that improved people's lives—the first electric locomotive, the first mainstream refrigerator, the first jet engine, new types of plastic, the first fluorescent light, the first garbage disposal. The company made money, showing a profit every single year of its existence and delivering a dividend to investors every year since 1900. And it did all that while famously taking care of its employees, providing them with good wages, good benefits, and, often, lifetime employment. "When [my dad] got a job with General Electric, that was it. I mean, that was the dream," said Bernie Witkowski, who eventually joined his father—and uncles and cousins—as a GE employee in Schenectady. "When I was brought up, that's what we heard all the time. 'Oh, when you get out of high school, you go to GE, you go to GE.'" When Reg Jones, himself regarded as one of the most capable executives in the country, spoke of the "spirit of General Electric" during the 1978 centennial of Edison's invention of the light bulb, he cited loyalty, along with moral integrity and innovation, as the key element of that spirit.

Indeed, though there were occasionally fierce strikes, the way GE did business epitomized the "tripartite contract" that Father Ed Stanton, the Youngstown priest, had articulated: a true partnership between a company, its employees, and the communities in which GE operated.

Nowhere was that clearer than in Schenectady, where GE had actually been founded in 1892. (The new entity was created following the merger of Edison General Electric Company and Thomson-Houston Electric Company.) As GE grew, so did the city, and by the late 1920s both were booming. GE employed nearly thirty thousand people in Schenectady, from executives and engineers to factory hands, with a sprawling campus that occupied more than a square mile. High above it, atop—fittingly—the engineering building, was GE's iconic "meatball" logo, thirty-six feet in diameter and visible from a mile away. It came to symbolize Schenectady itself.

The power of the company—and the community—was on full display during the Second World War, when Schenectady became an essential part of the war effort, producing powerful turbines for allied ships; crucial components for airplanes; large motors for tanks; and lamps and lighting systems for bases and vehicles. Meanwhile, amid all of it, the innovations continued, including new materials like silicone and molded plastics that proved vital during the war and became an essential part of American life after it.

For all their efforts, the residents of Schenectady and the surrounding area got not only the satisfaction of improving the world, but also solid, secure, middle-class jobs. People worked at GE for their entire lives—and saw generations of family members do so as well. The number of employees in Schenectady peaked during the massive war effort, but even as Jack Welch took over the company in 1981, GE remained Schenectady's biggest job provider, employing nearly twenty-five thousand people.

Despite all that—despite GE's powerful impact, its rich legacy, and its healthy, $1.5 billion profit in 1980—Jack Welch believed, as he took the reins from Reg Jones, that the company essentially needed to be reinvented. For starters, there was its financial performance. Yes, it was nice that GE invested in research and was loyal to its employees, but it had done so, Welch argued, at the expense of its shareholders. In 1971, GE's stock had traded at twenty-two times its earnings; a decade later that ratio had dropped to eight times earnings. What's more, someone who bought stock in the company in 1971 and held on to it had actually *lost* ground to inflation over the course of a decade. Simply put: If shareholders came first, then Welch believed GE had an obligation to show better growth and stronger profits.

At the same time, Welch was also insistent that the company, like American business in general, had gotten slow and soft, that it was falling behind. The world was changing, becoming more competitive, and it was crucial for GE to change, too. "National productivity has been declining, and, in industry after industry, product leadership is moving to other nations," he and Jones wrote in a coauthored letter to shareholders in 1980, shortly before Welch became CEO. "Companies that refuse to renew themselves, that fail to cast off the old and embrace new technologies, could well find themselves in serious decline in the 1980s. We are determined that this shall not happen to General Electric."

Over the course of 1981, as he settled into the chairman's suite at GE headquarters in Stamford, Connecticut, and began to put his stamp on the company, Welch made clear his ambition to reimagine General Electric. GE had long prided itself on its strategic planning capabilities and strict processes, but Welch saw these as adding cost and slowing the company down, and he was determined to dismantle much of that infrastructure.

Even more significant was his desire to fundamentally change what

GE did. In 1980, half of the company's profits came from what it referred to as core manufacturing—everything from jet engines to light bulbs. But making money in manufacturing was increasingly difficult, and Welch believed the company needed to focus more on the knowledge industries that were attracting so many young college grads to cities: technology, services, and finance.

Finally, there was GE's company culture. As kids, Welch and his friends had frequently played baseball and basketball in an abandoned quarry in Salem, Massachusetts, called "the Pit." His fire and competitiveness were already on display. Years later a buddy—who'd go on to become a respected Massachusetts judge—recalled Welch reaming him out midplay on the basketball court for letting a bigger opponent score. Welch didn't hold back on saying what he wanted—and what he wanted, more than anything, was to win.

That was the culture Welch was determined to see inside GE. It was a culture in which candor ruled the day, competitiveness was key, and the only goal that mattered was coming out on top.

Sometimes, unfortunately, that required tough choices. Within a few months of taking over as CEO, he met with the company's strategic planning department, the group he believed was slowing things down so much. "Take a look around you," he said, "because you won't be seeing each other anymore." Of the team's two hundred positions, he eliminated all but a dozen.

*   *   *

In early December 1981, as the American economy fell more deeply into recession, Jack Welch went to the dais inside an ornate ballroom at the Pierre Hotel in New York City to address analysts from Wall Street's leading investment firms. He was nervous. This was his first opportunity to talk, publicly, to the investment community about GE, and he wanted his presentation to be a rousing success.

Normally at such events, a CEO would share with analysts a company's financial results and its successes during the previous year. The analysts would then take the detailed numbers they got and plug them into whatever formulas they had for valuing a stock, and everyone would be happy.

But Welch wanted to do something different—he wanted to talk about the future; he wanted to talk about his *vision* for GE. The message he hoped to convey was remarkably similar to the mindset that many of those fast-track Boomers had come to adopt: Success in America, success in the world, was no longer guaranteed. In the 1980s, there would be winners and there would be losers, and if you wanted to come out on top—indeed, if you wanted to survive—you needed to compete. Ferociously. There was no longer room, Jack Welch believed, for mediocrity.

As he spoke to the analysts, Welch made clear that his GE would not be mediocre; it would be a winner. Standing at the dais, he unveiled the company's new operating philosophy: It would be either number one or number two in whichever industry it was in, whether that was nuclear reactors or washing machines. And if it wasn't? Well, it needed to be prepared to do something about it. "The managements and companies in the '80s that don't do this, that hang on to losers for whatever reason—tradition, sentiment, their own management weakness—won't be around in 1990," he said.

As Welch spoke, he looked out at the crowd and mostly saw blank expressions. *What is Welch doing?* their faces seemed to say. *Isn't he going to give numbers? We usually get numbers.* The CEO continued speaking.

He had no intention, Welch said, of letting GE become one of those doomed companies, and the key to avoiding that was going to be culture. He would create an atmosphere where all of GE's employees would feel comfortable stretching, trying to be better than they ever thought they could be. "Only the limits of their creativity and drive would be the ceiling on how far and how fast they would move," he declared.

If they did that, they would create a new and mighty company. For years analysts had expected GE, because of its massive size and breadth, to only grow in line with America's gross national product, but Welch had other ideas. *His* GE would be "the locomotive pulling the GNP, not the caboose following it." GE would become "the most competitive enterprise on Earth," Jack Welch said. It would be a company on the fast track.

When the speech was over, the analysts applauded politely, and Welch knew he'd bombed. Walking out the door, one analyst was over-heard to say, "We don't know what the hell he's talking about." They were numbers guys. Why hadn't he given more numbers?

Of course, in his own way Jack Welch was a numbers guy, too, maybe even more than the analysts were. And the number that mattered to him most was GE's stock price. That day it went up all of 12 cents. He was lucky, he thought to himself, that it hadn't gone down.

CHAPTER 8

People Like Us

By the early months of 1982, as Ronald Reagan instituted his new vision for America and Jack Welch struggled to explain his new vision for GE, the number of well-educated young professionals gravitating toward cities around the country only continued to grow. They remained just a sliver of the overall urban population, and a sliver of their own generation, but in the neighborhoods where they settled an identifiable young professional culture was beginning to crystallize. They were members of a small but growing tribe.

Kathy Kehoe was among them. Kehoe had grown up on New York's Upper East Side, attending a private high school in the city before going to all-female Smith College in 1967. Her experience there was very much of its time: frequent marches and protests, whether about Vietnam or civil rights or any number of issues. During the spring of her junior year, in 1970, Kehoe and other students had gone on strike to protest the killings of four Kent State student protesters by the National Guard, ultimately shutting down Smith for a period of days. Similar strikes had taken place at elite schools across the country.

In time such political activism came to an end, but the sense that such protests engendered—that Kehoe and others of her generation were important and powerful—didn't. It was a feeling they would carry forward with them. "I never felt like there was anything I couldn't do," she said later. "There was a sense we could change things. We could make things better."

After graduating from Smith in 1971, Kehoe moved back to New York and began a job as a teacher, one of the professions that young women were still actively being steered toward in the early 1970s. But as the decade progressed and more women hopped on the career fast track, Kehoe found herself thinking more ambitiously—she'd taken on a leadership role at the school where she taught, and her abilities in the classroom convinced her, correctly, that she had the talent to do many different things. She enrolled in an MBA program at Columbia, and by the early 1980s she was building a brand-new career in the world of advertising.

In 1981, when Kehoe went back to Smith for her tenth college reunion, the school's president reported that the class of '71 had sent more of its members—all women, of course—to graduate school than any class before them. Kehoe realized that a lot of people were on the same track that she was. They'd started law school or business school in their late twenties, and now, with the world opening up, they were deeply focused on their careers.

And the best place for an ambitious young professional, female or male, to make their mark in this new world? It was in a large city, for the simple reason that cities were where the best jobs were. America's industrial heartland—places like Youngstown—might be struggling mightily in the deepening recession, but the "ideas industry"—the postindustrial economy—was now becoming a reality, and cities were where the best opportunities lay. New York, for example, which in the early '70s had lost nearly six hundred thousand manufacturing jobs, was in the midst of what one observer called the biggest economic shift since the Industrial Revolution, with more than half of its economic output now being generated not by blue-collar workers who manufactured products, but by white-collar workers who processed ideas and information in fields like finance, law, media, marketing, and technology.

In Manhattan, you'd see them in two geographic areas. One was near Rockefeller Center, where, within a few blocks, there were three major broadcast TV networks, the largest cable TV companies, the world's biggest book and magazine publishers, and major ad agencies, as well as the new headquarters of IBM and AT&T. The other epicenter was the financial district in Lower Manhattan, now the world's financial center, where technology was bringing about a massive spike in the number of transactions done every day. On any given morning, in both parts of New York, you'd see well-dressed young professionals—many of the women now wearing sneakers with their power suits—scurrying to get to their offices.

While New York was leading the way, the same phenomenon—an increase in good-paying, white-collar jobs requiring a bachelor's degree or higher—was happening in cities across the country: Chicago, Atlanta, Washington, DC, San Francisco. "It's the archetypal post-industrial city," the *Los Angeles Times* wrote of the changes taking place in San Francisco in the first half of the 1980s, "one with an economy based not on steel plants or breweries, but on silicon chips, corporate headquarters, international trade, banking, law. And its residents represent that."

The rise of the postindustrial economy was only intensifying the gentrification of certain neighborhoods within cities. In New York, changes were obvious not only on the Upper West Side, but in SoHo, the Seaport, Chelsea, Tribeca, and Hell's Kitchen, as well as across the Hudson River in Hoboken and Jersey City. In Boston, neighborhoods like Back Bay, the South End, and Charlestown were being taken over by young professional couples whose dual incomes allowed them to afford the fast-rising real estate prices. (In the South End, the percentage of college graduates jumped 188 percent in a decade.)

One of the most symbolic shifts was happening in the Bay Area. In the late 1960s, San Francisco's Haight-Ashbury had, at least for a time, become the epicenter of the counterculture, ground zero for 1967's

Summer of Love. At the time, the Haight was filled with a fascinating mix of people—hippies who'd arrived from all across the country, but also blue-collar workers, Blacks, and Latinos. As the '60s—both literally and symbolically—came to an end, the Haight struggled. Crime went up; property values (never that high to start with) went down. But as the '70s went by, more and more young professionals—enamored of the great housing stock and the cheap real estate and, of course, the iconic name—had begun moving in, and now, fifteen years post–Summer of Love, the Haight was unrecognizable.

In 1970, the median property price in the neighborhood was $46,000. By 1980 it was $150,000. And as young, college-educated white people moved in, blue-collar workers and people of color were pushed out; the percentage of Blacks in the Haight dropped from 33 percent in 1970 to just 20 percent in 1980.

For the Baby Boomers who were planting roots in such neighborhoods across the country, the appeal was consistent. The lovely and varied architecture. The ability to walk places. The cosmopolitan feel of urban living. All of it was in direct contrast to what so many of them had grown up with. When a reporter asked a young man why he and his wife had chosen to buy a brownstone in the Hell's Kitchen section of New York rather than a house in the suburbs where they'd both grown up, he simply sighed. "The sameness," he said. "I just can't be part of the sameness again."

The great irony? The more that people like that couple moved into city neighborhoods around the country, the more all those neighborhoods were beginning to look and feel exactly the same.

To walk around gentrifying neighborhoods in New York, DC, Boston, San Francisco, or Philly was to begin to see many of the same things. Restored town houses and lofts, all with the same "original features" (brick walls, hardwood floors, high ceilings). Dessert shops. Video stores. Fitness clubs. Restaurants that served amazing brunches. Gourmet markets, all carrying twenty-three different kinds of mushrooms. Not all the old places were gone. You'd still see laundromats and pawnshops and the like, but every month it seemed like there were fewer and fewer of them. In Manhattan, the stretch of Columbus Avenue that developer Bob Quinlan had once tricked out-of-town flight attendants into moving to now featured an array of upscale retail tenants, including a chic children's boutique, an organic food shop that sold New York's best muffins, and a pricey toy store owned by TV anchor Tom Brokaw's wife, Meredith.

But it wasn't only the businesses that seemed the same; it was also the people: young, fit, well-educated, well-dressed, well-spoken. Kevin Starr, a historian and columnist for the *San Francisco Examiner*, wrote about the gentrification of Berkeley, which, like other places in close proximity to universities in the early 1980s, was developing into a very specific type of community, attracting not just academics, but other people who "take ideas seriously," as Starr put it—journalists, lawyers, physicians, businesspeople.

"Taste and scholarship are in evidence everywhere," Starr said. "In the selections in bookstores, in the decorative motifs of smaller restaurants, in home furnishings and other evidence of personal preference. Some of this has a 'boutique' feel to it; but much of it is possessed of natural vigor that arises out of youth, optimism, and some meditation upon the issues of culture and one's place in the world."

For a certain type of educated person it was, no doubt, an inviting atmosphere. Then again, if the original appeal of the Back to the City movement had been the rich mix of people and experiences one found in urban settings, that was less and less the case.

How well all these young professionals blended with any old-timers who remained in the neighborhood varied from person to person and place to place. In some cases, there was friction. One young professional who lived in Boston's Back Bay—an interior designer who'd purchased a distressed brownstone in 1975 for $27,000 and spent two years renovating it into a showplace—refused to let a reporter use his name as she wrote about the changes taking place in Boston. The last time his name had appeared in print, he explained—for a design spread on his home—he got a rock thrown through his window and threatening phone calls from his neighbors. Some of the people in the neighborhood, the man snorted, were "derelict, alcoholic men, waiters in tacky restaurants, and bag ladies." Their feelings for him—or people like him—weren't any warmer. "They're hotty totty, snooty. Mustn't fraternize with the lower classes," a woman who lived in a nearby $15-a-week boardinghouse said of the upscale interlopers. "They don't care about the neighborhood."

In other locales, at least some of the veterans were trying to be more flexible. Milton Levine, proprietor of a junk shop on Eighth Avenue in New York's gentrifying Chelsea section, confided that he was simply adapting to what the new crowd wanted. "It's all just starting," Levine said in 1982. "But with all the conversions and the loft people coming in, I feel the pressure." He was ditching the dime novels he'd always sold in the back of his store, he said, in favor of "first editions, sci fi—you know, the classy stuff." More generally, he was rebranding his merchandise from "junk" to "antiques." "I can cope with trying to clean up my act," he said. "I'll probably have as much fun selling $400 oak tables as I do with $40 Formica."

*   *   *

The growing concentration of young professionals in city neighborhoods wasn't just a signal of where an educated segment of the Baby Boom generation wanted to live; it was also emblematic of *how* they wanted to live. The trends, tastes, and values that had started bubbling up in the second half of the '70s—a focus on career success, an interest in fitness, a sophistication about food and fashion and products, a desire to be "professional" and live an "elevated" type of adulthood—were deepening and broadening. A specific type of cosmopolitan, young professional lifestyle was essentially being codified among a small group of people.

In many respects, the desire to live a certain way wasn't really surprising. After all, the members of this tribe had so much in common. Most of them were white, from middle-class backgrounds, graduates of good—in some cases, elite—colleges. All of them were part of the largest, most influential generation in American history. It was only natural that their attitudes, sensibilities, and ambitions would rub off on one another.

And it was only magnified by what was happening in the country. The economic anxiety that had first sparked the focus on career success was only getting deeper; if you didn't understand the stakes, you just needed to keep your eye on the unemployment rate, which, as 1982 dragged along, rose every month. Nothing was guaranteed, as it seemed to have been for their parents. On the contrary, no one else was looking out for you, which meant you shouldn't be embarrassed—in fact, it was practically a requirement—to look out for number one. What's more, the messages being sent from on high—from the White House, from Wall Street, from corporate corner offices—were increasingly in alignment: The country needed to get off its ass and start competing again.

*   *   *

By the early months of 1982, the fitness business that Jane Fonda launched in Beverly Hills a couple of years earlier had become a success far beyond what she could have imagined. Within months TV personalities like Barbara Walters and Merv Griffin were asking to come and film classes at her studio for their shows. Out-of-towners—not just from across the country, but from around the world—were calling up and asking if they could get in while they were in LA. Attendance at almost every class was at capacity.

Fonda was aware that she'd tapped into *something*, and she started to expand. She opened a second studio in Encino, then a third in San Francisco. And in 1981, she took the basic elements of the Workout and put them together in a book published by Simon & Schuster. *Jane Fonda's Workout Book* debuted that fall. By January it was in the top ten of the nonfiction bestseller list; by March it was number one.

Not long after the book was published, Fonda had been approached by a young guy named Stuart Karl, a blond-haired California surfer type with a sharp entrepreneurial streak. After dropping out of college in the mid-'70s, Karl became a waterbed salesman; then, sensing a need, he launched a trade magazine *about* the waterbed industry. It was successful enough that he began buying and launching other titles, including one called *Video Store* magazine, targeted to the owners of video rental stores, which were starting to pop up across the country as more and more people bought VCRs.

The more Karl learned about the home video industry, the more he saw yet another opportunity. Nearly all the videos that companies were producing were movies; hardly anyone was getting into informational, non-entertainment videos. So in 1980, he launched Karl Home Videos, with a goal of filling that niche. (Among his early efforts: an interview with John Lennon and a video first aid kit.)

Karl's wife, Deborah, had read *Jane Fonda's Workout Book*, and she told her husband it was a natural to be turned into a video. Karl finagled a meeting with Fonda, but she wasn't impressed. A video? Who'd watch it? She didn't even own a VCR. What's more, she'd won two Academy Awards. She couldn't step in front of a camera to do exercises.

But Karl kept coming back, and finally Fonda agreed. The video wouldn't take her long to shoot, she figured, and any income that was generated—she wasn't expecting much, but who knew?—could go right to Tom Hayden's political operation, CED. In the early months of 1982, Fonda spent a few days shooting the video, and that April, *Jane Fonda's Workout Video* began appearing in stores.

Fonda might have been unsure whether anyone would want to watch a workout video, but there was, by that point, no question about the fitness movement itself (as the growing sales of her book proved). New fitness clubs were continuing to open across the country—in Boston, no fewer than eight new clubs appeared between 1978 and 1982—and for young professionals, there was a deepening link between working out and professional success. A young Boston nightclub owner named Patrick Lyons, who belonged to two different clubs and lost sixty pounds over a couple of years, talked about how exercise kept his mind sharp and helped him make decisions. Meanwhile, at the Women's Athletic Club of Boston, the promotional materials described the facility as being for "socializing, exercising and making contacts." At least 75 percent of its members, the club's manager boasted, had not just bachelor's degrees, but graduate degrees. They were, in a word, achievers.

* * *

If Jane Fonda was tapping into young professionals' growing lust for fitness, a young Yale graduate named Richard Thalheimer was tapping into something else: their growing love of high-priced toys.

Thalheimer, thirty-four years old in 1982, was in many ways the perfect man for the job. He'd grown up in Arkansas in a family of merchants—the Thalheimers owned the largest department store chain in the state, one acquired by Dillard's in the late 1960s—and Thalheimer had shown an early knack for retail sales. As a kid he worked in the toy department of one of the family's stores, demonstrating the newest products to other wide-eyed kids, and by high school he was selling the *Encyclopaedia Britannica* door-to-door. It was invaluable experience—he learned how to get people's attention, listen to them, get them excited, and ultimately get them to buy.

Thalheimer finished high school in 1966 and went to Yale, where he not only continued selling encyclopedias, but—homing in on the burgeoning interests of his fellow Yalies—also sold embroidered T-shirts and yogurt machines. He was successful enough that, while still an undergrad, he was able to buy himself a Porsche. By the time Thalheimer was an upperclassman, Yale, like so many other elite campuses, was swept up in anti-war protests and conversations about the counterculture, but—save for attending a march or two—he largely stood apart from what was happening. "My activities selling somewhat put a difference of opinion between me and my fellow students," he'd say later, "because they were not into capitalism. They were into anti-war protests. But I was from the South. I was from a public high school. That was very different from the prep school environment that Yale had at the time."

After graduating from Yale, Thalheimer moved to San Francisco, where he earned a degree from University of California Hastings College of the

Law while creating a new company—Thalheimer Business Systems—that focused on selling copier products to merchants in San Francisco's financial district. Within a couple of years, he realized that going door-to-door to meet merchants individually was inefficient, and so he started taking out small ads in magazines and selling his products through mail order. He made one other shift, too: He changed the name of the business to something a little punchier, the Sharper Image.

In 1977, Thalheimer—still in love with toys, although now more focused on the grown-up kind—went to the annual Consumer Electronics Show in Las Vegas and came across a product that would change his life: a new-fangled digital watch that was waterproof, shock resistant, and absolutely perfect for the growing legions of runners in America (of whom Thalheimer was one). Seiko had created the market for such a product, but its was expensive: $300. In contrast, Thalheimer figured out he'd be able to sell the Realtime watch for $69.99.

But how to market it? He approached a fellow San Franciscan named Walt Stack, who was a legend in the local running community largely because he did a seventeen-mile run every day over the Golden Gate Bridge, waving to people and showing off his tattoos in the process. Stack tried out the watch and gave it his seal of approval, and Thalheimer created an ad for *Runner's World* magazine that said: "If it's good enough for a legend like Walt Stack, it's good enough for you." The ad, which cost $300, worked, and Thalheimer doubled down. Over the course of the next year he upped his ad budget to $1,000 per month, and by the end of the year he'd sold so many watches that he had profits of $300,000.

Now, four years later, Richard Thalheimer had transformed Sharper Image into a mini-mail-order empire with luxurious offices in San Francisco and sales on track to hit $60 million in 1982. The key? As he thought about what had made the Realtime watch such a hit, Thalheimer realized it wasn't a product that anyone, even a hard-core runner, necessarily *needed*. But for a certain type of customer—notably, one who had a little bit of money to spend and a big desire to spend it on himself—it sure was a cool thing to show off to your friends. And that, in essence, had become Richard Thalheimer's model as he expanded. He began seeking out more products that checked those boxes, including early versions of the cordless telephone and the radar detector. In 1979, he'd put them all into a catalog, and by 1981 that Sharper Image catalog was being sent out to millions of people across the country—all of whom had enough money to buy stuff they didn't need but couldn't resist.

In addition to the innate appeal of high-end toys, Thalheimer believed there were several other factors driving Sharper Image's growth. He knew who his customer was—male professionals between the ages of twenty-five and fifty with "upscale incomes," as he put it, of between $25,000 and $40,000. And he had a keen grasp on the kinds of things they were willing to spend their money on. This included more than two hundred electronics and toys that Sharper Image now carried, from a voice-activated light switch ($34) to a pillow shaped like a BMW ($42) to a crossbow with a telescopic sight ($298) to a Spanish-made suit of armor ($2,450). (Thalheimer liked the last one so much he proudly displayed it behind his desk in Sharper Image's San Francisco headquarters.)

Of course, maybe most importantly there was Thalheimer's timing. There were more and more people just like himself, young professionals with money in their pockets, and if once upon a time they'd talked about peace and love and ending the war, now a growing number of them were focused on something else: stuff that made them happy, stuff that made them look cool.

"It was a time when people were aspirational," Thalheimer said. "Young males, age thirty to forty, were really into this idea. It was almost an aspirational philosophy: He who has the most toys wins."

*   *   *

Richard Thalheimer was selling expensive toys to boys, but the gestalt he was tapping into was, in fact, broader than that. By 1982, among this tribe of young professionals that Thalheimer had targeted, what you owned was becoming a way of defining who you were.

"I think it was certainly a sign of, okay, I'm successful, and because

I'm successful and doing well, I deserve to have nice things," Kathy Kehoe would say of the attitude toward consumption taking hold. "I think we were very conscious of brands. You had to have certain shoes, and you had to have certain clothing. In New York, you had to shop at Bergdorf Goodman. So the brands were omnipresent."

Finding just the right brand—one of the markers of *quality*—was becoming important in every consumer category. Gucci briefcases. Coach bags. Cartier watches. Ferragamo shoes. The fine craftsmanship and materials were nice. But part of the appeal of owning any of them was that most people didn't.

All of it, of course, was so different from what a generation had bought and owned in the late '60s and '70s, when long hair and blue jeans had signaled what you stood for. But the world had changed, and in an era when *Dallas* was the most popular show on TV, a generation's goals had changed even more.

One of the people who influenced what was being worn was a man named John T. Molloy, a native New Yorker who had dubbed himself "America's first wardrobe engineer." Molloy had somehow crafted a career out of offering clothing advice to various corporations, including General Motors, U.S. Steel, and Merrill Lynch. In 1975, he shared his secrets in the bestselling book *Dress for Success*, followed a year later by an even bigger bestseller, *The Woman's Dress for Success Book*. Molloy was hardly the first person to observe that what you wore conveyed something about your status, but he brought to the table a unique twist. He didn't believe being well-dressed had anything to do with taste; it had to do with science. Over the course of nearly a decade he'd surveyed thousands of people on how they reacted to different looks and different types of clothing, and he used that research, not his own eye or sense of style, to make recommendations. And what that research told him was that the key to making it was to dress like someone who was "upper middle class"—*that* was the power spot in America.

As for how, exactly, to pull that off, part of it was absolutely avoiding things that made you look merely "middle class" or, God forbid, "lower middle class." The latter included anything polyester, as well as bright colors like yellow, green, orange, or pink. Instead, the focus should be on suits that were blue (which conveyed authority) or gray. Molloy was particularly doctrinaire when it came to advising the millions of women who were now trying to climb the corporate ladder. Their number one goal should be to avoid looking like someone who belonged in the secretarial pool, and so they needed to embrace what amounted to a uniform: a conservative skirted suit (preferably blue), paired with a light-colored blouse (preferably white). They should wear plain pumps, never boots, and accessorize with an executive gold pen and a leather attaché case.

Molloy's advice generated plenty of grumbling and outrage from critics—it was superficial, it was elitist, it was sexist, it was, from a fashion standpoint, just plain dull, they cried. But he was undeterred— "Class-conscious conformity is absolutely essential to…individual success," he wrote—and to look around law firms or executive suites or investment banks was to see that, knowingly or not, millions of fast-trackers were following his advice.

One of the brands that had benefited from what Molloy was selling, as well as from the country's embrace of conservatism more generally, was Brooks Brothers, the storied clothing chain that had long been a favorite of blue bloods everywhere (and that had been mentioned prominently in *The Official Preppy Handbook*). Though it was the oldest continually operating clothing business in America—its first store had opened in 1818—Brooks Brothers appeared, in many ways, to have been made for this particular moment. Preppiness was hot, and if what you wanted was well-made, conservative blue or gray suits paired with white shirts or blouses—none of it polyester—Brooks was the place to turn. The business, which had more than two dozen stores around the country, had seen its sales jump 34 percent between 1980 and 1981, and that year it had been the crucial asset in the sale of its parent company to Allied Stores Corporation for $230 million.

But the allure of "quality" was hardly limited to what you wore or carried with you to the office. You needed the right stuff in every part of your life, and quality brands were prospering. European cars were certainly one beneficiary. In the late '70s and early '80s, luxury foreign carmakers like Mercedes, BMW, and Volvo were beginning to see an uptick in sales in the US. The underwhelming quality of American cars was one factor, but so was the fact that European vehicles telegraphed performance and affluence. (It was surely no coincidence that all three of those European brands had also received a stamp of approval in *The Official Preppy Handbook*.)

BMW, in particular, was making significant inroads with young buyers. In the 1950s an American car importer named Max Hoffman had begun selling the cars in the US, and by the mid-1960s he was successful enough that he sold his other auto businesses to focus on BMW exclusively. A decade later, with sales still growing, BMW bought the North American business back from Hoffman and started emphasizing a marketing message that focus groups had suggested would resonate with a new generation of car buyers: performance and quality.

"From the beginning we looked at where the market was and where we thought it would go," a company exec would later say. "What we saw was a new generation of car buyers coming up that was interested in product and quality. Did we see the whole Baby Boom phenomenon? No. But we did pick up on attitudes and a strong interest in product name and image."

Whether it was fitness, fashion, cars, or food, the aspiring professionals living in large metro areas were increasingly aware that they had a different sensibility than the masses did. One evening in 1981, a young New York lawyer named Marissa Piesman was having dinner at her apartment with her friend Marilee Hartley, a writer and editor. The two women were neighbors in Manhattan's Chelsea neighborhood, and they found they enjoyed many of the same things. As they sipped white wine and ate the soft-shell crab that Piesman had cooked, Hartley blurted out an idea: The two of them should write a cookbook for young professionals just like themselves. It would be filled with recipes for dishes, like the soft-shell crab they were eating, that were sophisticated and delicious, but that were fast and easy to make for busy young people.

They started working on the book at night and on weekends, and a few months later came up with a name. "I had a friend from Seattle who drove cross-country to visit," Piesman said later. "In Chicago she said she heard this word—'Yuppie.'" It was exactly the audience Piesman and Hartley were trying to reach, and that became their working title: *The Yuppie Cookbook*.

*   *   *

With its massive size and comfortable upbringing, the Baby Boom generation had long been the object of Madison Avenue's affection. Its seventy-five million members had the ability to make or break not just individual products, but entire categories. And the ad industry had been innovative in trying to reach them. One of the most iconic campaigns aimed at Boomers was "the Pepsi Generation," which debuted in 1963 and was a mainstay of Pepsi's marketing for a couple of decades. What helped the approach stand out was that it didn't sell a product, per se—it sold a mindset. You didn't drink Pepsi because of the taste…you drank it because it said you were young, free, adventurous, and open to new things.

By the late 1970s and early 1980s, the focus on Boomer consumers had only deepened as they moved into adulthood and saw their needs— and incomes—increase. Companies began tailoring products to appeal to grown-up Boomers—Levi's, for instance, came out with a new style designed to fit bodies now slouching toward middle age.

But there was a growing recognition among marketers that not all Baby Boomers—not all members of the Pepsi Generation—were created equal when it came to purchasing power. Not only did college-educated young professionals have more disposable income than their less affluent peers, but they also—as the organizers of the conference on the Back to the City movement had noted in 1977—had influence. Their habits and tastes became, over time, the habits and tastes of the mainstream. "They are the biggest single factor in anyone's marketing calculation," ad exec Jerry Della Femina said of affluent Boomers in 1981. "They are the people who make or break products."

By 1982, the value of capturing the attention of those high-end Boomers began to show itself not only in specific marketing campaigns, but also in the strategies of certain media properties more broadly. In 1981, *Rolling Stone*, for nearly a decade and a half the bible of youth culture and rock and roll, had changed its look, morphing from a tabloid into a sleeker magazine. The strategy wasn't complicated: *Rolling Stone* wanted to make sure it was capturing more upscale readers and, by extension, more lucrative advertisers. (Said a media buyer at the time, talking about why he loved *Rolling Stone*'s transmogrification: "I'm very interested in the 28-year-old college graduates who are interested in politics and travel.")

Magazine publisher Condé Nast was working on a relaunch of *Vanity Fair*, the iconic magazine from the 1920s, for the same reason: It wanted to create a vehicle to reach educated, affluent young professionals that the ad world was increasingly hungry for. Editorially, the magazine would be built on first-rate writing and pictures from the world's top photographers, but the pitch to advertisers was different—it was all about luxury. "You see a rush of premium products," the magazine's publisher said. "It's the Gucci, the BMW, the Sevilles, the Mercedes that are selling. So, from a marketing point of view, *Vanity Fair* couldn't have better timing." Meanwhile, magazines that were already catering to that affluent audience—*Town & Country*, *Bon Appétit*, *Gourmet*—were busy adding readers and ad pages. To an extent they were all following the same strategy the *New York Times* had pioneered in the mid-1970s: Give high-end readers the information they want and need, and high-end advertisers are sure to follow.

By 1982, a version of that playbook had come to television as well. The previous year, RCA hired the much-heralded TV producer Grant Tinker to become CEO and chairman of its broadcast subsidiary, NBC. RCA was desperate. Despite NBC's rich legacy as a broadcaster, its performance had been a disaster through much of the mid- and late '70s, with the network routinely finishing behind ABC and CBS in both ratings and profits. In 1981, NBC showed earnings of just $48 million, less than a quarter of what each of the other two networks was bringing in.

In turning to Tinker, then fifty-five, NBC was gambling on a completely different approach. Smart, sophisticated, genial to a fault, he was best known at the time for two things: his nineteen-year-marriage to Mary Tyler Moore (which ended the same year he joined NBC), and overseeing the company they'd cofounded, MTM, the producer of critical and popular hits like *The Mary Tyler Moore Show*, *Rhoda*, *Lou Grant*, *Taxi*, and *The White Shadow*.

At MTM—and now, at NBC—Tinker's approach boiled down to one word: quality. In contrast to much of what was on television— sitcoms with broad jokes and canned laughter, predictable cop and private eye shows, good-ol'-boy hits like *The Dukes of Hazzard*, America's second-most-watched series in 1981—Tinker set out to build an NBC lineup known for class, sophistication, and wit.

One of the shows that he and his young, innovative head of programming, Brandon Tartikoff, commissioned was *Family Ties*, which had been pitched to them by a TV writer named Gary David Goldberg. Goldberg was a thirty-seven-year-old Brooklyn native whose life journey epitomized that of a certain segment of the Boomer generation. In the late '60s and early '70s, he and his future wife, Diana Meehan, spent more than a year hitchhiking around the country before settling in Berkeley and opening a day-care center. Within a few years they'd relocated to Southern California, where Goldberg broke into the TV business, writing scripts for an array of shows, from *M*A*S*H* and *The Bob Newhart Show* to *Lou Grant*.

The premise for *Family Ties* was both autobiographical and culturally timely: two former hippie parents (played by Meredith Baxter-Birney and Michael Gross) raise kids whose values and sensibilities owed more to Ronald Reagan than Haight-Ashbury. Son Alex (Michael J. Fox) was a dyed-in-the-wool Republican obsessed with business, while daughter Mallory (Justine Bateman) seemed mostly focused on shopping. The show was "totally autobiographical in concept," Goldberg later said. He and Diana had inspired the characters of the parents, while their "daughter

Shana was as smart as Alex but could shop with Mallory." *Family Ties* debuted in September 1982, airing on Wednesdays at 9:30 p.m.

By that point, Tinker had already struggled through a first year at NBC that couldn't have gone worse—the network's ratings had actually gone *down* and were, in fact, the lowest of any network in twenty-five years. But the following season Tinker's approach started to get traction, in part by targeting Thursday nights and putting together a strong lineup: *Fame*; a smart new sitcom called *Cheers*; *Taxi* (which had come over from ABC); and the rich, innovative cop show *Hill Street Blues*. In its promos and marketing, NBC consciously pushed the quality of the programming: "The best night of television on television."

When you looked at the national ratings in the 1982 season, NBC still seemed to be tanking; it remained in third place. But that wasn't Tinker's strategy. Where he wanted to win was in what the industry called "A" and "B" counties—mostly large metro areas with plenty of affluent professionals. Those were the people advertisers most wanted to reach, and Tinker started delivering them. NBC finished the 1982 season ranked first in New York and Chicago, a close second in Los Angeles and Philadelphia. "I subscribe to the city mouse, country mouse theory," Tinker said, "that city folks spot things, including good programming, first."

Advertisers were happy. "NBC certainly seems to be reaching more of the viewers we're interested in reaching," one ad executive said. "We have a hunch that they're not taking viewers away from *The Dukes of Hazzard* so much as bringing people to the TV universe who weren't here before."

The biggest sign that NBC was on to something? In the 1982 season, critically praised *Hill Street Blues* became the first prime-time drama ever to be sponsored by Mercedes. The overall ratings for the show were modest, but the luxury carmaker loved the sophisticated young city mice who were watching.

CHAPTER 9

The American Recession

O n the evening of October 13, 1982, with John Cougar Mellencamp's ode to the heartland, "Jack & Diane," at the top of the music charts and the St. Louis Cardinals ready to play the Milwaukee Brewers in Game 2 of the World Series, Ronald Reagan went on national television to deliver what his administration billed as a "nonpartisan" speech about the economy. Despite the focus on consumption that prevailed in certain places, there was general anxiety about the country's economic state, and the Reagan team knew it. The truth was, the economy was making them anxious, too.

From the beginning of his administration, Reagan—the former actor, the Great Communicator—and his advisers had paid attention to their messaging. Ever since television had become a dominant factor in American life in the 1950s, and even more so now that cable TV was starting to get traction, the presidency had increasingly become about communication, controlling the narrative, as the professionals put it, and so the Reagan team thought long and hard about their strategy. Even before they got into office, they'd more or less plotted out a high-level messaging plan for the first two years of Reagan's presidency. In Phase

One—roughly his first year in office—they'd focus on selling Reagan's economic plan, his combination of tax cuts, deregulation, and reductions in the growth of government spending. In Phase Two—January to August 1982—they'd pivot to "the New Federalism," their effort to scale back the federal government's influence and return power and programs to the states. In Phase Three—from September 1982 up through the midterm congressional elections that November—they'd focus on social issues like school prayer and abortion, which were so important to the Christian Evangelicals in their base. While nearly every incumbent president saw his party lose ground in the midterm elections, the Reagan camp believed they could buck history. Their mandate in 1980 had been so strong, and if their plan came together, they'd not only hold on to Republican control of the Senate, but at worst—*at worst*—lose just a few seats in the Democratic-controlled House. And if they got lucky, perhaps they could turn the House of Representatives Republican for the first time in more than thirty years.

Phase One of the strategy worked masterfully, as Reagan passed his economic plan—the biggest tax cut in US history—and saw his approval ratings among the American public climb into the 60s (sympathy about Reagan's shooting had helped). He was popular personally, and his policies had support. But in Reagan's second year, an uncertainty had crept into the minds of many Americans about the president, and for one simple reason: the economy.

Many people were truly in desperate straits. The high interest rates the Fed had maintained in order to bring down inflation had brought economic activity to a near standstill in some sectors, and the overall economy was in the worst shape since 1930. Unemployment was above 9 percent. Businesses were failing—twenty-five thousand would shutter in 1982, the most since the Great Depression. Home foreclosures were at their highest rate since 1952, and the country was seeing 430 bankruptcies every day. The overall state of things was so bad that a handful of economists had started using the term "depression," believing the country was either headed for one or even potentially in one already.

By September 1982 there were faint signs of progress—inflation had at last begun to moderate, and the Fed had started to bring down interest rates. But Reagan's approval was in the low 40s and still falling. The Reagan team now feared the worst: They could get wiped out in the midterm elections in November, and if that happened, Reagan's economic agenda—the entire conservative revolution Reagan hoped to lead—could be imperiled.

And so the decision was made to send Reagan on the road and have him campaign more aggressively for congressional candidates—and himself—than any president before him in a midterm election. The overall theme? "Stay the course." It was the message FDR had used two years into his own administration, with the country growing impatient about why his New Deal policies hadn't yet ended the Depression. As Reagan crisscrossed the country, he reminded people that he'd inherited a brutal economic situation; he hadn't caused it. He said Democrats didn't have any new ideas—they just wanted to go back to what hadn't worked before. Harkening back to Linda Taylor and long-ago tales of welfare abuse, Reagan even wondered aloud whether part of the reason unemployment was so high was because some people didn't *want* a job.

"Every time I find myself in a city on a weekend I'm away...I look in the Sunday paper at the help-wanted ads," he told a crowd in Ohio. "And you look at them in the great metropolitan centers, and you count as many as 65 pages of help-wanted ads. And you say, 'Wait a minute. You know, 9.8 percent unemployment, but here are employers. They're advertising for people, and they can't get the jobs filled.'"

Mostly, Reagan tried to emphasize the positive: Yes, there were dark clouds, but brighter skies were ahead. Unfortunately for him, in early October, news broke suggesting the opposite. The Bureau of Labor Statistics reported that the unemployment rate for September had climbed to 10.1 percent, the worst since 1940. Growing even more anxious, Reagan's team made the decision to try to bypass news reporters—who seemed to focus overwhelmingly on the bad news—and take their message directly to the American people with a national TV address.

Speaking from the Oval Office on October 13—CBS and ABC carried the speech, while NBC opted to stick with its World Series coverage—Reagan began by acknowledging the fear some people were feeling. He quoted letters and messages he'd received from Americans who were struggling, and he said he heard them. "Millions of other men and women like you stand for the values of hard work, thrift, commitment to family, and love of God that made this country so great and will make us great again," the president said. "And you deserve to know what we're doing in these very difficult times to bring your dream, the American dream, back to life again, after so many years of mistakes and neglect."

From there he doubled down on the direction he was leading the country—the real cause of America's problems was too much government, he again declared—and said that despite the harsh stories and harsh economic numbers, his plan was working. Inflation, Reagan reiterated, had been caused by decades of runaway government spending, but his economic plan had reversed that, and now inflation was falling. (Reagan's cause-and-effect wasn't necessarily true. The drop in inflation had come because of the Fed's tight-money policy. What's more, government spending hadn't gone down under Reagan; with his tax cuts, he'd simply stopped paying for some government spending, letting the budget deficit rise to a record level.)

Reagan continued, saying that most economic indicators—inflation, interest rates, the stock market—were now going in the right direction. The only marker that wasn't improving was unemployment. But that was understandable, because unemployment was always the last thing to turn around before an economic recovery.

Reagan finished the speech on a note of resolve and with his characteristic optimism: "Throughout our history, we Americans have proven again and again that no challenge is too big for a free, united people. Together, we can do it again. We can do it by slowly but surely working our way back to prosperity that will mean jobs for all who are willing to work, and fulfillment for all who still cherish the American dream. We can do it, my fellow Americans, by staying the course."

Was it enough to ease an anxious country? To stop a bloodletting in the midterms? On Election Day, the Democrats picked up twenty-five seats in the House—far more than the Reagan administration and the GOP had hoped for. The only silver lining for the Reagan camp was that the president's campaigning and televised speech had at least helped them hold on to control of the Senate.

The mixed result was, in many respects, fitting, given that the recession of 1981–82, now eighteen months old, wasn't impacting every American equally. In truth, how much you were affected by what was happening was dependent on who you were, where you lived, your level of education, and what you did for a living. If you happened to be one of those people who lived in a nice part of an educated, affluent "A" county, surrounded by connoisseurs of *Hill Street Blues*, you were likely doing all right. But if you lived in lots of other places in America—say, the heartland of Jack and Diane—your prospects were potentially a whole lot different.

*   *   *

Few places were feeling more pain than Youngstown, Ohio, where five years earlier "Black Monday" had kicked off a string of steel mill closures. In the fall of 1980, when then-candidate Reagan campaigned there, promising economic growth for everyone in America, Youngstown's unemployment rate was an already high 13 percent. By August 1982, it had climbed to a barely believable 21 percent, the worst in the entire country.

The impact of years of struggle—fifteen thousand steel industry jobs had now been lost—was felt every single day. People were lined up to sell their plasma for $10 a pint. The downtown department store, Higbee's, for so many years a hub of economic activity in Youngstown, had been forced to close. Meanwhile, business was brisk at the thrift store run by the Salvation Army, which also opened a soup kitchen and ran an addiction rehab facility. "We're seeing people in here who've been laid off after working all their lives," said the Salvation Army officer who ran the facility. As the holiday season approached, the mother of a nine-year-old girl in Youngstown said her daughter still believed in Santa Claus but would have to learn the truth that Christmas. The girl's father had been laid off seven months earlier, and he'd just undergone bypass surgery. Santa wouldn't be coming.

The Mahoning Valley had not sat idly by, hoping for some kind of savior, when the mills began closing. In fact, in the years after the factories shut down, an unlikely mix of labor and religious leaders—including Father Ed Stanton, who talked about the tripartite contract between a company, its employees, and the community—had come together to form an organization called the Ecumenical Coalition of the Mahoning Valley. Its purpose wasn't just to provide economic and spiritual support for the laid-off workers; the group put together a plan that would have allowed the community and the steelworkers to take over the closed mills and begin operating them as an employee-owned business.

But after a couple of years, the project was abandoned when the obstacles it faced were ultimately deemed too large to overcome. The federal government had backed off loan guarantees that were necessary for the deal's financing. The labor unions grew skeptical of the idea. And even though it could have saved thousands of jobs and bolstered the collapsing Mahoning Valley economy, the local chamber of commerce had come out against the plan, believing it bordered on socialism. By the fall of 1982, with little hope that anything was going to change in their community, thousands of people had simply left Youngstown and the Mahoning Valley altogether.

The troubles in the steel industry, which in the mid-1970s had employed a half million people in the US, were also beginning to devastate other communities in Ohio, as well as in Pennsylvania and the Midwest. The combination of foreign competition, outdated factories, and now an economic downturn decimated the industry completely. By the end of 1982, American steel was operating at just 35 percent of its capacity, and several hundred thousand jobs had been lost.

The news was similarly dark in communities around the Midwest and the South that depended on the US auto industry. The high interest rates and general economic anxiety that had followed the Fed's tightening of the money supply had driven car sales to their lowest point since 1960, and between the summer of 1981 and the fall of 1982, more than 185,000 autoworkers had been laid off. In Michigan, the unemployment rate was above 15 percent for nearly the entire year; in the city of Flint, it topped 20 percent.

If the industrial Midwest was seeing tremendous economic pain, it wasn't the only place. Farm foreclosures had reached levels not seen since the 1930s, devastating the center of the country. And in large cities across America, in neighborhoods that weren't being gentrified by college-educated knowledge workers, the pain was equally acute.

Chicago, for instance, despite the presence of Yuppies in the Loop and other prospering neighborhoods, was in the midst of a twenty-year economic downturn. Factories that had once provided jobs to many Black workers had closed, the positions shipped to the suburbs, the South, or overseas. White flight had sucked away many in the middle class. In struggling neighborhoods, Black and Latino residents were unable to get mortgages as banks either discriminated against them or closed down entirely. In Kenwood-Oakland, a mostly Black neighborhood on the South Side, many houses were abandoned or boarded up, and one-third of the lots were completely vacant. The unemployment rate was 30 percent, maybe higher—an accurate count was tough to come by. The average household income was $4,000 a year—a quarter of Chicago's average. When a reporter asked Robert Lucas, the director of Kenwood-Oakland's community organization, about the area's economic problems, Lucas looked at him and said, "We haven't got any economic problems here. You can't have economic problems if you don't have an economy."

The personal stories of hardship from across the country could be heartbreaking. In Detroit, a credit counselor reported that he was seeing twice as many clients each month in 1982 as he had in previous years. The typical person requiring help was three months behind on their mortgage and hundreds of dollars past due on other bills. The counselor talked of one client who'd come in, desperate to hold on to his house.

The good news was the client had just been called back to work at his auto industry job on an every-other-week basis. The bad news? All but $14 of what he'd make each week would have to go to covering his past-due mortgage. But he told the credit counselor he'd find a way to make it work, to cover everything else on fourteen bucks.

In Aliquippa, Pennsylvania, a forty-seven-year-old steel industry truck driver who'd lost his job choked up as he talked to an interviewer about his circumstances. Only a few years before, he and his family had lived a blessed, middle-class life, he said, with a nine-room house, two cars, and a boat. Since his unemployment benefits had run out, the man and his wife had lost their home and were living in government housing, receiving a welfare check of $126 every two weeks. "I've felt like killing myself," he confided. "I cry at night."

Not all of the pain was being caused by the worst economy in fifty years. Some it was the result of Reagan's budget policies. Academics looking at the cuts the Reagan administration had made to social programs concluded that the most devastating impact was on the poorest cohort in America—households headed by women with children. Though two-thirds of those women worked, many struggled to stay above the poverty line, and the reductions Reagan made in Aid to Families with Dependent Children only made the situation more difficult. According to research from the University of Chicago, a typical working welfare mother with two kids in New York would now see her income drop from 119 percent of the poverty line to 90 percent; a working welfare mother with two kids in Texas would see her income drop from 63 percent of the poverty line to 48 percent.

Would things turn around? There was always hope. Reagan remained upbeat that his policies would eventually spur reinvestment in America's industrial base and bring back middle-class, family-sustaining jobs. But some people had begun to wonder. In early 1982, U.S. Steel, which in 1979 had shut down its Ohio Works factory near Youngstown, announced it was going to demolish the mill completely. That April, hundreds of people showed up to watch the detonation. In a bit of unintended symbolism, the company set up a concessions tent serving food, but only for its executives and their spouses; steelworkers themselves were forced to stand behind a wall.

As the explosions went off and the mill's towers crashed to the ground, onlookers understood something intuitively. The older workers, who'd achieved middle-class lives because of the mills, knew it wouldn't be the same for the next generation. "The hurt don't come for us," an older worker said. "It comes for the young guys."

*   *   *

In many ways the recession of 1981–82 only exacerbated the small crack that had appeared in the economy in the 1970s. In the immediate post-war years, all boats—all income levels—had risen together in America. But people rising and falling in unison no longer seemed to be the case. Now, if you were a person who went to college, then your economic prospects were probably better than okay. But if your education stopped at high school? Well, that was a different story.

The disparity in how the downturn was impacting different parts of, and different people in, America was striking. While the unemployment rate in Youngstown topped 20 percent in 1982, in well-heeled Stamford, Connecticut—home of several corporations and scores of executive jobs—it was just 3.5 percent. While nationwide the blue-collar unemployment rate was 16 percent, the rate among white-collar workers was 5 percent. As for educational differences, the rate among people with a four-year college degree or higher was just 3 percent, compared to 8 percent for those with a twelfth-grade education and 12 percent for those with an eighth-grade education. Unfortunately, three in four Americans had never gone past high school.

What was particularly interesting was that the broader trend—that those who worked with information and ideas were generally doing fine, while those who made things with machines were often not—was playing out not just in different geographical regions, but within individual cities. Nowhere was that clearer than in New York City. Between

1980 and 1982, even as the national economy went into a tailspin, New York had actually seen a net gain of forty thousand jobs. The key word, though, was "net," since the statistic masked the fact that the city had actually lost thirty-five thousand jobs in manufacturing, transportation, and utilities while gaining seventy-five thousand jobs in services, finance, insurance, and construction.

The transformation also had a geographic dimension. Between 1978 and 1982, Manhattan had added 150,000 jobs, while the four more-working-class New York boroughs—Brooklyn, Queens, the Bronx, and Staten Island—had collectively added just six hundred jobs. "We have a Wall Street, Madison Avenue and Broadway recovery," the Bureau of Labor Statistics commissioner for New York said in mid-1982. "Job growth has been concentrated in Manhattan, and mainly from the lower tip of the island to 59th Street, and between Broadway and Lexington." He was clearly troubled by what was happening, asking, "Can you really have a healthy New York economy with such concentration [of jobs]?"

Another tell of what was happening was the surprisingly robust state, even as America's manufacturing sector was decimated, of the small but growing luxury retail market. In 1982 the Reagan tax cuts had kicked in in earnest, giving a small break to middle- and working-class Americans and a very large one—in many cases, upward of tens of thousands of dollars per year—to those near the top of the income scale. The hope of supply-siders was that wealthy people would save and invest the money, providing needed capital to American industry. It remained unclear whether that was happening, but what was obvious was that wealthier Americans were buying lots of stuff with their excess cash. While thousands of people in Ohio and Michigan were visiting soup kitchens, and two-thirds of all Americans reported feeling anxious about losing their home or business in the coming months, people who were well off were spending freely on things like travel, high-end real estate, jewelry, gourmet food, fine wine, and furs. "We've found the very wealthy are spending more money than ever before," a car importer in California said, noting that he kept selling out of Mercedes that cost $35,000 each.

The affluent market seemed to be thriving in places across the country where there were a growing number of high-income, two-career couples. In Houston, the retailer Frette was having no trouble selling silk sheets that went for $1,500 a set. In San Francisco, a store was selling plenty of imported baby strollers at $800 each. At gourmet food stores in Atlanta, DC, and the Bay Area, shoppers weren't batting an eye at high-priced products like gourmet chocolate, caviar, or sun-dried tomatoes that went for $15 per pound. In suburban Chicago, the buzzy restaurant Le Francais reported that business was brisk.

Some nights, the owner said, couples flew in from out of town just to have dinner.

* * *

For the young professionals who'd migrated to cities over the previous decade, living now in increasingly homogenized neighborhoods, the recession was a mixed bag. Some of them were among those at the top of the economic pyramid, for whom life was good. Others couldn't help but feel disappointed, even though they had good-paying jobs and knew their own economic situations were far better than those of the laid-off factory workers or foreclosed farmers or single working mothers.

In the summer of 1982, *New York* magazine ran a cover story titled "Downward Mobility," which chronicled the economic anxiety and frustration that at least some Baby Boomer professionals were experiencing. On the surface, many of them seemed to be living well—they'd embraced the young professional lifestyle of dining out several times per week, going to museums and shows, joining a health club, and taking Caribbean vacations. But, in truth, they weren't flourishing as much as it might have appeared, or at least as they might have wanted. Some were struggling to buy a house or rent an apartment. Others were disappointed that, given their relatively large salaries, they hadn't been able to afford a vacation home. Compared to the lives many of them had known as kids in the '50s, '60s, and early '70s, when even middle-class families had felt secure, they had a sense they were somehow falling behind.

"If anyone would have told us we'd be making $60,000 a year, I would have thought we'd be living like millionaires," said a young Manhattanite whose husband was a lawyer. "That's not true." Another New Yorker, a college professor who was married to an MBA holder, bemoaned making $70,000 a year as a couple but still not being able to afford a house.

"I wouldn't even want the kind of house we *can't* afford," the professor said. "My father sent us to private school and summer camp. We lived in a large, seven- or eight-room apartment and had a cottage in the country. I had everything I wanted, and we were hardly rich. I don't see how we'll ever be able to do the same for our kids." Not that they'd given up looking. As the magazine put it, they were typical of the couples "who spend their Sunday mornings at home, nestled up with a calculator, the *New York Times* real estate section, and smoked salmon from one of the shops near Columbia."

In a different time, perhaps, the response to that economic anxiety might have been different, more political. In an affluent country like America, shouldn't a professor and a business executive be able to afford a good house and provide a decent life for their kids? Shouldn't elected officials be able to figure that out?

But that wasn't the reaction. In response to the frustration they felt, young professionals had started to do two things. One, ironically, was to spend even more money, particularly on seeming luxuries like eating out and quick weekend getaways. If they couldn't afford the really big things they wanted, like a nice house, they'd comfort themselves with high-quality indulgences that were still affordable to them. "If you're stuck in an apartment because you can't afford a house, you might as well buy a Betamax or stereo," said sociologist Paul Blumberg, who'd written a book called *Inequality in an Age of Decline*. Another expert, economist Eliot Janeway, called the young professionals populating New York "well-dressed paupers."

But spending money on indulgences was just one strategy for dealing with economic frustration. The other was far simpler, and far more emblematic of how the world was beginning to shift: to redefine your life around making money. As kids, the Baby Boom generation had been told they could do whatever they wanted; they didn't have to make widgets just to earn a living; they should find careers that were fulfilling. The reality was turning out not to be so simple. Some of those Boomers who'd chosen spiritually rewarding but lower-paying jobs like teacher, social worker, or editor were now going back to school and making a detour into higher-paying professions.

"There are people who are happy to make $20,000 to $25,000 a year in publishing because they love books," one disgruntled young editor observed. "I don't happen to be one of them." He was now finishing up his MBA at NYU's business school.

CHAPTER 10

Bob Greene

The dichotomy was striking. Even as large parts of America struggled through the worst economic pain in half a century, in other places there was a growing emphasis on money, success, and status. And nowhere more so than the White House.

With tax reductions that heavily benefited the wealthy and cuts to social programs that hit hardest on the poor and working class, with his decision to fire the federal air traffic controllers, Ronald Reagan was constantly battling the perception that he was a "rich person's president"—someone who, deep down, cared only about the interests of his well-off Republican donors and the successful business executives who filled his administration. Reagan's advisers knew the image was harmful to him politically—it was one of the reasons, no doubt, that his poll numbers had been dropping for more than a year—and they were constantly trying to counteract it. In the fall of 1982, Reagan had campaigned at an array of fairs and ethnic festivals across the country, and whenever possible his communications team tried to set up photo ops of him working on his ranch in California. Their goal: to portray the president as a regular guy comfortable in boots and on a saddle, a man who loved beer and kielbasa.

Their challenge, alas, was that many of the other signals the administration sent telegraphed just the opposite. For instance, even as farm and house foreclosures around the country hit numbers not seen in decades, Nancy Reagan had spent $800,000 (all of it donated) on a stately renovation of the second and third floors of the White House, then another $200,000 (also donated) on new White House china. Critics called it offensive and tone-deaf, but the Reagans' defenders—and there were many of them—pushed back: The White House was home to the leader of the richest, most powerful nation on earth. It should not be a dump.

Then there was the social swirl around the First Couple. In great contrast to Jimmy and Rosalynn Carter—who reputedly frowned on hard liquor in the White House and were often embarrassed by Jimmy's beer-swilling, ne'er-do-well brother, Billy—the Reagans believed in going first-class when they entertained, and they entertained often. They hired consultant Letitia Baldrige, the social secretary who'd helped bring such glamour to the Kennedy White House. They put a premium on making White House social events feel exclusive and elite, making sure attendees radiated power and success, with a guest list heavy on deep-pocketed GOP donors and Hollywood stars like Frank Sinatra, Gregory Peck, and Jimmy Stewart. The women looked fabulous in designer gowns; the men looked dashing in tuxedos. The hottest ticket in town? An invitation to one of the Reagans' informal White House movie screenings, where a silver bowl filled with popcorn was placed before each guest. Getting yourself on the list immediately transmitted something about your status—you were in the club. One Sunday morning, on the set of ABC's *This Week with David Brinkley*, regular panelist George Will leaned over to Secretary of State Alexander Haig and said, "How'd you like the movie last night?"

When it came to the perception of whose side he was on, maybe most significant of all was Reagan's own rhetoric. In his speeches, when he talked about welfare hustlers like Linda Taylor, or wondered aloud why the unemployment rate was so high when there were so many want ads in the newspaper, or said that the country would have jobs "for all who are willing to work," it seemed to imply something about the people who were struggling—that maybe they didn't really *want* a job, that their plight was their own fault, that they were lazy or manipulative or somehow lacking. The between-the-lines message ignored the reality of the economic conditions in places like Youngstown or inner-city Chicago, where jobs had literally vanished, but it was a point that resonated with plenty of people. Reagan, meanwhile, only reinforced the notion that some Americans were looking for a handout with the stories he'd tell. He'd talk frequently about his own search for work as a young man in the Depression, noting that "in those days, of course, there weren't any provisions as there are now for unemployment insurance." The subtle suggestion? Don't complain. You don't know how good you have it.

Of course, if Reagan's words and tone implied that poor people might be lacking in character, they also implied the opposite: People who were financially successful were, almost by definition, virtuous. And not just virtuous, but in a period when the country was struggling economically, patriotic. Clearly, *they* weren't part of the problem.

And so it was that the cultural tone began to shift—having money, or pursuing money purely for the sake of it—was not in any way something to hide. Old-money families—the Preps—had generally kept quiet about their riches. *It's offensive, Muffy, to draw too much attention to one's finances.* But now, in the same way that young professionals were becoming more overt about their desire for career success and the toys and lifestyle that came along with it, in the same way that Jack Welch was obsessed with *winning*, money was becoming something to celebrate, even boast about.

One place you saw it was in New York's social scene. In the '60s and '70s, at least some of the high-society crowd who attended the city's most important charity balls had shown an interest in what was happening in the broader world—in avant-garde artists and, occasionally, radical activists. During great social change, being in the company of such people was its own signifier of status. But now, with Ronald Reagan in the White House and a growing focus on success, the status signifiers were shifting. The new era, and the new crowd, was defined by money, often big money, and by being seen at the right events.

One of the new stars of the social world was Susan Gutfreund, second wife of John Gutfreund, the man in charge at Salomon Brothers and part of the new wave of bosses on Wall Street. Susan was a classic climber, a woman who wasn't above telling tales about her background (she told people she'd been "raised in England," leaving out the fact that she was an Air Force brat whose family had bounced around). But she knew how to get herself noticed—and to spend money. On tours of the Manhattan duplex penthouse she and John lived in, she was known to point out the million-dollar living room rug as well as the double Jacuzzi and the refrigerator filled with champagne. Her rise said something about her, but also about the growing money and clout of Wall Street (though some would grumble that, as an investment banker, John Gutfreund merely *worked* for the people with real money). John himself, who'd been a private person in his first marriage, seemed thrown by the new environs his second wife had led him into, once saying of the high-society world: "The relationships seem to be mostly based on the idea that we're all affluent." Which, of course, was exactly correct.

Despite the struggles in the rust belt and the farm belt and the inner city, there actually seemed to be more affluent people than ever—or at least people who wanted to appear affluent. Experts who offered lessons in etiquette were seeing a decided uptick in business. In Palm Beach, the Breakers Hotel offered the first-ever Emily Post Summer Camp to teach upscale, old-school manners to young kids. Meanwhile, something of an arms race had started in the rarefied world of high-end interior designers. Joan Kron reported in a book she wrote on status and home decor that the going rate among the well-off to get a room redecorated by a top designer was now well into the six figures—two or three times what it had been just a few years earlier.

Pop culture was driving part of the shift as well. While Grant Tinker at NBC was trying to attract rich people by putting on shows that were "smart," at the other two networks executives were trying to attract the masses by putting on shows about rich people. Seeing the cultural juggernaut that *Dallas* had become for CBS, for instance, ABC fired back with *Dynasty*, an even more over-the-top nighttime soap about rich people behaving badly. Chronicling the misadventures of yet another oil family, the Carringtons, who lived in a forty-eight-room mansion in Denver, the show, debuting a week before Reagan's inauguration in 1981, had been slow to get traction. But following the introduction of Joan Collins's scheming Alexis in season 2, the American public was hooked, and at the end of the 1982–83 season, *Dynasty* was the fifth-most-watched show in the country—and heading to number one.

For the young professionals living in gentrifying neighborhoods, building their careers, and trying to define themselves as adults, the growing focus on wealth was impossible to ignore. Stuart Samuels, a documentary filmmaker who had helped Jerry Rubin launch his networking salons, would look back at the attitude shift and make an observation that seemed to sum up not only fictional characters like J. R. Ewing and Blake Carrington, but real-life people focused on success in cities across the country.

"The '80s were defined by winning and losing, in every area of your life," he said. "You didn't have to justify making money or getting ahead of anybody. It wasn't so much greed as entitlement."

*   *   *

In the spring of 1983, if you happened to be walking on a certain block of Fifty-Fourth Street in New York City around seven o'clock on any given Wednesday evening, you'd likely see a group of young people lined up outside the famed nightclub Studio 54. But the crowd wouldn't be dressed as they had been at the height of the disco phenomenon half a dozen years earlier. There'd be no tight pants and open-collared shirts; you'd see instead dark power suits and nice leather briefcases. John T. Molloy would have approved.

And if you poked your head inside the club? You wouldn't hear the pulsing *thump thump thump* of the *Saturday Night Fever* soundtrack; you'd hear classical music. The lights would be up, not down. And the people wouldn't be dancing; they'd be sipping white wine and Perrier and chatting amiably with all the other young professionals in the room. Overseeing all of it? Jerry Rubin.

The "networking salons" that Rubin had launched in his apartment in 1981 continued to grow in popularity, so much so that Rubin's neighbors, miffed that hundreds of people were coming into their building every week, started complaining. The crowds got so large that Rubin, who by early 1983 had reconciled with his wife, Mimi, decided to move the weekly salons to another venue. First was the Underground, a trendy downtown New York club. Then came the iconic Studio 54, now being run by Jerry and Mimi's friend Mark Fleischman (who'd bought the club after co-owners Steve Rubell and Ian Schrager had been sent to jail for tax evasion). It was an arrangement that made sense on both sides: The Rubins needed a large venue for their ever-more-in-demand post-work soirees, while Fleischman was hungry to have someone inside the club in the early evening hours, since things didn't really start rolling at Studio 54 until ten or eleven o'clock at night.

The salons—officially produced by what was now called Jerry Rubin Business Networking Salons, Inc.—had become Rubin's prime focus, and they were a successful venture. On Wednesday evenings from 5:00 p.m. to 10:00 p.m., Rubin hosted his regular open-to-the-public salons at Studio 54, each one being attended by more than a thousand people. Guests paid $8 and handed over a business card (further fattening Rubin's Rolodex) to get in the door. On Thursday evenings, Rubin hosted a second event for a more exclusive group he'd created called the 500 Club. Each club member paid $175 a year.

Keeping all this organized—and keeping the events full—was a formidable undertaking. While the gatherings were no longer being held in their home, the Rubins still used the apartment as an office, installing multiple phone lines for Jerry and Mimi and whatever extra help they could wrangle to reach out to people, trying to make sure just the right crowd showed up during any particular week.

Early on Stu Samuels, who'd spent much of the '60s and '70s deeply involved in the counterculture, looked at the events through an intellectual lens: The weekly gatherings would be a new form of much-needed communication, he thought, mixing people from different worlds—finance, fashion, media, law, you name it—in a way that would create powerful new interactions. But before long even he admitted it was something else—either a place to do deals (one attendee would boast to a reporter of getting a "five-figure finder's fee" for helping launch a telecom merger at a Rubin event), or, even more commonly, a place to get laid. "Within six months, it was a dating place," Samuels said.

Whether it was money or sex or status that was getting people to show up at his events, Jerry Rubin was convinced he had created exactly the right thing at exactly the right time. He began talking of expanding, creating signature Jerry Rubin networking events in all of America's major cities. "My company will be one of the most important service companies of the 1980s," he boasted that spring. "I expect to be located in thirty cities and be a multimillion-dollar business by 1985."

His continuing evolution had been fascinating. In 1980, when he'd publicly embraced capitalism and first gone to work for a Wall Street firm, Rubin had talked of helping to raise money for small "socially aware" companies that would help change the world. Free enterprise was merely a different means to the same end he'd always focused on: a better, fairer, more just society. But now, three years later, talk of changing the world seemed to have disappeared. His goal was success—and he seemed more prepared than ever to do what it took to get it.

Rubin had lost touch with many of the people he'd protested alongside in the '60s, but one person he'd stayed close to—though it wasn't always easy—was Abbie Hoffman. In 1974, Abbie had gone underground following his arrest on cocaine charges, getting plastic surgery and taking on a new identity, Barry Freed, as he evaded law enforcement. Still, he and Jerry had found ways to keep in touch. Mimi Rubin would later remember that when she and Jerry moved in together in 1977, one of the first things they did was fly to Florida to spend time with Abbie and his girlfriend, Josie Lawrenson; the couples would see each other often during that period.

In 1980, as Jerry was reinventing himself as a capitalist, Abbie made the decision to turn himself in to authorities, ultimately serving four months in prison. Upon his release, he returned to a life of public activism, now focusing mostly on the environment and U.S. involvement in Central America. One day, looking for support for one of his causes, Abbie asked Jerry and Mimi if he could have access to the giant database of names the two of them were amassing through their networking events.

Their answer was straightforward: no.

The list, thousands of names long, was their one real asset, they said, a thing they'd worked hard to create, the key to their success. They couldn't just give it away, even to a friend.

Abbie got furious and stormed off. Their friendship, he said, was over.

*   *   *

One evening in March 1983, Jerry welcomed a special guest to Studio 54: Bob Greene, the widely read syndicated newspaper columnist.

For the duo, it was something of a reunion. Greene's first big break in the newspaper business had come shortly after he graduated from Northwestern University and raised his hand to cover the Chicago 7 trial for the *Chicago Sun-Times*, where he worked part-time. Covering the trial, he not only got to watch Rubin, but got to talk with him numerous times.

Greene, based in Chicago, was thirty-six now, and in the intervening years he'd become one of America's most high-profile journalists, with a column that appeared in the *Chicago Tribune* and more than two hundred other newspapers across the country, a monthly spot in *Esquire* magazine, and more than twenty appearances a year on ABC's *Nightline* program. He blended Baby Boomer irreverence with an aw-shucks earnestness about small-town America that struck his critics as phony and cloying, but that his regular readers across the country loved.

Greene was visiting New York when he heard about the networking salons Rubin was holding, and it seemed to him to be a natural column. Like so many other people, Greene was intrigued by the unexpected turn Rubin's life and philosophy had taken.

At some point prior to going to Studio 54, Greene found himself having drinks at a bar on Columbus Avenue in New York with a group of colleagues, including Betsy West, the ABC producer whose mother had once paid for karate lessons when she first arrived in New York. West had moved to Chicago for several years and was now back in New York working at *Nightline*. As they were talking about Rubin, Greene would later remember that someone—possibly West—had cracked, "I hear that Rubin isn't going to be the head of the Yippies anymore. He wants to be head of the Yuppies."

Despite being from Chicago, Greene had never heard the term before, and he asked what a Yuppie was. "A young urban professional," he was told.

That night at the event, as Greene interviewed him, Rubin was in classic form, expounding on the changes happening within their generation and the importance of his latest venture, with Greene dutifully writing it all down.

"What we stress is business achievement and success," Rubin told him. "Our generation has become very business-oriented, very ambitious. When you're ambitious in the business world, your day does not end at 5 o'clock.

"I really haven't changed that much," he continued. "It's the generation that has changed. Now people are into business and success and accomplishment. But I'm still trying to bring people together. Someone has said that what I'm actually doing is sponsoring business be-ins."

Greene noted all the business cards that were collected at the door every Wednesday, and Rubin explained what he did with them. "I make an 'A' pile, a 'B' pile, a 'C' pile, and a 'D' pile," he said. "In the 'A' pile would be presidents of corporations; the piles put people in descending order of importance and success in the business world. When I'm finished, I go through the 'A' and 'B' piles again and choose people to be my co-hosts at a future party. I invite those people to invite their own friends. That assures me of keeping the quality of our guests high."

In the column he'd write about his evening with Rubin, Greene made reference to the funny line he'd heard from Betsy West—or someone—in the bar, writing: "While [Rubin] and Abbie Hoffman once led the Yippies—the Youth International Party—one social commentator has ventured that Rubin is now attempting to become the leader of the Yuppies—Young Urban Professionals."

Greene's column appeared in the *Chicago Tribune* on March 23, and in the two hundred papers that syndicated his column within a week or so after that. For many of the thousands and thousands of readers, it was, in all likelihood, the first time they'd heard the term "Yuppie," and its impact wasn't small.

"A funny thing happened once the column was syndicated around the country," Greene would say a couple of years later. "All of a sudden, Yuppie was part of the language. It was as if people had been grasping for a term to describe the huge population hump that had been the student generation in the late '60s and '70s—the generation that had become something else in the '80s. Yuppie was the word for it."

"Yuppie" was the word, although how many people around the country were searching for a term to describe an educated and ascendant group of Baby Boomers was harder to say. Sure, it was nice for Jerry Rubin that he might be dreaming of creating one of the most influential companies of the '80s, but at that moment many Americans were still anxious about making their mortgage payments and still uncertain about Ronald Reagan and his supply-side economics and still wondering when, if ever, the economy was going to get back to what it had been so many years ago.

PART III
1983–84

CHAPTER 11

Attack of the Young Professionals

The unemployment rate dropped.

On Friday, February 4, 1983, the Bureau of Labor Statistics in Washington, DC, released its monthly economic report. The big headline of the day: After hitting a rate of 10.8 percent—a post–Great Depression high—in December, unemployment in January fell to 10.4 percent, the first decline in more than a year. There were caveats, to be sure. January had been mild, allowing more construction projects to move forward than in a typical winter. What's more, the number of "discouraged" workers—people who'd grown so frustrated at the sorry state of the economy that they'd given up looking for work completely and were no longer counted as unemployed—had climbed by three hundred thousand people. All of which meant that the drop could be a mirage.

On the other hand, there were plenty of additional indicators that an economic recovery really might be taking hold. Inflation in January had fallen to an annualized rate of 3.7 percent, the lowest since January 1973, before the Arab oil embargo and a decade of steeply climbing prices. On top of that, consumer spending had grown for the fourth month in a row, and the stock market had been rising for five straight months, with investors feeling more bullish about the country's economic future.

For Ronald Reagan, all of this was, of course, welcome news. Only a week before the January unemployment numbers had been released, Reagan's approval rating had dropped to a new low—just 38 percent—closer than ever to the bottom-feeding spot Jimmy Carter had found himself in during the final year of his term. No one had to tell the Reagan camp what that had meant for Carter's reelection prospects.

Of course, if the slowly recovering economy was good news politically, it was also, in the minds of Reagan's economic advisers, potential vindication. The policies they'd staked the Reagan presidency on—the "supply-side" theory of substantial tax cuts for the wealthy—had never been tried before, and the truth was that even the most committed of them had never been 100 percent sure it would work. With nearly every major economic indicator now at least pointing in the right direction, perhaps, at last, they could breathe again.

On the campaign trail in the fall, as he'd rallied voters to support his policies and Republican congressional candidates, Reagan had urged people to keep their faith in the new path he'd charted for the country. On the stump in the final week before the election, the president actually started quoting Scripture to indicate what he believed was coming.

"There's a passage in Psalms that says, 'Weeping may endure for a night, but joy cometh in the morning.' America has endured a long, terrible night of economic hardship, but now we're seeing the first welcome burst of sunshine, the dawn of a new day for our country. America is entering a new season of hope, a genuine hope which springs from the vitality of the American spirit. We will put strong wings on weary hearts."

* * *

By the spring of 1983, four and a half years after she'd broken her foot and begun working out with Leni Cazden, Jane Fonda was the unquestioned queen of fitness in America. *Jane Fonda's Workout Book* had been at the top of the bestseller list for more than eighteen months, with no signs of slowing down, and the workout video that Stuart Karl had persuaded Fonda to make had turned into a phenomenon, becoming the first nontheatrical video to top the sales charts. It persuaded many people to buy their first VCR.

For Fonda, the success was gratifying. The more books and videos she sold, the more she got letters from women telling her how "doing Jane," as they put it, had transformed them. Sometimes it was physically—they'd lost weight or bounced back from an illness—but other times it was something deeper, a new confidence, deeper courage. Beyond that, the sales were more than accomplishing what Fonda had first set out to do with the workout business: raise money for Tom Hayden's political organization, CED. By 1983 the book and video were pulling in tens of thousands of dollars per month in royalties. Ironically, Hayden hated everything about the Workout. He saw it as an exercise in pure vanity, and the couple would later say it was the beginning of a strain in their marriage.

From a cultural standpoint, Fonda's book and video were transformative. Fitness, which in the '70s had been a niche pursuit—the domain of the "physical elite"—had become mainstream. Workout style—headbands, spandex, leg warmers—was suddenly ubiquitous.

Membership at fitness clubs was at an all-time high—and growing. Not every new member was necessarily a young professional, but it was the Boomers' involvement, their focus on fitness and health, that had powered the movement overall.

Typical of the scene in large cities were clubs like Boston's Back Bay Racquet Club, which had opened in 1979 and now boasted more than two thousand members. To walk through the club—a plush, mahogany-paneled place with ten racquetball courts and dozens of exercise machines—early in the morning or at the lunch hour or right after work was to come face-to-face with young professional Boston. There were technology professionals and architects and lawyers and surgeons and money managers. What linked them was not just a desire to be in shape, but a particular kind of striving. "It's another embodiment of the American way of getting ahead," the club's exercise physiologist would say. "They're not accumulating dollars in the office. They're trying to accumulate [weight] plates on a Nautilus machine."

Perhaps most significantly, the concept of the American body was changing. Among women, the new ideal owed much to Fonda and others leading the fitness revolution: lean and athletic, with well-toned arms. Among men the focus was on pure muscle. In 1982, Sylvester Stallone, already in good shape (and famous) from the first two Rocky movies, committed to an extraordinary training regimen that left him with a newly cut physique and a body fat percentage of just 2.6 percent. Stallone showed off his new look in two monster hits that year—*Rocky III*, which exceeded the commercial success of the first two installments of the franchise, and *First Blood*, in which Stallone played John Rambo, a Vietnam vet with PTSD who has to rely on the brutal skills he learned as a Green Beret in order to survive a manhunt. In addition to presenting Vietnam vets in a different light—near the end of the film, Rambo breaks down as he recounts how much he sacrificed in the war and how little recognized he and other vets were by the American public—it presented a new kind of movie hero. Until that final monologue, Rambo hardly talks, instead relying on his physical strength and fitness to save himself. His body spoke for him.

*   *   *

Bob Greene's column about Jerry Rubin and the Yuppies was published in newspapers around the country in the last week of March 1983. But Greene wasn't the only social observer who'd taken an interest in what was happening with a certain segment of the Baby Boom generation. The embrace of cities. The focus on money. The obsession with success in every aspect of their lives. In April, not long after Greene's column, the *New Yorker* published a cartoon by artist Roz Chast titled "Attack of the Young Professionals!"

"Watch in horror," the caption to the three-panel drawing said, "as they...turn your neighborhood into an overpriced, high-rent boutiqueland!...talk about their investments right in front of your eyes!...dress for success even while sleeping!" Chast had clearly been spending time on the Upper West Side.

In Philadelphia, as the broader economy showed increasing signs of life, a twenty-seven-year-old writer named Cathy Crimmins was noticing the evolution of her generation as well. One detail that kept popping out was the way people her age were starting to talk. Suddenly, phrases like "interface," "pencil you in," "bottom line," and "prioritize" were showing up in people's everyday conversations. All this business language, she noticed, was now being used for personal stuff. It was as if a new species had been born, she thought, one that couldn't distinguish between their jobs and the rest of their lives.

Crimmins had one foot inside and one foot outside this blossoming, hyper-professional world. Her own life had followed an arc typical of a certain segment of her generation. She'd grown up in suburban New Jersey in the late '50s and '60s before going to an all-women's liberal arts school, Douglass College. She'd missed the anti-war movement by a few years, but the countercultural vibes were still strong enough for her to not get too caught up in thinking about work or a career. She'd "taught macrame and hung around with potters," as she'd later put it, for a few years before enrolling in a graduate program in medieval literature at the University of Pennsylvania. It was there, as she was finishing her degree, that she smacked head-on into the real world. There were, she realized, maybe five jobs for medievalists in the country, and those jobs were filled. So off she went to earn a living, first writing copy for a seed catalog, then working for a corporate consulting firm.

The more she became immersed in the professional world, the more Crimmins noticed how her friends were changing, how the world was changing, how she herself was changing. People with whom she'd once smoked weed and drunk wine now seemed to be disciples of John T. Molloy and Jerry Rubin, wearing pin-striped suits and carrying slim briefcases and talking about building their "networks." When her friends called her, it wasn't to say hello—it was to see if she knew of any good job openings. And the ambition wasn't limited to their professional lives. Crimmins noticed her friends—and herself, to some degree—working hard to be chic and cosmopolitan when it came to the food they ate and the clothes they wore and how they decorated their homes. Everybody, a friend observed to her, suddenly seemed to be *aspiring.* They were *aspiring professionals.*

For Crimmins, the clearest sign that the world was changing came one day when she had lunch with her boss, and the woman, just a few years older than Crimmins, shared some tough news: The previous evening her husband had announced he was leaving her. Crimmins blanched. The news was obviously a blow. The woman and her husband had gotten married when they were still in college, and after graduation Crimmins's boss supported her husband while he got his MBA. The couple had then moved around the country as the young man climbed the corporate ladder, with Crimmins's boss dutifully finding whatever job she could in whatever city they happened to land in.

But the night before, over a candlelit dinner no less, her husband had told her he wanted out. He'd met another woman at work who was not just beautiful, but ambitious. "I've got a fast-track career," he said. "And now I need a faster-track relationship."

"It was the first time I heard the phrase 'fast-track,'" Crimmins would later recall. "And I realized something was happening."

Crimmins had done some freelance writing, and she decided she had an article idea on her hands. She came up with her own name for this new business-obsessed species—young aspiring professionals, "YAPs." She talked to an editor friend at a new alternative newspaper, the Philadelphia *City Paper*, who recognized the phenomenon she was talking about and gave her the green light to write the piece.

Crimmins's story—titled "The YAP Syndrome"—was published in *City Paper* in April 1983. On the cover, the paper ran a photo of the publisher's girlfriend posing in a business suit...and sneakers (of course). Meanwhile, Crimmins hilariously spelled out a phenomenon that was happening not only in Philadelphia, but in cities across the country. As she'd write:

"Typical YAPs are 25 to 40, well-educated, well-motivated, well-dressed and well-exercised. Fast-track YAPs eat out regularly, see a hair stylist at least every six weeks, make wise investments, and, with their disposable income, hire people to do things they don't have time for due to the demands of a hectic career."

Crimmins pinpointed some of the status details that differentiated the tastes and choices of this burgeoning group—from city townhomes to gourmet food stores to "better baby" flash cards for the YAP offspring she dubbed "Lap-YAPs." She touched on the YAPs' focus on work, as well as their obsession with high-priced clothing and appearance.

"The YAP Syndrome" touched a nerve, generating buzz around Philadelphia when it was published. One of the people who read the story was Larry Teacher, cofounder of a small, Philly-based book publisher called Running Press. The runaway success of *The Official Preppy Handbook* three years earlier had book publishers looking for ways they could put their own spin on the concept, and with YAPs, Teacher figured he had a winner. Crimmins began working on what amounted to a YAP version of the *Preppy Handbook*.

*   *   *

As it happened, at nearly the same time that Crimmins was writing about YAPs in Philadelphia and Roz Chast was mocking young professionals in the *New Yorker* and Bob Greene was hanging out with Jerry Rubin at Studio 54, a Berkeley-based writer named Alice Kahn was trying to make sense of the exact same phenomenon in the Bay Area.

Kahn, originally from Chicago, had arrived in Berkeley in the mid-1960s, where her boyfriend (and future husband) was enrolling in graduate school. It was a time of flower children and peace marches and drugs, and Kahn, in her mid-twenties, was thrilled to be in the middle of all of it. "I came to Berkeley in the era of Dustin Hoffman's *The Graduate*," she said later. "We wanted to get out of the rat race, out of the plastic, out of the boredom and mediocrity, just as Benjamin did." She taught English to high school kids, hoping to radicalize their young outlooks on the world. But after getting laid off, she turned to something she thought would be more useful to society: She became a nurse.

Still, in the back of her mind, Kahn always had a desire to write, and in the early 1980s, after a decade in nursing, she began contributing humorous essays to the alternative newspaper *East Bay Express* while still holding on to her day job in health care. By early 1983, Kahn, too, couldn't help but notice—and honestly, be annoyed by—the changes that were taking place among Baby Boomers, specifically the way their new lifestyles and tastes and money were transforming what had once been the capital of the counterculture. Just how much Berkeley and the Bay Area had changed was driven home to her when she saw the results of a survey the *East Bay Express* had done of its own readers. While the paper maintained a lefty, crunchy vibe, its readers, the survey responses indicated, were anything but. "Instead of a scraggly bunch of old hippies and die-hard lefties," Kahn recalled, "we have a bunch of mysteriously rich people who travel a lot, exercise a lot, work a little and are up to their ears in lifestyle."

Kahn decided it was a great topic for a piece, and that June *East Bay Express* published her satiric essay entitled "Yuppie!"

"Going beyond the usual chitchat about life, death and human sexuality," she wrote in the introduction to her piece, "I wish to address the problem experts are calling 'the plague of the baby boom generation.'

"I am not referring to herpes or AIDS, for only fundamentalists see meaning in these cruel diseases. I am speaking of the menace that is stalking our streets, threatening to ruin our neighborhoods, overtake our towns, and wreak havoc with the economy. Lock up your daughters, for this menace lurks on every corner. We who have survived the hippies, the yippies, and even the junkies wonder: will we survive the ultimate? I am speaking, of course, of the YUPs, the Young Urban Professionals. Like mutant rats, they multiply without even reproducing."

To illustrate what was happening, Kahn concocted a fictional Yuppie couple she named "Dirk" and "Bree." "Both are 32.2 years old," Kahn wrote. "They have combined education of 39.4 years, a combined weight of 265 pounds, and combined income before taxes of 77,500 dollars and 23 cents. This last bit of data is the key to appreciating the YUP's potential to wreak havoc. They're young, they're restless, and they gotta spend."

From there, Kahn, like Crimmins, went on to hilariously eviscerate nearly every aspect of the educated young professional lifestyle, from workout videos, espresso makers, bed-and-breakfasts, and an obsession with wine, to high-end kitchen stores, BMWs, antique furniture, and their focus on their careers. ("Each spent brief periods of time unemployed," Kahn wrote of Dirk and Bree. "During those times they made the following pact with the Great Spirit: get me a professional job and I'll do whatever they ask.")

She hit on the three "ences" she said seemed to guide all Yuppie behavior—"convenience," "indulgence," and "obedience"—as well as, importantly, the impact this new crowd and their upscale tastes were having on Berkeley and the surrounding area. "The YUP...suffers from severe agoraphilia," Kahn wrote, "love of the marketplace, adoration of Macy's, intercourse with boutiques. While it's a fun leisure time activity for the yuppies, we all pay a higher price for the way they squander their surplus income. And the demand for stores that service the needs of the YUPs radically alters our neighborhoods. We complain as we lose our local service shops, our hardware stores and shoe repair shops, our bourbony taverns for blurry-eyed old-timers. These essential services are replaced by sofabed emporiums, new wavish T-shirt zones, friendly neighborhood high technia, and food specialty shops of every description (with appropriate names of endearment)."

Like Crimmins's piece on YAPs, Kahn's essay set off a storm among those who read it. The *East Bay Express* was inundated with letters, including some from readers for whom the article hit a little too close to home. One of them got hold of the paper's readership survey and accused the publication, not inaccurately, of a certain level of hypocrisy, while another reader wrote, "How can you make fun of people who eat croissants?"

Kahn, too, got the attention of the book publishing world. Later in the summer, after her essay was reprinted in an LA-based alternative weekly, she received a call from someone working at a publisher on the East Coast. They loved her story and wanted Kahn to write what amounted to a Yuppie version of… *The Official Preppy Handbook*. Kahn got to work on an outline and sample chapter, only to get a call a few days later from her contact at the publisher: Editors in another division of the company had just commissioned their version of a Yuppie handbook. Kahn was out of luck. But the author of the competing book wasn't Cathy Crimmins with her send-up of YAPs. It was yet a third entry among the writers dying to mock pretentious young professionals.

* * *

When Marissa Piesman and Marilee Hartley had come up with the idea of a Yuppie-oriented cookbook a year or two earlier over soft-shell crab, there was one detail they overlooked: Neither of them was an authority on cooking. As the publishers and agents who rejected their proposal asked: Who, exactly, were *they* to write a cookbook?

But in 1983 Piesman and Hartley were introduced to two fellow New Yorkers, Connie Berman and Roseann Hirsch, who worked as book "packagers"—creating ideas for books, then working with both writers and publishers to get them into print. Berman and Hirsch were also skeptical of the cookbook idea, but they loved the notion of something focused on the young professionals they were seeing all over New York. Why not, they suggested, do a Yuppie version of… *The Official Preppy Handbook*?

Piesman and Hartley got to work, with plenty of inspiration and ideas from the book packagers, who, truth be told, were even closer to the world of Yuppies than they were. "They really had a huge thumbprint on this book," Piesman said later. "They were both wealthier than us; they were older than us. One of them lived on Park Avenue in a huge apartment. The other owned a way cool restaurant in the Village. And we were, like, schleppers."

Piesman was, to say the least, an unlikely Yuppie. She'd grown up in the Bronx, where her mother was a schoolteacher and her father was, literally, a Communist. "He didn't really believe in money, and he didn't believe in making money," she said. "We were a very anti-materialistic family."

But it was that upbringing, she thought, that later gave her the distance to see how things were changing. Piesman had gone to law school at Northeastern University in Boston before returning to New York to practice law, ultimately landing at the New York attorney general's office. While she wasn't making the kind of salary young associates were making at some of New York's most powerful law firms, she had moved up the economic ladder compared to her parents, and she was able to afford an apartment of her own in Chelsea.

By the summer of 1983, Piesman and Hartley had sold a proposal for what they were calling *The Yuppie Handbook*, and by the fall the two young authors—with their packagers—had turned in a manuscript, with publication set for January.

*   *   *

Cathy Crimmins's book *Y.A.P.: The Official Young Aspiring Professional's Fast-Track Handbook* came out first, arriving in bookstores in November. The cover featured an illustration of a young woman in a business suit, carrying a briefcase (stuffed with the *Wall Street Journal*) and wearing a pair of running shoes. Next to the drawing was a caption:

Q. Why did the YAP cross the road?
A. To get to the better side.

Inside, Crimmins followed the formula that had made *The Official Preppy Handbook* such a hit. The book was divided into multiple sections, each focused on a different area of YAP life, and each containing plenty of sidebars, quizzes, and fun photos and illustrations.

One section, titled "A Brief Scenario: The Birth, Education and Evolution of YAPS," gave a history of fictional YAPs "John" and "Susan"—and was more or less a history of the Baby Boom generation.

"Like most parents, Mom and Dad believed that their beloved John and Susan were gifted, intelligent, and certainly most likely to succeed," Crimmins wrote. "Neither parent had the slightest inkling that grown-up Boomers were going to face some tough job competition in the post-flower-child '80s. Yet as they were to find out, their positive reinforcement of overachievement had worked subliminally on John and Susan to prepare the little tykes for the dog-eat-dog world.

"Sure, Mom and Dad had been upset in the early 1970s, when adolescents Susie and Johnny railed against their parents' 'plastic' world. Johnny, who liked to smoke pot with friends and listen to Country Joe and the Fish, created his 'own major' in environmental sociology at Hampshire College and worked after graduation as a VISTA volunteer. Susie left to go 'cross-country' with her bearded boyfriend in a VW van.…But then John suddenly decided he wanted to go to law school. Three years after Susie moved to New York (with a BA in Modern Dance from Bennington), she was hired as a management trainee for Chase Manhattan Bank and began her MBA at NYU's evening division. Before they knew it, John and Susie had become YAPs."

Elsewhere, Crimmins delved into the various aspects of YAPness, including the YAP love of "original features" in their town houses; a list of YAP favorite foods (black beans, hummus, pesto, Perrier); the YAPs' love of gadgets and technology (including answering machines, call waiting, and beepers). She also identified various subspecies of YAPs: There was the SuperYAP ("Lines between this guy's worklife and homelife have blurred to the point that he no longer knows if he is making friends or networking, deciding on something or prioritizing"). The Hard-Edged, Dressed-for-Success Female YAP ("She usually comes with two sets of papers: an MBA from a prestigious institution, and a divorce decree from a foolish first marriage to a slow-track buffoon"). The Gay Male YAP ("Responsible for YAPifying more urban townhouses than all other types put together"). And the Minority YAP ("Bright, alienated; when speaking uses perfect diction, but peppers conversation with minority slang to emphasize his roots").

In the late fall, Crimmins began doing press to promote the book. Chatting with a reporter from the *Philadelphia Inquirer*, Crimmins explained the background of the book and laid out the various tenets of YAPness.

YAPs were Baby Boomers, she explained, which meant they came of age in the 1960s, when individuality was celebrated, and they didn't like to admit to the conformist tendencies of their parents. "They like to think that eating croissants, buying an historically certified building, or shopping in an old firehouse protects them from conformity," she cracked.

While YAPs engaged in various types of behavior, Crimmins said, ultimately it wasn't very complicated.

"All you really need to be a YAP is a good, healthy dose of overachiever's anxiety," she said. "Of course, owning a Cuisinart and seeing a good hair stylist doesn't hurt."

CHAPTER 12

Simon Says

As the economy began to revive, Michael Milken found himself sitting at the very center of a corporate finance revolution—both figuratively and literally. A year earlier, four years after he'd first moved Drexel's high-yield department to Southern California, Milken and his brother Lowell, a lawyer who was his chief confidant and top lieutenant in the business, purchased (along with several other investors) an office building at the corner of Wilshire Boulevard and Rodeo Drive in Beverly Hills. The building—which the Milken group leased back to Drexel, making Milken the landlord of the firm he worked for—could not have signaled success more clearly: an elegant, sleek structure at the most prominent intersection in one of the richest enclaves in all of America. But what was truly fascinating was the way Milken asked that the desks be arranged on the floor he occupied. In order to see the other Drexel traders at any given moment, and so they could all see him in case they needed a thumbs-up or thumbs-down on any given trade, the desks had been set up in a giant X, with Milken at the very center. He was not only the man in charge, but literally the man around whom everything in their world—the world of junk bonds—revolved.

By now, the zeitgeist shift Jerry Rubin had sensed three years earlier—that money and financial interest would capture people's passions in the '80s—was only intensifying. The various forces that had been bubbling up over the previous several years—looking out for number one, new energy around capitalism, new aggressiveness on Wall Street, Ronald Reagan's faith in free enterprise and free markets, young professionals' obsession with success—were coalescing into something bigger. And among the people creating this new moment, the thing that was being used to measure almost everything was financial success.

By such a yardstick, few people were doing better than the guy at the center of the X, Mike Milken. Traditionalists might still have viewed junk bonds with suspicion, but the market that Milken had almost single-handedly created had exploded in size, and Drexel's dominance of it had only grown. In 1983, the firm was responsible for $4.6 billion in new junk bond offerings, more than three times what they'd underwritten in 1982. Not only were there more deals than ever, but the deals themselves were getting larger and larger, as Milken helped companies, many of them new ventures, find financing they couldn't have gotten through traditional means like bank loans. More and more, too, Milken was helping businesses that were themselves shaking up the status quo. Among Milken's clients were John Malone, as he expanded his burgeoning cable TV empire; Bill McGowan, as he launched upstart long-distance phone carrier MCI; and Ted Turner, as he launched the world's first twenty-four-hour all-news channel, CNN. Milken was, in a very concrete way, helping to create a new America.

Such deals were making Milken, and those who worked with him, rich. "No one who has been with me for five years is worth less than $20 million," Milken told a trader he was trying to woo to Drexel. And money, of course, was why nearly all of them were there. As for Milken's motivation, that was harder to say. Money was clearly part of it—he was, by now, extraordinarily wealthy—but he and his family continued to live relatively modestly, in Encino. What seemed to drive him instead was the desire to upend the entire system. The more research he did, the more financing deals he put together, the more success he had, the more he was convinced that the traditional Wall Street way of doing things— of cozy relationships and credit rating agencies that looked more at a company's past than its future—was not just inefficient, it was elitist. Great ideas, great companies that could revitalize the economy and give people jobs, were never getting a chance, because they weren't part of the old boy network. His approach, in contrast, was democratizing. Did you have a good idea? Did you have the chops to pull it off? Did the numbers work? Then he'd help you raise money. It was the ultimate meritocracy.

The higher pursuit was perhaps what made him so obsessed. He not only got to the office each morning at four thirty, but had his head buried in stock tables and spreadsheets while driving there. He was so distracted that he kept getting into car accidents, finally asking an associate to pick him up in the morning and take him home at night. In the mornings, she'd remember, there was no conversation as Milken devoured the latest information. But at night, after the day's work was done, he'd be laughing and giggling.

Milken's reputation within the broader world of finance was only growing. His relationships with key investors and knowledge of the world—he kept in his head not only who purchased original-issue bonds, but to whom the bonds had subsequently been traded—made his power immense. "Michael *is* the market" became a common refrain when it came to junk bonds. There was no better proof of that than the limos that had begun to line up outside Milken's Beverly Hills office in the early morning hours, as CEOs, financiers, and other heavy hitters came to meet, and try to do a deal with, the driven thirty-seven-year-old. And the more power he gained, the more his ambition grew. One day, it was said, Milken sat in his office and told a colleague that his dream was to boost his net worth by a factor of ten, into the billions of dollars. Then, turning to the view of western Los Angeles outside his window, he asked: "What do you think it would cost to buy every building from here to the ocean?"

Milken's dominance had elevated Drexel's status among Wall Street firms—it now ranked sixth when it came to underwriting—but it wasn't the only Wall Street firm that was thriving. As 1983 progressed, there was a new, more manic energy on the Street. The bull market that had begun the previous August contributed to it, as did New York's status as the world's financial capital. But more than anything it was the new aggressiveness embraced by the investment banks. Once, firms had made most of their money in the rather genteel, relationship-driven business of underwriting new stock and bond offerings for corporations. Now, investment banks were increasingly using their own money to play the market, buying and selling securities with the sole goal of making a profit for themselves. And it was working. In 1983, nearly half the profits at leading Wall Street firms would come from trading.

The heightened influence of the traders coincided with—and contributed to—the new mindset taking hold within corporate America that prioritized stockholders above all else. The shift was having a clear impact on how CEOs at the largest companies made decisions: Under constant pressure from shareholders to show growth not just in the long term but quarter to quarter, corporations were avoiding investing in areas like new technology and new production techniques, whose payoffs came down the road; instead, they were looking for ways to make their balance sheets shine right away.

One method of doing that? Acquiring another company and shifting its revenues and profits to your own financial statement. Corporate mergers, which had happened in waves over the previous century, had started heating up again in the mid-1970s, and by the early 1980s—spurred on, in part, by the Reagan administration, which seemed uninterested in antitrust concerns—corporate America was in the midst of an M&A boom. In 1975 there had been fourteen corporate mergers or acquisitions that had a value in excess of $100 million. By 1983 there were ten that had a value in excess of $1 *billion*.

The deals were greeted with cheers on Wall Street—they drove up stock prices, and investment banks earned massive fees arranging and administering the transactions. But in embracing such "paper entrepreneurialism," as economist Robert Reich called it, CEOs were abandoning what had made the American economy strong over the decades: innovation and investing in American workers. "To invest in new products or processes ties up resources far too long for the tastes of industry," Reich wrote in *The Next American Frontier*, a book that appeared in 1983.

As an example of the downside of this approach, Reich cited RCA, which a few years earlier said it didn't have the $200 million it needed to further develop technology for videocassette recorders, and was therefore ceding the market to Japanese companies (which were investing heavily in VCRs). But that same year, Reich noted, RCA spent $1.2 billion to acquire a middling finance company so it could show investors profits immediately. "Paper entrepreneurialism," Reich argued, "has replaced product entrepreneurialism as the most dynamic and innovative occupation in the American economy."

Perhaps nothing would better illustrate the trend Reich was talking about—a greater focus on finance than on actually making things—than the extraordinary deal former US cabinet official William Simon pulled off in the summer of 1983. Eighteen months earlier, Simon, a successful Wall Street player who served as Treasury secretary under Presidents Nixon and Ford, put together a group of investors to purchase the greeting card company Gibson Greetings from RCA for $80 million. There was nothing particularly unusual about a group of investors buying a company, but what was unique was the way this deal was financed. Simon and his partners put up only $1 million in cash—borrowing the remaining $79 million. And the collateral they offered in exchange for the loans? Not their own assets, but Gibson Greetings itself. This approach, a leveraged buyout (LBO), wasn't invented by Simon, but it had never been used to finance such a large transaction.

From a financial standpoint, it would turn out to be an act of genius. Just a year and a half after buying Gibson Greetings, Simon and his group took the company public—at which point the market put its worth at a staggering $290 million, three and a half times what they'd paid for it. Simon's windfall was astounding: After risking just $330,000 of his own money, he now had cash and stock worth $66 million—a 20,000 percent return on his investment.

What was equally remarkable was that Simon and his partners hadn't changed the way the company was run in any significant way. The spike in value had come about mostly because of the failure of a couple of Gibson's competitors and the overall energy of Wall Street's bull market. Simon himself seemed to be of two minds about what had happened. On the one hand, he readily acknowledged that he and his partners had been in the right place at the right time. "We were just darn lucky," he said. On the other hand, looking at the stunning success of the LBO approach, he couldn't understand why more people and companies weren't doing it.

Simon's windfall was, not surprisingly, the talk of Wall Street. If someone could make $66 million in one deal, what did it say about you if you were making only $500,000 or a million bucks a year?

Just as important, Simon's success would only affirm the changing view of what a corporation was. No longer was a company seen as a group of people creating goods and services to be consumed by other people. It was, instead, simply a financial asset, one that could be bought, sold, traded, leveraged, broken apart, or disposed of, without too much thought about anything other than the bottom line.

*   *   *

One night in January 1983, GE chairman Jack Welch was out to dinner with his wife, Carolyn, at a restaurant called Gates not far from their home in Connecticut. As the couple chatted, Jack was trying to explain to Carolyn some of the nuances of his vision for GE, and he found himself grabbing the cocktail napkin his drink had been sitting on top of, taking out a pen, and starting to draw.

The speech Welch had given at the Pierre Hotel in New York some thirteen months earlier—the one that had left the stock analysts scratching their heads—was not the only time Welch had puzzled people about where he wanted to take GE. In fact, even as he'd set off on making major changes, communicating his vision had been a struggle throughout his nearly two years at the helm. The concept of being number one or number two in any business GE was in was simple enough, but how exactly did that impact things on a day-to-day basis? What's more, Welch was always offering exceptions to the rule. In some lines of business—consumer appliances, for instance—being number one or number two might not even matter, given how competitive that market was and how low the profit margins were. In other cases—financial services, as an example—you didn't even have to be number one or number two, because of the trillions of dollars being spent.

As Welch tried to explain all this to Carolyn, he drew three circles on the back of the napkin, each representing one of the major categories of GE's business: core manufacturing, technology, and services. Within each circle, he then filled in the actual industries GE was in. Inside core manufacturing, for instance, he put lighting, major appliances, motors, turbines, and transportation equipment. He did the same for the other two circles.

The businesses inside the circles, he explained to Carolyn, were where he wanted the company's focus to be. Any business that fell outside one of those three circles—and there were many of them—represented marginal performers or low-growth markets. Those entities, Welch said, the company would either "fix, sell, or close."

Welch liked what he'd drawn—it was the closest thing yet to capturing his vision—and over the next few weeks he started to share it with his underlings at the company. The cocktail napkin—or at least a version of it—became the guide for explaining where GE was going.

When he took over as chairman and CEO, Welch readily acknowledged there was nothing deeply wrong at the company. It was an iconic American corporation, the tenth-largest in the world by market size, ninth in terms of annual profits. What's more, nearly all of its individual lines of business were profitable. But Welch was adamant that simply looking at where GE stood right now was a mistake. The company needed to be looking at where the world was headed and where the winners—and losers—would be in that new world. His GE would be the home of only winners.

By the middle of 1983, it was crystal clear just how aggressive Welch was willing to be in his pursuit of that new, more modern, more "competitive" General Electric—and how devastating that would be to tens of thousands of GE workers and the communities in which they lived.

In towns and cities around the country where the company had operated for decades—in some cases since the days when Thomas Edison himself was alive—Welch was overseeing the elimination of a staggering number of positions, through either jobs being sent overseas or business units being sold or operations just shutting down. GE's air-conditioning business, for instance, which was profitable but whose 10 percent market share paled in comparison to other GE appliance businesses, was sold to Trane Company, impacting the twenty-three hundred people who worked in that division in Louisville, Kentucky.

In Erie, Pennsylvania, the company closed a foundry that had made metal casings for seventy-two years, while shipping nearly four hundred jobs in its diesel engine division there to a nonunion shop in Grove City, Pennsylvania.

In Fort Edward, New York, a town of fewer than ten thousand people on the banks of the Hudson River, GE cut more than nine hundred jobs, a third of them going to Juárez, Mexico, where workers were making 78 cents an hour.

Even GE's spiritual home of Schenectady, New York, wasn't spared: Five thousand jobs there were eliminated, and union ranks were only half of what they'd been a decade earlier. All told, between 1981 and 1984, Jack Welch would cut seventy thousand of General Electric's four hundred thousand jobs.

What was ironic, given how competitive Welch was as a person, was how often he chose *not* to compete in a particular business, how rarely he seemed to choose the "fix" option when the choices boiled down to fix, sell, or close. One example was GE's consumer housewares division, the unit that manufactured and sold toasters, fans, clocks, and dozens of other products. It was a foundational part of the company, not only producing profits, but putting GE's name into millions of American households. While the division remained the market leader, by 1983 its earnings had slipped thanks to sharper competition from more technologically advanced Japanese companies. That year, GE formed a task force to figure out how the unit could innovate and better compete with the Japanese. The head of the group was proud of the progress they were making, but one day in November, while he was in the middle of a presentation, the task force leader got a call. He excused himself to take it, then came back a few minutes later and ended the meeting. Welch had just sold the entire division to Black & Decker.

Not surprisingly, the deep cuts rankled many within GE. In 1982, Welch started hosting roundtable conversations with employees every other week, getting together for coffee with about twenty-five of them at a time and fielding their questions about what was happening. One of the most common queries was why, even as Welch was cutting tens of thousands of blue-collar jobs, he was simultaneously spending vast sums on new amenities at GE's corporate headquarters in Connecticut—including a million dollars on a new fitness center and more than $25 million on a new guesthouse and retreat center. His response? "A headquarters building is filled with specialists who make nothing and sell nothing," he said, which meant they didn't usually feel the natural sort of camaraderie that people who worked together in a plant did. The fitness center was a place for them to bond. As for the guesthouse and retreat center? It was meant to convey—to guests, to executives, to potential high-level hires—that GE was a "world-class company." Indeed, Welch was insistent that GE had to have the "best people in the world" and pay them that way—in its *executive* positions.

Another issue workers raised was a quality that had long been crucial to GE's culture: loyalty. GE's history was replete with people who'd joined the company right after they'd finished school, spent four decades working there, then continued to stay connected to the company even in retirement. For much of its hundred-plus years, General Electric had considered its employees its greatest asset. When Welch's predecessor, Reg Jones, had spoken of the "spirit of GE," he included loyalty as central to it.

But now, in a new era where the only thing that mattered was the verdict of the market, Welch had an entirely different view: He believed the idea of loyalty within a business setting was ridiculous, a kind of sentimentality that GE, or any company, couldn't afford. If there was once an implicit agreement between a company and its employees that it would provide lifetime employment, that contract was now void, he said. As for any tripartite understanding among a company, its workers, and the community? Over. The only thing that mattered was whether the business was winning in the marketplace. If it was, then workers who were willing to compete could hold on to their jobs. And if it wasn't? Then the jobs disappeared. None of this was personal, Welch tried to emphasize, telling GE's workers (and perhaps himself) over and over again: "We didn't fire the people. We fired the positions, and the people had to go."

For the actual human beings who once occupied those positions—not to mention the communities they were part of—Welch's explanation was, of course, a distinction without a difference. They were all suddenly faced with questions about how they'd move forward, and bewildered that all the years they'd spent working for GE had seemingly meant nothing.

In 1981, GE announced it was shutting down a plant in Ontario, California, not far from Los Angeles, which for decades produced metal steam irons. The iron had actually been invented in Ontario in the early 1900s by an entrepreneur named Earl Richardson, who after a few years had sold the rights to the product, along with the name of his company, Hotpoint, to General Electric. GE wasn't losing money at the plant, and it wasn't getting out of the iron business. It was, it said, simply transitioning to making plastic irons, and the Ontario plant wasn't set up for that, and so one thousand people—sorry, one thousand positions—were being let go.

Couldn't the Ontario factory simply be refitted to make plastic irons? Perhaps, but that didn't address the issue of labor cost: The plastic irons were being made at GE plants in Singapore, Brazil, and Mexico, where workers' wages were a fraction of what they were in California. As Mary McDaniel, the president of the United Electrical Workers local, said simply, "They can make a bigger profit out of the country than here."

On the day the Ontario plant closed, a handful of workers held a pot-luck lunch on a stretch of grass near the factory. The group dug a hole, buried one of the final irons they'd made, and put up what amounted to a grave marker: "Here lies Ontario's metal iron," it read. "Born 1902, Murdered 1982."

*　　*　　*

The moves that Welch was making—indeed, his entire approach and philosophy—weren't going unnoticed in corporate America. If Ronald Reagan's firing of the air traffic controllers had been a quiet signal to workers about who now had power, Welch's moves were a cannon blast. Or maybe, as one observer had noted, that wasn't quite right. Cannonballs took out buildings and people. Welch was more like a neutron bomb—taking out only the latter while leaving the former untouched. Thus was born a nickname, one Welch couldn't stand: "Neutron Jack."

In 1984, *Fortune* magazine would put Welch first on its list of the "toughest bosses in America." He'd received twice as many nominations as any other CEO. "Managers at GE used to hide out-of-favor employees from Welch's gunsights so they could keep their job," the magazine said. "According to former employees, Welch conducts meetings so aggressively that people tremble."

Welch complained that the barbs hurt, but ultimately, he wouldn't be swayed by any of them. Why should he be? Under the new rules that were in play, he was doing precisely what was expected; he was making money for the people he believed he did owe some loyalty to: stockholders. Between 1981 and 1983, as tens of thousands of longtime GE employees got pink slips, GE shareholders saw the value of their stock nearly double.

CHAPTER 13

Hart

What ultimately tips something into becoming a phenomenon isn't always easy to say—and the ascendance of Yuppieness to the highest echelons of the cultural conversation was no exception. Part of the reason lay in the sharp observations of people like Roz Chast, Cathy Crimmins, Alice Kahn, Marissa Piesman, and Marilee Hartley. They'd exaggerated various traits for comic effect, but what they'd noticed about the habits, tastes, and values of a particular cohort of Baby Boomers rang true. The Yuppie phenomenon was also a case study in the copycat nature of media. When one outlet latched on to a particular trend, scores of others did the same—which only served to reinforce it. Finally, there was timing. The Boomers who met the definition of being Yuppies were a small minority, but their ambition and materialism and focus on self-fulfillment and success perfectly represented the rising cultural forces at that particular moment.

Marissa Piesman and Marilee Hartley's *Yuppie Handbook* was officially published in early January 1984, a couple of months after Cathy Crimmins's book on YAPs. In concept and execution, the two books were remarkably similar (as both were similar in format and tone to their inspiration, *The Official Preppy Handbook*). Like Crimmins, Piesman and Hartley had divided their book—which showed a quintessential young professional couple on the cover, he wearing a gray pin-striped suit and L.L.Bean hunting boots; she in a blue Ralph Lauren suit and running shoes—into chapters about various aspects of Yuppieness, from Yuppie cars and kitchen items to Yuppie dogs and movies.

As for what, precisely, a Yuppie was, Piesman and Hartley offered their definition at the beginning of the book:

> Yuppie or Yuppy ('yup-e) pl. Yuppies: (hot, new name for Young Urban Professional): a person of either sex who meets the following criteria: 1) resides in or near one of the major cities; 2) claims to be between the ages of 25 and 45; 3) lives on aspirations of glory, prestige, recognition, fame, social status, power, money or any and all combinations of the above; 4) anyone who brunches on the weekend or works out after work. The term crosses ethnic, sexual, geographic—even class—boundaries. Adj.: Yuppiesque, Yuppie-like, Yuppish, a la Yuppie. See also *fast trackers, baby boomers.*

Where *The Yuppie Handbook* and *Y.A.P.* differed, mostly, was in the attention that was paid to them. *Y.A.P.* had gotten a moderate amount of press upon its release two months earlier, but—likely because it came from a bigger publisher, Pocket Books, a division of major publishing house Simon & Schuster—*The Yuppie Handbook* hit the publicity jackpot right away.

In the beginning of January, two of America's most widely read magazines, *Time* and *People*, ran pieces on the Yuppie phenomenon, centering on *The Yuppie Handbook* (and saying not a word about YAPs). Just like that, a term that had originated in the Midwest some half a dozen years earlier—and that a growing number of people had been reading about over the previous months—got massive exposure.

"Who are all these upwardly mobile folks with designer water, running shoes, pickled parquet floors, and $450,000 condos in semislum buildings?" *Time*'s story began. "Yuppies, of course, and the one true guide to their carefully hectic lifestyle is *The Yuppie Handbook*. Tongue firmly in chic, authors Marissa Piesman and Marilee Hartley tirelessly chronicle the ways of the Yuppie, along with its lesser-known subspecies the Guppie (Gay Urban Professional) and Puppie (Pregnant Urban Professional)."

The piece went on to give a breezy overview of both Yuppieness and Piesman and Hartley's book. It noted Yups' "twin goals of making piles of money and achieving perfection through physical fitness and therapy"; their obsession with esoteric gourmet foods; the "Yuppification" of neighborhoods in cities across the country; and their fondness for Woody Allen, *Casablanca*, and *Chariots of Fire*. "Long the darling of the advertising world, these fast-trackers are now united under a sassy name and invited to smile along at their own trendiness."

The *Time* and *People* pieces exposed millions of magazine readers to the basic concept of Yuppieness. What's more, they put Yuppieness on the radar of hundreds of other journalists around the country, many of whom, of course, were well-educated Baby Boomers with Yuppie tendencies themselves. Whether they were laughing, cringing, or simply nodding along, it was little wonder that dozens of them soon began writing their own stories about the rise of the Yups.

Over the course of the next several weeks, stories about Yuppieness (and *The Yuppie Handbook*) began popping up all across America—the journalistic equivalent of a hit single climbing up the charts. One of the first was in the *Boston Globe*, which in mid-January did a long feature story headlined "Good Morning, Hub—What's Yup?" The piece cataloged the various things that made a Yuppie a Yuppie while also touching on well-educated Boston's prominent place in the Yuppie universe. As an example, it cited a class being offered by the Cambridge Adult Education Center that simultaneously hit the Yuppie passions of tech and exotic travel. The course, called "Tropical Computer," convened in the Virgin Islands and consisted of mornings spent learning about word-processing skills and afternoons relaxing on a sun-kissed beach.

Baltimore. Memphis. Muncie. Tacoma. Grand Junction, Colorado. As January and February passed, newspapers across the country ran their own pieces on what was happening with this well-educated segment of Baby Boomers. Some of the stories also mentioned Cathy Crimmins and her term "YAP." Others framed Yuppieness as a successor to Preppiness. Still others localized the trend, by either interviewing local young professionals, or, even better, creating a new acronym that incorporated their own city's name. In upstate New York, for instance, the *Rochester Democrat and Chronicle* coined "Yurp"—young urban Rochester professional—and highlighted all the places around town Yurps could be observed.

Many of the initial stories hewed closely to what was in *The Yuppie Handbook*, but a few attempted to go a little deeper. In Memphis, a columnist and critic named Donald La Badie wrote about his encounters with Yuppies on a recent excursion to New York. La Badie talked about Yuppie sightings at a Tom Stoppard play on Broadway and a New Year's Eve dinner party in Manhattan, where La Badie overheard a young stockbroker and a young lawyer discussing a recent de Kooning exhibit. Their focus wasn't on the artist's paintings, but on how the show itself would raise the price that de Kooning's work would now fetch.

La Badie also caught a glimpse of Yuppies' obsession with food at a restaurant in Greenwich Village called Centanni. Until recently, the place had been a well-kept secret, beloved by regulars who formed a tight bond with the staff. But after a recent rave review in the *Times*, an entirely new, more well-heeled crowd had begun flocking in. One might have thought that was good news, but La Badie noticed one of the restaurant's veteran waiters looking glum, and he asked him what was wrong.

"I lost all my friends," the waiter said. "I get bigger tips, but these people—they look through me like I wasn't there. It's no fun no more."

*   *   *

For all the hype Yuppieness was receiving in the early months of 1984, it could have been yet another here-today-gone-tomorrow media fad—the sociological equivalent of the Hula-Hoop or Pet Rock or so many other ephemeral, Boomer-centered phenomena. But then came the 1984 presidential campaign, and everything changed.

Throughout much of 1982 and 1983, Democrats had been optimistic about their chances of regaining the White House. Ronald Reagan's approval ratings were low, the Democrats had done well in the midterm elections, and the misery of the recession was palpable in many places across the country. The '84 race would, Democrats believed, be a referendum on Reaganomics, and if that were the case, the American people might be glad to reverse course and put a Democrat back in charge.

Going into the primaries, Jimmy Carter's vice president, Walter Mondale, was the clear front-runner to win the nomination; he had a double-digit lead over other Democrats in national polls and a string of endorsements from unions and party insiders. Mondale not only had name recognition, but was a classic New Deal liberal with a strong record when it came to labor, civil rights, social programs, and other issues that had been central to Democratic orthodoxy for generations. That said, a host of other candidates were willing to take him on: Senators John Glenn of Ohio, Alan Cranston of California, and Fritz Hollings of Florida; civil rights leader Jesse Jackson; former Democratic presidential nominee George McGovern; and former Florida governor Reubin Askew.

And then there was Gary Hart. In December 1982, Hart, the forty-six-year-old senior senator from Colorado, made a trip to New Hampshire for the first of what would become hundreds of meetings with activists, insiders, and Democratic party honchos. Officially, Hart was merely exploring a run for president in 1984; in truth, his mind was mostly made up to get in.

On one level, Hart's candidacy seemed like folly. His name recognition was nearly nonexistent outside of Colorado; he wasn't tapped into any sort of national network of donors or supporters; he was only two years into his second Senate term.

But Hart believed the time was right for a campaign like the one he wanted to run and for a candidate like himself. Support for Mondale

175

might be broad, Hart believed, but it was thin—few people seemed passionate about putting Fritz Mondale in the White House. Even more significantly, there was a history, at least in recent years, of unexpected outsiders becoming the Democratic nominee. George McGovern—whose first presidential campaign Hart, not coincidentally, had managed—came from nowhere to win the nomination in 1972; and four years later Jimmy Carter, despite being a little-known governor from Georgia, won not only the Democratic nomination but the presidency. Why couldn't Hart do the same?

Also on Hart's side was the fact that he presumably knew how to connect with voters in rural places like Iowa and New Hampshire, the two starting points of the primary season: He'd grown up in a small, religious community in Kansas, after all, before going to a church-affiliated college in Oklahoma. After earning degrees from Yale Divinity School and Yale Law School, he spent time working in the federal government and in private law practice before running McGovern's '72 campaign. Two years later, at age thirty-eight, he knocked off a two-term incumbent Republican to become a US senator from Colorado.

What most distinguished Gary Hart, though, was the fact that he wasn't a traditional New Deal Democrat. While he was a decade older than the oldest members of the Baby Boom generation, he shared a sensibility with those who'd come of age in the 1960s. He was liberal on social issues like women's rights, abortion, and the environment, but he wasn't afraid to question Democratic Party orthodoxy on things like defense (he didn't want to cut spending, just refocus it) and the economy (where he questioned the clout of Big Labor and put a premium instead on innovation and technology). As he launched a presidential run, he overtly emulated the idealism—and to some extent, the personal style—that had made Jack Kennedy a hero to the Baby Boomers. Like Kennedy, Hart was handsome (*Playgirl* had named him one of the ten sexiest men in America in 1979), and he peppered his speeches with JFK-isms like "We can do better." Maybe most significantly, he consciously presented himself as the candidate of the future, the one with "new ideas."

Hart had traveled the country extensively in 1983, without necessarily having much to show for it when it came to support for his candidacy: His national poll numbers had never risen above 3 percent. Indeed, there seemed to be a persistent question of how long he could keep going, particularly as Mondale continued racking up money and endorsements. But along the way, particularly in New Hampshire, Hart had gotten the support of a small but passionate group of young activists and Democratic party operatives, who were attracted by the freshness of his approach.

One of them was a young political strategist named Susan Berry Casey, who signed on to be co-organizer of Hart's New Hampshire operation. "Those of us who became involved with Hart thought he was a candidate with a message that was right and ripe for the time, a message that could touch people," she said later. "His message of change, of hope, of idealism was directed toward those formed by the experiences of the '60s and '70s."

The first sign that something was really happening with Hart came in December. His polling in Iowa and New Hampshire started to tick up, and political reporters began to pay more attention to him. Mondale was still the heavy favorite, no question, but to a handful of journalists Hart had become the "keep your eye on" candidate.

In late February, at the Iowa caucuses, the first official contest for the nomination, Hart proved those reporters right. While Walter Mondale easily won the night with nearly 45 percent of the vote, Hart finished a surprising second with 15 percent. Hart's performance was so far above what many people had expected that the media quickly made *him* the story, not Mondale (who'd simply done what he'd been expected to do). Hart's confidence, bordering on arrogance, only added to the buzz. "I told my daughter that if we finished second in Iowa," he boasted, "we were going to win the nomination."

A week later, in the New Hampshire primary, Hart backed up his bravado: He won that race with 41 percent of the vote, twelve points ahead of Mondale. Just like that, he was Mondale's main opponent, and an avalanche of Hart coverage started in the media. Who was he? What did he stand for? Why was he surging?

The Mondale campaign found itself faced with a decision. Did it continue to ignore Hart, trusting that all the support they'd lined up over the previous year would still pay off? Or did it go after Hart directly, trying to stop his momentum? For a couple of weeks they chose the former path, but after Hart continued to surge—he won contests in Maine, Vermont, and Wyoming, and on Super Tuesday, in early March, took six contests to Mondale's three—they had no choice but to engage. Mondale's hold on the nomination was now officially at risk.

As the campaigning continued, one strategy Mondale embraced was to say that Hart lacked compassion for people who'd lost their jobs and been struggling over the last several years. Hart didn't empathize with those steelworkers in Ohio or autoworkers in Michigan, Mondale said. Another tactic was to publicly question whether Hart was even up to the task of being president, suggesting there was little substance behind his so-called "new ideas." "Where's the beef?" Mondale asked at a debate, parroting the popular Wendy's commercial.

Privately, meanwhile, Mondale campaign aides started talking to reporters, trying to poison the well about whether Hart was really an *authentic* Democrat. He had, they pointed out, limited appeal to the traditional Democratic base—he did okay, not great, in white union households, and he had virtually zero backing in the Black and Latino communities. Hart's biggest support, the Mondale operatives noted, was actually based on age and class: He was the candidate of the affluent young professionals everyone had been reading so much about—*Yuppies*.

And so began a spate of Gary-Hart-Is-the-Yuppie-Candidate stories. The *Wall Street Journal.* The *Boston Globe. Time.* CBS News. They all did pieces noting that Hart's campaign had risen based on the support of young professionals—Yuppies who wanted nothing to do with old-school Democrats like Walter Mondale.

"Yuppies have become the strike force of the Hart campaign," CBS News reporter Bob Simon said in a piece that aired nationally in late March. Simon used the story as an opportunity to introduce evening news viewers to what, precisely, a Yuppie was—and to let a handful of

Yuppies explain what they saw in Hart (and themselves). "We're fairly sophisticated and educated and well-read," a young woman in Connecticut said, "and I think that's who Gary Hart appeals to."

In the *New York Times*, reporter Steven Roberts went even deeper in a piece headlined "Hart Taps a Generation of Young Professionals." Roberts noted specific voter outcomes—in Florida, Hart had won among young voters, college grads, and those making $50,000 a year or more—and did interviews with half a dozen young professionals in Illinois who were enamored with the newly famous senator.

"I like his generational appeal," said a twenty-six-year-old who worked in banking. "He appeals to people who grew up with Vietnam and Watergate. I think the events bred cynicism into a lot of young people, and Hart represents an attempt to address that cynicism and overcome it. It's a very Kennedy-esque appeal."

Others seemed drawn to Hart's independence, the fact that he wasn't tied to the old ideas of the Democratic Party. A young lawyer named Richard Toman explained to the *Times* that his grandparents had emigrated from Czechoslovakia to Chicago, where his parents now operated a bakery. While the older members of his family were FDR Democrats—loyal to the party because it had connected them to a culture and country they weren't familiar with—his own attitude was different. "Do I need the Democratic Party? Probably not. I can make enough waves and get things done anyway." His choice was Hart.

To still other young professionals, Hart's appeal seemed not much different from that of Perrier or nouvelle cuisine or hardwood floors. Supporting him was trendy, it was chic, and it signaled that you were not part of your parents' bland middlebrow world. "We're part of the 'Me Generation,' and people don't want to take on the titles others had," said a young woman who worked in advertising and was running as a Hart delegate to the Democratic National Convention. "The establishment is Republican and the working class is Democratic, and being independent sounds a lot cooler."

The impact of Hart's candidacy—and of all the stories about Yuppies' support for Hart's candidacy—was twofold. First, it took the term "Yuppie" from the features section of the newspaper and put it onto the front page, broadening even more the number of people who understood what a Yuppie was. (Nodding to the fact that there were young professionals who didn't live in cities proper, some journalists used the less geographically specific term "Yumpie"—young *upwardly mobile* professional.)

Second, and maybe more importantly: It signaled a shift that was taking place, announcing that the massive Baby Boomer generation—or at least the well-educated portion of it—had arrived politically. Those Boomers, who had questioned all the rules in the '60s and turned inward in the '70s, were now ready to exert their influence at the ballot box in a real way, and the generation's leaders, the Yuppies, were showing the way—with their support of Gary Hart.

Within the political classes, people were scrambling to understand whatever they could about the new demographic. Richard Darman, a young special assistant to President Reagan, was reading *The Yuppie Handbook* and telling anyone who'd have anything to do with Reagan's reelection campaign in the fall they needed to do the same.

Meanwhile, in an editorial that was published on a Sunday that spring, the *New York Times* was announcing the dawn of a new era.

"This truly is the Year of the Yuppies, the educated, computer literate, audiophile children of the Baby Boom," the *Times* wrote. "They are part of a huge generation. Nearly eighty million were born between 1946 and 1965—compared with about fifty million births in the previous 20 years. Beyond numbers, 1984 will be the year in which all can vote for President. By definition, not all baby boomers are Yuppies. But the Yuppies are numerous—20 percent of the vote in New Hampshire, 10 percent in Illinois. And they possess atypical affluence and influence: These are the people who created the counterculture. They still listen to rock music, still wear wire-rimmed glasses. Does their politics of the left also endure? Or does turning gray mean, as for other generations, turning right?"

The answer, the editorial continued, likely depended on the issue. Citing a recent survey, the paper said Yuppies "strongly favor the equal rights amendment and freedom of choice on abortion, and oppose employment discrimination against homosexuals." But on other issues, they were more conservative or more self-absorbed. They were less concerned about unemployment than other age-groups, and more inclined to favor further cuts in federal spending. As for social welfare issues, they were less likely than older Democrats to support income maintenance programs.

The important point, the *Times* concluded, was that no matter what their positions were, as a political force, they were here to stay.

*   *   *

On the campaign trail, Mondale and Hart, along with the third remaining candidate, Jesse Jackson, battled one another as April and May went on. In many ways, it was a proxy fight for the soul and future direction of the Democratic Party. Would it continue, as Mondale and Jackson advocated, in the New Deal–Great Society tradition of FDR and LBJ, using government to help meet the needs of labor unions, people of color, and the working class? Or would it transform itself, as Hart argued, so that it was focused on a new economy and new ideas?

Mondale's and Hart's differences on policy, particularly around economic issues, were telling. When it came to the millions of manufacturing workers who'd lost their jobs in recent years, Mondale said the country needed to revisit its trade policies so such jobs could be protected; Hart suggested such jobs were never coming back and advocated for retraining of workers. On the issue of the bailout that the federal government had given to Chrysler several years earlier, Mondale said it was exactly the right thing to do since it saved so many good-paying union positions. Hart called it a mistake, saying that government should be supporting new technology and new industries, not propping up struggling companies in dying industries.

Which side you agreed with, and which candidate you supported, likely depended on what your background was and what you did for a living.

181

"Hart's people have christened his core constituency as 'Yuppies,' young urban professionals," the *Indianapolis Star* wrote in an editorial that framed the race as a battle between new and old. "Like Hart himself, these people have college degrees, and many of them, like him, have graduate school degrees. They are doing well in the professions, the sciences, academia, the media. The future, understandably, looks very bright to a Yuppie who is moving upward in the microchip industry or in computer software, and the word 'new'—it doesn't really have to be attached to anything in particular—has a welcome ring to such a Yuppie.

"Such people are liberal, on the whole, but not in the 'old' sense. Mondale is perfectly right when he accuses Hart and his 'new' constituency of lacking 'compassion.' The word 'compassion' is another code word. It means re-distributing the income to the various parts of the 'old' constituency: urban blacks, old people, minorities generally, out-of-work teenagers. The college-educated Young Professional does not thrill to that program."

If there was a turning point in the race, it came in the first half of April, when Mondale won the delegate-rich New York and Pennsylvania primaries in consecutive weeks. The race ground on for two more months, with Mondale finally amassing enough delegates to secure the nomination in early June. He'd formally accept the nomination the following month at the party's convention in San Francisco.

Still, if Mondale had won the battle to be the candidate that fall, there was a feeling among many Democrats—among anyone who was paying attention—that he and his supporters might not be winning the broader war that was taking place.

As the *Star* wrote, "[Yuppies] are a growing constituency....However the race comes out, Hart has demonstrated an important thing conclusively: the growing weakness of the old liberal coalition as it rapidly passes into history, into the past."

CHAPTER 14

Where You're Going, It's Michelob

Gary Hart's campaign may have marked the political arrival of a particular group of Baby Boomers, but certainly not the entire generation. In truth, many, if not most, Boomers were struggling. The economic malaise of the '70s had fallen hardest on younger workers without college degrees—including many of those who'd fought in Vietnam—and the same was true of the tremendous difficulties inflicted by the recession. In the auto and steel industries, in manufacturing in general, younger workers were the first to be laid off and the last to be rehired (assuming there was any rehiring being done at all). Compared to where their parents' generation had been at the same age two and three decades earlier, blue-collar Boomers were lagging.

Bruce Springsteen was paying attention to what was happening. The musician had grown up in a working-class household—his mother was a legal secretary; his father held a series of blue-collar jobs—and most of the people Springsteen hung around with, even as his star rose in the world of rock and roll, were from the same background. When he came into money following his successful 1980–81 *River* tour, he confessed to being embarrassed about buying his first new car, a Corvette: He didn't know anyone who didn't live paycheck to paycheck.

Springsteen's earliest records had a romantic feel to them, focusing mostly on life at the Jersey Shore, but as he matured, he'd begun exploring deeper themes and embracing a more sober point of view. "The River," the title song from his 1980 album, inspired by the real-life experiences of his older sister and her husband, told the story of a teenage couple who get pregnant and get married, then run head-on into the economic reality of late 1970s America: a lost job, lost hope, lost dreams. His 1982 acoustic album *Nebraska*, mostly recorded in his bedroom, went further still, chronicling the lives of people who were not only down on their luck, but desperate enough to resort to crime. "Down here it's just winners and losers and don't get caught on the wrong side of that line," Springsteen sang in *Nebraska*'s second song, "Atlantic City," and in many ways that line summed up the entire album: All of *Nebraska*'s characters were people who'd ended up on the wrong side of the line.

The new album Springsteen released in June 1984, *Born in the U.S.A.*, was a sharp musical and sonic departure from *Nebraska*, an upbeat rock and roll record that showcased Springsteen's E Street Band. But many of its songs had been written at the same time as *Nebraska*, and the theme of people struggling against forces outside their control carried over to the new record. The heart of the album lay in its opening and closing numbers. The first song, "Born in the U.S.A.," was inspired by conversations Springsteen had been having over the previous couple of years with Vietnam vets he'd met (including Ron Kovic, author of the memoir *Born on the Fourth of July*). Thematically, it was not far afield from the Sylvester Stallone vehicle *First Blood*, telling the story of a young American who'd gone off to fight in Vietnam and returned home to find not much waiting for him: no job, no hope, no future. The song's chorus—Springsteen bellowing "Born...in the U.S.A.!," a line he'd cribbed from a movie script he'd been asked to write music for—was simultaneously ironic, plaintive, and outraged: *Yeah, I'm an American. For whatever that's worth.*

The album's closing song, "My Hometown," was similarly dark—the first-person story of a young man forced to move his family out of the town where he'd grown up because there's no economic future there. The song had autobiographical elements—a textile mill in Springsteen's hometown of Freehold, New Jersey, had closed in the '60s, costing thousands of people their jobs—but it could just as easily have been about Youngstown or any of a dozen American cities that had been upended in the late '70s and early '80s.

Born in the U.S.A. was released at the beginning of June, and within three weeks it was the number one album in the country—elevating the singer to new heights. In late June, Springsteen—sporting a muscular new physique thanks to a couple of years spent working out in his local gym—kicked off a nationwide tour, playing to arenas filled with ten thousand to twenty thousand fans each night, many of them thrusting their fists in the air as they screamed, "Born...in the U.S.A."

On the surface, the song and Springsteen's massive popularity signaled a potential reprioritizing of the American working class. The reality was exactly the opposite.

*   *   *

Gary Hart's campaign had lifted the Yuppie phenomenon to an entirely new level. By the summer of 1984, the media had evolved from merely explaining what Yuppies were to demonstrating how to live like one, and even running think pieces on what they meant. (Whatever battle had existed among the terms "YAP," "Yuppie," and "Yumpie" had now been settled; "Yuppie" was the winner.) Meanwhile, reporters across the country were still looking for Yuppies in their own backyards, including places far removed from the Yuppie hotspots of New York, Boston, DC, and San Francisco.

Lincoln, Nebraska—the state capital, population 175,000—was one of those places, and the epicenter of Yuppieness there was Nebraska's forty-one-year-old governor Bob Kerrey. Kerrey was "an early Hart supporter," the local paper, the *Star*, noted, "and the embodiment of all that is Yuppie—young, successful, well-dressed, politically committed, hard-working, athletic. Many of his followers at the Capitol reflect the same values." Kerrey, in true high-achiever fashion, was in the middle of a relationship with Oscar-winning actress Debra Winger, but how did other Lincoln Yuppies spend *their* spare time? Well, there were several Yuppie hangouts in Lincoln, and at one Yuppie gathering that summer, guests passed the evening watching Kerrey's and Hart's speeches at the Democratic National Convention in San Francisco before settling in for a screening of the previous year's Boomer-focused big hit, *The Big Chill.* Of course, the clearest marker of Lincoln Yuppieness was inclusion in the *New York Times* Co-op, a group of sophisticated young Lincoln professionals who paid to have the paper bused in every Sunday morning from Omaha.

Around the country, the focus on Yuppies—specifically, the Yuppie obsession with achievement and materialism—engendered some pushback. That May and June, Yuppieness was a common topic among university commencement speakers, who feared what forces graduates might be susceptible to. At Cornell, president Frank H. T. Rhodes told the class of '84 that aspiring to a Yuppie lifestyle was a shallow pursuit destined to lead any young person down a path of misery. "Yuppieness depends on the prestige of gaining; happiness on the satisfaction of giving," he said. "Yuppieness depends on the trophy of achievement; happiness on the rewards of commitment." At Stanford, President Donald Kennedy told graduates to be wary of focusing too much on a high-powered career in a big city, lest they miss the real magic of America and life. "Touch bottom often" in your country, he told them. "Yuppiedom does not conduce to a realistic view of the human condition or American society.… This is a great, diverse country. Its genius does not reside in the practice of law or medicine or in the cultivation of urbane tastes and high culture." If you needed direction, Kennedy advised the graduates, "visit Newark, Ohio, or Bend, Oregon, or Munising, Michigan… and relearn the arts of living in communities of manageable size."

It was a quaint, lovely sentiment—and completely at odds with the direction the culture was moving. It was becoming clear that Yuppieness was not merely a fad, nor was it only a political phenomenon. What was happening was something more fundamental than that—a once-in-a-generation shift in power. But the shift wasn't to the Baby Boomers writ large; it was to a particular segment of the generation. Those who'd gotten good educations at Cornell and Stanford and other top schools. Those who had—or would have—good salaries. Those who were committed to success.

To many of them, that shift felt exactly right. They'd worked hard and followed the rules (mostly), and where they hadn't liked the rules—whether it was smoking weed or opposing an unjust war—they'd simply forged their own paths and gotten everyone else to follow along. They'd been smart in their choices, picking professional fields—business, law, medicine, media, technology—that were headed up, not down. Was it sad what was happening to blue-collar workers in America? Of course, but the world needed to move forward.

The growing confidence of this group—their ascendance—could be seen in an array of places. One area was business. Around the country, corporate execs were reporting that underlings in their twenties and thirties were a new breed. On one hand, with values rooted in the '60s, they were more egalitarian, less enamored of strict corporate hierarchies and certainly more open to the contributions of women (because many of them were women). At the same time, they were ambitious and impatient. They wanted to succeed now, and if they couldn't succeed in this company, they had no problem moving on to another one, and then another one, and then another one. Like Jack Welch, they saw the idea of loyalty in the world of work as silly and passé. "They don't see any corporation as a place where they will stay for the rest of their career, and they're likely to move on if they don't achieve what they want in a certain time frame," one manager observed. "They are more committed to their profession than to the company." Lawrence Daniele was a twenty-four-year-old Cornell-trained engineer who told a reporter he was obsessed with "making it." Though he'd started his career at Hewlett-Packard, Daniele was concerned that it would take too long to move up in management, so he quit to launch his own computer graphics firm.

Others were making similar moves—becoming entrepreneurs, many in the growing world of tech. Mitch Kapor had followed a quintessential Boomer journey: Raised on Long Island, he was involved in anti-war protests at Yale in the '60s before working as a DJ and teaching transcendental meditation in the '70s. But by the early '80s he'd gotten interested in tech, and in 1982 he cofounded a software company called Lotus. The following January, the company released a product called Lotus 1-2-3 for PCs that integrated graphics, database management, and spreadsheet analysis. In its first year it brought in more than $50 million in sales, and Kapor, age thirty-three, became a millionaire.

Then there was Steve Jobs, who'd cofounded Apple Computer with Steve Wozniak in 1976. Jobs, too, had a '60s sensibility, and what made him stand out in the tech world was his belief in what computers could achieve. Yes, they could crunch numbers and process data, but he saw them even more as a tool for unlocking human creativity. In early 1984, Apple aired an ad during the Super Bowl unveiling a new computer, the Macintosh, that Jobs believed would change everything. Within five months Apple had sold 70,000 units, and by the end of 1984 it would sell 250,000 units. The tech revolution was spreading.

The success of young tech entrepreneurs was a signal of where the broader economy was going—the ideas industry was growing; manufacturing was not. Their rise was emblematic of something else, too. Like so many of their Boomer counterparts, the tech execs had a deep belief not just in themselves, and not just in business, but in the intersection of the two: They were what they did. And that made being successful all the more crucial.

*   *   *

Perhaps an even greater sign of the shift that was now taking place was the way so many elements of the country were pivoting to appeal to, and align with, Yuppies and Yuppieness. There was a growing feeling that, no matter what sort of organization you ran or activity you were involved in, success in America in 1984—and likely beyond—meant catering to this smart, educated cohort with its upgraded tastes, fast-track values, and growing incomes.

One place you saw the impact clearly, as Yuppie fever spread around America, was in advertising and marketing. In some instances, the appeal to Yuppies was comically superficial, as small businesses across the country slapped the term on anything and everything that might be of interest to the young professional set. A Delaware bar advertised "Yuppie cocktails." An investment firm in Boston created the "Yuppie portfolio." A New Jersey bank marketed a "Yuppie mortgage."

But in corporate America and on Madison Avenue, where there was a deepening understanding that Yuppies were *the* key demographic you needed to target (a conclusion reached, in part, because many of the decision-makers were themselves Yuppies), the approach was more sophisticated. It wasn't just a matter of placing a trendy word on a product or service; it was about telegraphing to young professionals that you understood their lives, their priorities, their needs.

A telling example was the strategy adopted in 1984 by the iconic American brand Alka-Seltzer. The product—a fizzy concoction designed to deal with indigestion or a Sunday morning hangover—had been part of American life for fifty years, and its marketing had always reflected the times. In the '50s, the company had introduced TV viewers to Speedy, a wholesome, animated 3D character who sang the Alka-Seltzer jingle ("Plop plop fizz fizz oh, what a relief it is") while promising a quick reprieve from what ailed you. In the '70s, the brand had created a hugely popular campaign featuring a series of comic middle-aged characters who overindulged in one thing or another and uttered a series of catchphrases—from "Try it, you'll like it" to "I can't believe I ate the whole thing"—that made their way into pop culture.

By the early '80s, though, that approach had grown tired, and Alka-Seltzer, thanks to heightened competition from other antacid products, was struggling. The solution landed on by its new ad agency, McCann Erickson? To position the product as one meant not for schlubby middle-aged gluttons, but for the growing number of ambitious young professionals.

In a series of slick TV commercials that it rolled out in the second half of 1984, Alka-Seltzer unveiled its new slogan: "For the symptoms of stress that can come with success." One fast-moving spot paid homage to an array of ambitious business types: The young executive gunning to become vice president by the end of the fiscal year. The vice president intent on being a senior vice president by age thirty-nine. The high-powered board chairman working hard to appease company shareholders. The campaign was perfectly reflective of a new national vibe and perfectly pitched to the young professionals who saw themselves as different—more ambitious, more sophisticated, healthier—than those who'd come before them. "The executive lunch that begins with two martinis is as much a relic as the weekly hangover," an Alka-Seltzer marketing executive explained as the campaign debuted. "Many business people don't even order wine at lunch anymore—it's spritzers and Perrier."

Another brand anxious to tap into the shifting zeitgeist was Michelob. The beer had always been more of a premium product than its Anheuser-Busch stablemate, Budweiser, and in the '70s it had built its identity around the idea that it wasn't an everyday beer ("Weekends were made for Michelob" was the ubiquitous jingle). But now, as the economy continued rebounding from the recession and journalists cranked out stories about Yuppies, the brand's ad agency, Ted Bath Worldwide, positioned Michelob as a beer not for special occasions, but for special *people*. "Where you're going, it's Michelob" was the new slogan, and the brand's new campaign reflected upwardly mobile ambitions and sensibilities to a tee. In one quick-cutting TV ad, a young professional was seen driving his sports car (European, of course), working the phones in his busy office, then hustling through the airport, where he would eventually hop on…the supersonic, superluxury Concorde. The ad finished with our hardworking Yuppie hero walking on a tropical beach alongside a beautiful young woman as a song played underneath:

There's a style in your life no one could ever deny
You're moving up, moving up
You're always the one, the one who's eager to try
You're on your way to the top
Where you're going, it's Michelob

The National Coffee Association, the trade group promoting coffee, not only published a booklet titled *The Achiever's Handbook* (which noted, miraculously, that most of the "achievers" surveyed by the association started their day with a cup of joe); it also hired a young psychologist to tour the country and advise students and young corporate employees on career success. She no doubt knew what she was talking about: She was a thirty-one-year-old Yale PhD who'd published three books on the topic.

Then there was American Express. As the credit card of choice for young professionals, Amex had been on a phenomenal tear; in 1983 alone, the number of American Express cardholders increased by more than 20 percent over the previous year, in part because of Amex's success in marketing its cards to women and new college graduates. But the company wasn't content to stand still as it did battle with competitors Visa and MasterCard. In the mid-'60s, Amex had created the Gold Card for its highest-spending customers; nearly two decades later, it decided that gold was no longer rich enough. In the spring of 1984, the company debuted the American Express Platinum Card, inviting the top 5 percent of its cardholders to pay $250 per year for the über-exclusive new card. Platinum did come with some extra benefits—it got you into various private clubs around the country if you were traveling—but American Express understood that the real point of having a Platinum card was that, well, so many people did not. "We're not just offering a piece of plastic," an Amex executive said. "We're offering an identity."

*   *   *

In many respects, companies like American Express and Michelob were lucky: They already had products and brand identities that naturally

191

appealed to aspirational young professionals. Their marketing campaigns merely needed to emphasize the point. But as the power of Yuppies grew, other companies understood that they had to do something far more dramatic if they were going to tap into the cultural moment: remake their business strategies completely.

That was the position the US auto manufacturers found themselves in. The industry had begun making a comeback from the darkest days of the recession in 1981 and 1982, but there was a giant hole when it came to their consumer base: affluent young American professionals. In the country as a whole, foreign cars accounted for about 25 percent of new-car sales in 1983. But among young professionals—a group projected to spend a quarter billion dollars a year on cars—the number was far higher, 40 percent. The generation that had purchased cheaper imports like Volkswagens and Toyotas and Datsuns in the '70s was increasingly trading up to those cool, identity-affirming, message-sending makes that had been touted in *The Official Preppy Handbook* and *The Yuppie Handbook*: Volvos and Saabs and BMWs. Detroit needed a way to fight back.

And so began what amounted to Operation Yuppie inside the big three American automakers, as research analysts tried to uncover what young professionals didn't like about American cars, and engineers and designers scrambled to figure out how to create vehicles that would match the Yuppie sensibility.

In the fall of 1984, all three major US automakers unveiled new cars they said were aimed specifically at the millions of young professionals ages twenty-five to forty-four who made $30,000 per year or more. At GM, it was a line of cars that hit dealerships as the Oldsmobile Calais, the Buick Somerset Regal, and the Pontiac Grand Am. All boasted what GM, and car writers, called "European flavoring"—sleeker lines, tighter handling, higher-performance engines, high-tech features in the passenger compartment. At Ford, the company didn't just go for "European flavoring"; it went for a European car, importing the Merkur line of vehicles from West Germany. Commercials—and the car-industry press—made a big deal about the shift, but whether the overt appeal to young professionals, who by now had spent a generation rejecting American cars, would work was another question. As a sales manager at a BMW dealership in Fort Worth, Texas, said, "A domestic car that looks like a BMW is still just a domestic car."

Another category where companies were remaking themselves to attract more young professionals was retail. The Yuppie preference for designer labels and "quality" products made it clear that serving the vast middle, as so many brands had done for so long, was no longer the way toward big profits. "Upscale" was the new buzzword and new strategy.

For decades the Spiegel catalog thrived as a mass-market retailer, selling everything from clothing to dinette sets to water heaters. (In the '60s and '70s, it got an added level of fame as a ubiquitous game show prize.) But by the middle of the '70s, the company had started to struggle, squeezed by discount stores like Montgomery Ward on one end and more-upscale catalogs on the other.

Finally, management made a decision: It would streamline its inventory, putting its emphasis on clothing and housewares, and it would abandon the budget-conscious shopper, focusing instead on more-affluent customers. From the company's perspective, it wasn't necessarily a difficult decision: According to its numbers, there were twenty-six million households in the US that included women (Spiegel's main customers) between the ages of twenty-one and fifty-four and that made more than $38,000 a year. Yes, that was the same sector of the market that competitors like Saks and Bloomingdale's and Marshall Field's were going after, but all the retailers were focused there for a reason: The demo represented more than 60 percent of America's disposable income.

By the summer of 1984, the once-utilitarian Spiegel catalog had morphed into a glossy, high-end statement publication with slick paper, luxurious photos, and the feel of a fashion magazine. And where it once peddled polyester slacks for under $10, it now sold $550 black onyx cuff bracelets and $185 skirts by French designer Jean-Charles de Castelbajac, as well as upscale offerings from Laura Ashley and Gloria Vanderbilt. Spiegel hadn't yet landed wares from Rolex and Ralph Lauren, but it was certainly trying. Meanwhile, it had started taking out ads for itself in real fashion magazines, hiring famed celebrity photographer Annie Leibovitz to take photos of appealing young professionals. It was all a long way from what had made the catalog a household name, but you couldn't necessarily argue with the results: The company was now pulling in more than $500 million a year in sales, the fourth-most-successful catalog in the country.

The pivot to upscale seemed to be happening everywhere. Levi's, for years the uniform of the counterculture, was rolling out more-sophisticated designs as young professionals turned away from jeans and toward a more professional look. Old-fashioned TV dinners got a makeover as food companies debuted new cuisines under new gourmet labels in an attempt to appeal to Yuppie tastes. Pillsbury, creator of that middle-American icon the Pillsbury Bake-Off, bought the fancy ice-cream brand Häagen-Dazs.

At Sharper Image, Richard Thalheimer already knew the power of the young professional market, but he was so confident in their spending prowess that he launched a new strategy: Sharper Image retail stores. By the end of 1984, there would be two in San Francisco, and one each in Houston, Denver, and Los Angeles. To an extent, they were the grown-up version of the toy department Thalheimer had worked in as a kid in his family's Arkansas department store, with scores of dazzling products displayed right in front of you.

For Thalheimer, figuring out where to place the new stores wasn't particularly complicated. When he got to a prospective location in a prospective city, he said, "I just stand on the street corner and count the number of people who walk by wearing suits and ties." The more Yuppies the better.

*   *   *

Perhaps the ultimate sign of the power that the young, city-based professional class was starting to have in 1984 was in the behavior of cities themselves. Once upon a time, American metropolises had thrived because they were centers of industry, providing jobs for the masses. As New York, San Francisco, and other cities had shown, the new playbook was different: Ignore the masses. Unless you attracted educated young professionals—as residents, as employees, as tourists—your city's future was bleak.

Certainly, the city of Boston understood that. In the winter of 1984, a development called Copley Place opened in Boston's Back Bay neighborhood. Built at a cost of $500 million and taking up nearly ten acres of prime Boston real estate, the new complex—much anticipated and trumpeted by Boston civic officials and business leaders—included two luxury hotels with two thousand total rooms; a nine-screen movie theater; fourteen hundred parking spaces; ten restaurants; and a hundred retail shops, the vast majority of which catered to the high end, from Gucci and Yves Saint Laurent to Louis Vuitton and Godiva chocolate. The centerpiece of the entire retail experience was Neiman Marcus, the luxury department store that had gotten its start in Dallas and was now fanning out into cities across the country.

"This is very much becoming a Yuppie town," a Boston University marketing professor said not long after Copley Place opened. "We have a lot of professionals, a lot of executives, to whom dressing well and dressing properly and having nicely furnished houses and apartments is considered important."

For longtime Bostonians, the arrival of Copley Place—as well as another new retail hub not far away called Lafayette Place—was a little jarring, given that the city, with its practical, unpretentious Yankee roots, had never been a place given to showy displays of wealth. But the powers that be believed not only that affluent Bostonians wanted such high-end options, but that having them was crucial to attracting even more affluent young professionals.

The phenomenon of cities suddenly trying to lure young professionals was hardly limited to Boston; it was happening in metro areas across the country. In Tampa that fall, a local mall announced an expansion that would feature additional restaurants and retail stores, none aimed at the traditional middle class. "We're going after the upscale Yuppie shopper," an executive said. "The Tampa Bay market is growing at an exciting rate. And the most dynamic growth is in the West Shore area. The expansion gives us the opportunity to bring in more upscale-type tenants to better serve the affluent market." In nearby St. Petersburg, a $72 million shopping and retail center called Pier Park was slated to open, and at a city council meeting officials had excitedly unveiled beautiful drawings of a completely remade downtown, with upscale shops and restaurants, as well as office buildings. Older longtime residents were frightened to death at what they saw—they thought it would drive up rents and take public money away from things the broader community needed, like improved public transportation—but city officials were committed to their strategy. "We need the young professionals because they have good salaries with disposable income for retail purposes, eating out and entertainment," a council member said. Added another official, "Those are the kind of people that are going to create 24-hour activity."

Philadelphia, meanwhile, was involved in a great debate. For decades there had been a gentleman's agreement that no building in the city's downtown would exceed the height of the statue of William Penn (the city's founder) that sat atop city hall. But in 1984, the Rouse Company— the developer that had transformed Quincy Market and Faneuil Hall in Boston—proposed the construction of two gleaming skyscrapers that would tower over poor little Billy Penn. To their critics, the buildings— called One and Two Liberty Place—were sacrilege: The no-skyscraper agreement was one of the things that made Philadelphia unique; what's more, the lack of showiness in the skyline was a reflection of the city's humble Quaker roots. To their proponents, the buildings were a necessary step forward: Not only would they show that Philadelphia was prepared to be a "modern" city, but they would attract even more of the kinds of high-paying postindustrial jobs—and the young professionals who filled them—that the city so desperately needed.

City residents opposed the project by a two-to-one margin, and Philadelphia's mayor, Wilson Goode, was besieged with letters against it, but ultimately the Rouse group, which technically didn't need special permission to move forward, broke ground anyway. Philadelphia was getting two skyscrapers.

Speaking out in favor of the Rouse plan was Steve Poses, the restaurateur who'd upended Philadelphia's restaurant scene in the late '70s with Frog and the Commissary. By now Poses's company had grown to more than five hundred employees, and Poses himself had evolved into a fascinating blend—equal parts socially aware liberal who volunteered in the community and 1980s entrepreneur. He made an effort to know each of his employees by name and was committed to being a caring boss, but he drove to work each day in a big black BMW and was duly focused on the bottom line in a competitive industry. "In the '60s, I was very much anti-business," he commented to a magazine writer. "I feel very strongly now about the role business can play in people's lives, and the satisfaction people can get out of work, which is not a thing I was at all in tune with in the '60s.... Entrepreneurs and employers are really key figures in creating opportunities for people."

The shift into savvy-businessperson mode was happening everywhere. In 1984, after her workout video had sold millions, Jane Fonda found herself with a dilemma: She wanted to grow the business even more, but she was being stifled. All the income was going to support the nonprofit that the workout business had been created to support, Tom Hayden's CED. Finally, Fonda made the call: The workouts had already funneled $17 million to the nonprofit. Wasn't that enough? She formally severed ties between the two organizations.

CHAPTER 15

Material World

As the fireworks began exploding in the sky over the Los Angeles Memorial Coliseum, Lionel Richie stopped, threw his arms in the air, and waved to the tens of thousands of people in the crowd as he left the giant stage at the center of the stadium.

On Sunday night, August 12, the 1984 Summer Olympics in LA were officially coming to an end with a notably over-the-top closing ceremony. Richie—dressed in a sequined blue jacket, white pants, and white shoes—danced all over the twenty-three-thousand-square-foot stage as he performed an extended version of his number one song "All Night Long" for the six thousand athletes who'd competed in the games, thousands of other spectators in the stadium, and millions more watching on TV around the world. The climax had come when dozens of performers—most dressed in white, many sporting headbands that nodded toward the fitness craze—bounded onto the stage. As the music blared, lights flashed, and Richie energetically played to the crowd, a handful of the performers dropped to the ground and began breakdancing, spinning on their backs, even their heads, as the stadium roared.

For the US, the games had been a triumph. To begin with, there was the economics of it. Over the previous decade the cost of mounting an Olympiad had become astronomical, and when the 1984 games had come up for bid, few cities around the world had been willing to take on the financial burden. But the approach of the LA organizers had been different: They brought in a sharp business executive, Peter Ueberroth, to lead the effort, and they vowed to fund the games without a dime of government money. Together Ueberroth and his team had not only managed to keep costs down by using existing event facilities all over Southern California, but found a way to bring in significant revenue through increased broadcast rights and a robust corporate sponsorship strategy that pulled in more than $125 million. The Olympics might be a celebration of amateurism, but there was no reason to ignore their commercial potential.

The United States was equally impressive in the competition itself. Four years after boycotting the games in Moscow, the US team topped the medal count for the first time since 1968 with eighty-three golds—more than four times what any other country won. The dominant performance had come in part because the Soviet Union, East Germany, and more than a dozen other Eastern Bloc countries boycotted the games in response to the Americans' 1980 boycott, but the watered-down competition didn't lessen the cheers or the pride.

That summer, a new feeling of patriotism spread across America. The country's showing in the Olympics was part of it, but there were other factors as well. Four years earlier, when he campaigned for president, Ronald Reagan had pledged to stand up to the Soviet Union and make America strong in the world once again, and in the eyes of many Americans he'd done just that. After a decade in which détente had dominated US-Soviet relations, Reagan built up US defenses and spoke bluntly about the Russians, deeming the totalitarian regime "the evil empire" in a speech he gave in March 1983. Many longtime diplomats cringed, but the public loved the show of strength. Seven months later, Reagan ordered American troops to invade the small Caribbean island of Grenada following a violent dispute there among that country's

Communist leaders. Reagan said he was fearful that six hundred Americans attending medical school on the island could become hostages, as had happened in Iran, and the US quickly seized control of the country. Reagan's decision to invade—which came just two days after more than three hundred US Marines had been killed in a barracks bombing in Beirut, Lebanon—was widely criticized by many in the international community, including Reagan's close ally Margaret Thatcher, but the president saw the episode as an opportunity to demonstrate American power (notwithstanding the fact that the People's Revolutionary Army of Grenada had all of fifteen hundred soldiers). "Our days of weakness are over," he said in a speech he delivered in Manhattan—and was said to have written himself—several weeks later. "Our military forces are back on their feet and standing tall."

Adding to the feel-good fervor around the country was the reinvigorated economy, which, broadly speaking, was now booming. Three and a half years into Ronald Reagan's term, inflation continued to fall, the number of new jobs being created continued to rise (6.5 million since the recession had officially come to an end in late 1982), and overall economic growth was clipping along at a pace not seen in decades.

Just two years earlier, the recession—even with its uneven impact—had created a somberness in the country, with a constant stream of negative economic data and devastating personal stories leading the network news most nights. Now much of that seemed to be fading, replaced by a frothiness in the culture and a newfound muscularity that matched the hard bodies being created in gyms across the country. It was a dual celebration of both wealth and self.

Looking back years later, Jim Kunen, the onetime Columbia student who'd written about his days as a revolutionary in 1969's *The Strawberry Statement*, would marvel at the shift that had taken place in America over the course of a decade, particularly as he looked at the attitudes, concerns, and values of the younger members of the Baby Boom generation.

"Vietnam ended, and people got into fern bars and brown rice and jogging," he said. "And the context was, people were not grappling with anything. They're not trying to figure out the moral thing to do. They're not trying to choose between two impossible choices—should I go to Vietnam, which is wrong, or should I let someone go in my place, which is also wrong?

"And in the wake of that," he continued, "in comes gliding a pleasure craft with Yuppies on it."

*   *   *

On Manhattan's Upper West Side, the influx of Yuppies was so steady that by the end of 1984, between Seventieth and Eighty-Sixth streets, fully half of all residents were between the ages of twenty-five and forty-four—a fact that was obvious whenever you peeked inside a bustling restaurant or tried to navigate through the sea of young professionals wandering along Columbus Avenue, a growing number of them pushing strollers, on a Saturday or Sunday afternoon. It was also evident in the real estate world, where agents were chattering about young Wall Streeters buying brownstones with their year-end bonuses and all the condo and co-op buildings that were being constructed in the neighborhood. In one of those buildings, an eye-catching high-rise on Ninety-Sixth Street called the Columbia, one-third of the units were said to have been purchased by lawyers. Neighbors dubbed it the Yuppie Housing Project.

The seemingly never-ending flood of young people only heightened the tension that had been building for a decade between the educated, upwardly mobile newcomers and the older working-class residents. Rent control had allowed some longtime Upper West Siders to stay put, but landlords, eyeing the money they could make leasing to the more affluent younger class, were getting creative in finding ways to evict lower-income tenants. One approach was to announce a major capital improvement: A building would invest in a pricey upgrade—a new boiler system, for example—then pass the cost along to residents in the form of an assessment, something many less-well-off occupants simply couldn't afford to pay. Another tactic was called a "personal use eviction," which allowed the owner of, say, a multiunit brownstone to force a tenant out if the owner wanted the space for himself.

One such evictee was a middle-aged man named Joe Mauri, who'd spent a dozen years living in a single room inside a brownstone on Seventieth Street. When Mauri, who was unemployed and paid $98 per month in rent, was informed by the new owner that she wanted to turn his space into a new sewing room for herself, he didn't have much choice but to prepare to exit. His first step, he told a reporter, was to give away his books, which were among his only possessions. "I won't have no need of them where I'm going," he said (which was, presumably, a shelter or the street).

Longtime business owners felt the gentrification squeeze as well, as mom-and-pop businesses got hit with unaffordable rent hikes, then saw their spaces replaced by trendy boutiques and dessert shops. The owner of Golden's Stationery on Broadway between Ninety-Fourth and Ninety-Fifth had only two years left on his lease, but his landlord refused to talk to him about a renewal; the building where Golden's had been in business for thirty years was likely to be torn down. The shop owner, who was fifty-nine, had always assumed selling the business would fund his retirement. No more. "It's all worth zero now," he sighed.

"A new breed is taking over, and there's a lot of hostility," an Upper West Sider said of life inside her co-op building. "People are separated by age and economic class. The senior citizens got insider prices, so there's a lot of resentment on all sides. At a recent meeting, one elderly resident shouted, 'Well, I'm not rich like you.' What are you gonna do?"

Exactly. What were you gonna do? Because the changes on the Upper West Side—and in other parts of New York, and in similar neighborhoods in other cities around the country—mostly reflected the changing economy, the shift to a postindustrial world. Since 1970, employment in manufacturing in New York had dropped by 20 percent, while employment in postindustrial fields had exploded. Real estate—up 25 percent. Banking—up 29 percent. Law and accounting—up 41 percent. Securities—up 64 percent. It was a new city.

*   *   *

With the economy improving, with the media continuing to write about the Yuppie phenomenon, the pull to live a certain way was hard to resist. In Philadelphia, Robin Palley—who'd made the conscious choice to reject suburbia and live in the city a decade earlier—still considered herself a committed '60s liberal. She reveled in the continued diversity of her block. She was active in union causes at her job. But her own habits were evolving. Once she'd been on the board of the Philadelphia Folksong Society; now she was a board member of a tonier theater company in Center City Philadelphia. She stopped being active politically, and found herself spending money on things that weren't so far removed from the conformist, materialist upbringing she'd been desperate to flee when she left for college in 1968. As she put it, "there was a period of time when it was all vacation, spend, dress-up stuff."

Others were feeling the same pull. After building her career in magazines and television, Mary Alice Kellogg—who'd helped popularize the term "fast track" with her 1978 book—struck out on her own as an independent journalist, with a particular focus on high-end travel. There was a large market for the topic among luxury magazines, and Kellogg was aware of the personal benefits as well. (As she'd later say with a laugh, "I wanted to be more comfortable!")

More broadly, the trends that educated Boomers had been embracing since the late 1970s were now becoming mainstream. Across the country there was a growing obsession, for example, with restaurants. More places were opening, and more young professionals were eating out with increasing frequency. And restaurants suddenly had more cultural significance.

In part, the buzz was simply a reflection of the busy professional lives of young achievers and two-career couples. Who had time to cook when you were spending so many hours a week at the office? But just as significantly, being sophisticated about food said something about who you were as a person. It was another way of distinguishing yourself from your Jell-O-mold-loving, meat-loaf-eating parents. "We had a 10-room apartment on Central Park West," a foodie explained to a reporter, "but my parents were totally ignorant about fine food. I live in a closet these days, but at least I've been to just about every great restaurant in Manhattan."

In San Francisco, the spate of new restaurants that had opened in recent years, many inspired by Alice Waters's Chez Panisse and Berkeley's Gourmet Ghetto, transformed the food scene, much to the chagrin of the old-time San Francisco restaurants like the Tadich Grill and Bruno's, which in the fall of 1984 found themselves in a labor dispute with their workers (the owners claimed they needed financial concessions because of the increased competition). Driving all the change were the changing demographics of the city itself: As one observer put it, "San Francisco is definitely being Yuppified."

The Yuppie ethos was transforming the way people ate at home as well. "The beautiful people have discovered pasta," Joe Pellegrino, the president of Lowell, Massachusetts–based Prince Spaghetti, said of the spike in pasta sales (especially fresh pasta). "The wine-and-Brie crowd and the athletes have decided we're the ideal meal. Now at cocktail parties you hear, 'Have you tried this red noodle or this green noodle or this or that marvelous thing.'" The change was crazy. "I used to be in the spaghetti business," he continued. "Now I'm in the *pasta* business."

One of the places where people were devouring pasta was a new Boston market called J. Bildner & Sons. It was the creation of Jim Bildner, a thirty-year-old Dartmouth and Case Western law school graduate who'd briefly worked in Washington, DC, before running for the legislature in his home state of New Jersey in 1979. Bildner lost the race but reconnected with his family's grocery business while he was there and found himself inspired. Within a few years he'd moved to Boston and acquired the local franchises of Ben & Jerry's ice cream and David's Cookies before launching his new, upscale market. While Bildner would always disdain the label, he certainly had the characteristics of a Yuppie. As he told a reporter from the *Boston Globe*, he ran four miles a day, worked 120 hours per week, drove a BMW, and wore tailored suits, tasseled loafers, and bow ties. And people who looked like him—other young professionals in Boston—felt right at home inside J. Bildner & Sons, which carried a range of high-quality, specialty foods in a setting of Italian marble floors and mahogany trim (with classical or jazz music playing through the sound system). "What we're selling is a lifestyle," Bildner said. "We're building stores for people who have limited time and appreciate good food."

The desire for a high-end life was becoming palpable. A young woman named Judy Langer owned her own research firm in New York, assessing consumer attitudes for a range of corporate clients. What she heard in focus groups was unmistakable. "I remember interviewing people who literally had their noses in the air," she said. "They thought of themselves as idealists, but it wasn't—*we're going to make the world a better place.* It was, *we can be who we want to be.* They saw the previous generation as old-fashioned, weighed down by their Depression-era thinking, where you can't spend and you can't enjoy life.

"To me it seemed conformist," she continued. "But they were very determined to succeed and very proud of themselves. The attitude was: *We've done well, we're proud of our success. If you've got it, flaunt it.*"

"Flaunt it" had certainly become the attitude in fashion. The dress-for-success movement that had sprung up in the late '70s now seemed turbocharged. It was not just what you were wearing—suits with padded shoulders, bold colors, strong silhouettes—but *whom* you were wearing, with designer labels like Versace, Armani, Gucci, and Chanel telegraphing to the world that you were someone. Around Wall Street, a handful of young men had even begun embracing a particularly old-style accessory—suspenders, or braces, as the British called them. Braces had had a moment in the countercultural haze of the late '60s, but those had been whimsically emblazoned with stars and stripes or hearts. These new braces were all grown up, and they sent a different message: I am sophisticated, and I am—or at least I will be—successful.

The spread of Yuppie behavior had created opportunities for the writers who'd first articulated—satirically—the distinct young professional mindset and lifestyle. Cathy Crimmins's "YAP" had lost out to "Yuppie" as the term for this influential new group, but she was continuing to write frequently about her generation, now for national magazines. Meanwhile, a Florida real estate developer whose new condo project, Serendipity, was geared toward Yuppies, engaged *Yuppie Handbook* coauthor Marilee Hartley to help promote it. As she chatted with local reporters about Yuppies and the tastes of upwardly mobile Boomers, Hartley was asked how many copies the *Yuppie Handbook* had sold. She said she wasn't sure, but she did know it had done well, and not just in the US. The book, she noted, was now in its fifth printing in Japan.

*   *   *

Perhaps nowhere was the new mood—optimism turbocharged by money and status—more tangible than on Wall Street. After eighteen months of a booming bull market, stocks had cooled off in 1984, but the new aggressiveness and swagger that had gripped the Street were only increasing.

The $80 million windfall Bill Simon had generated in the Gibson Greetings LBO was partly responsible for the vibe. Michael Milken's astonishing success in the junk bond market was another factor. As recently as 1982, eyebrows had been raised on Wall Street when the investment firm First Boston had earned a lofty $18 million in fees from U.S. Steel's acquisition of Marathon Oil. But just a couple of years later, Drexel was earning fees two and three times that with its junk bond financing of corporate takeovers.

The result was a shift. Making good money had always been the prime motivation for people working on Wall Street, but there had also been other rewards: influence, prestige, pride. But now money, big money, was the only measure that mattered—less because of what it could buy you than as a way of keeping score. "It's become, 'How much money am I making?'" one investment banker would say a couple of years later. "You had a sense of falling behind if you were not keeping up."

Wick Simmons, whose great-grandfather had cofounded the firm Hayden Stone, watched the shift taking place. "Yuppies started to come into the business," remembered Simmons, who by 1984 was heading retail sales for the firm known as Shearson Lehman, a descendant of his great-grandfather's firm. "It became all about me, not necessarily the firm. *I didn't come here to make Hayden Stone the best firm. I came in to make the biggest buck.* And if someone will pay me a dollar more over there, I'm going to look that way. It was the start of the loosening of ties between individuals, and much more about *me me me*—the what's-in-it-for-me generation."

A similar bottom-line sensibility was impacting the buying and selling of stocks themselves. More and more, professional money managers—the firms that oversaw the investments of massive pension funds and other institutional investors—were concerned only with a stock's short-term gains. Focusing on the longer horizon was a luxury no one felt they could afford, in part because the money managers themselves were often being judged on a quarter-to-quarter basis. That July, for example, when ITT Corporation announced it was cutting its stock dividend by two-thirds to invest heavily in the US telecom business, money managers began dumping the stock, lowering its price by a third.

It was the kind of thing that other Fortune 500 CEOs couldn't ignore, especially since their own compensation packages were increasingly tied to stock performance. The idea of sacrificing for the short term in order to be really successful in the long term? It was getting harder to do. As one investment banker would tell a reporter, "I don't think any company can afford a long-term investment today unless its managers own 51 percent [of the company]."

The live-for-right-now ethos was present not only in the way business was being done, but in everything about the Street. The cocktail of money and swagger had turned the financial district into one of the most active drug havens in New York, with deals for coke being done in parks, in restrooms, in bars. Law enforcement had begun paying attention, and one day two undercover agents—dressed as successful young traders—met a dealer at a bar in the neighborhood. What stood out was how familiar the dealer was to people there. He said hi to the bartenders and exchanged greetings with customers before sitting down at the table. He told his two prospective customers that he was looking for "long-term relationships," that he was very discreet, and that he worked only on Wall Street. A few moments later he walked into the restroom with one of the undercover agents and handed over a small packet of coke. When they returned to the table, the agents gave him a thousand dollars in cash, which he counted in front of everyone. Transaction completed.

Before the agents left, though, the dealer had a question for them. Did they have any deals coming up involving real estate? If they did, they should let him know—he wanted to make an investment. The drug business wasn't bad, but he was hoping, he told them, to "diversify."

The new Wall Street was bold and competitive—and for the best and brightest of the next generation, it was, by the middle of 1984, increasingly the place to be. Fifteen years earlier, graduates of the country's most elite colleges had often been concerned with trying to improve the state of the world. Now, the focus was different: How can I be as financially successful as possible?

In the early '70s, several of the large investment firms on Wall Street had created the position of analyst as a way of hiring promising young college graduates and grooming them for successful careers. There were only a handful of positions at first, but as the firms grew, the number of analyst jobs had started to increase. But now, what was really increasing was competition for those slots. At First Boston, four thousand graduates were applying for just one hundred positions. Among them: one-third of the senior class at Yale.

The appeal of the analyst position was obvious. The money was very good—typically around $40,000 per year plus bonus, well more than most twenty-two- or twenty-three-year-olds in America were making. But even more alluring was the long-term opportunity. Traditionally, analysts who'd spent a couple of years at the big investment firms had their pick of first-rate MBA programs—Harvard, Stanford, Wharton.

Or, for a select few, the "superstars" of any given analyst class, there was the possibility of not even needing an MBA and being promoted directly to associate, which put you on track to be a partner and share in all the riches now being created.

The downside of being an analyst? The actual job was pretty terrible. Indeed, the work was sometimes that of a glorified secretary—some research, some basic number crunching, proofreading lots of documents—and the hours were ridiculous. Take, for instance, a young analyst named David. A rower in college—an inordinate number of analysts seemed to have crewed—he'd joined his firm, he said, because he loved the idea of being in the thick of things, of seeing up close how American business and finance really worked. He acknowledged that the job was all-consuming; he routinely worked ninety- to one-hundred-hour weeks, and it wasn't out of the question to pull a "round-robin"—working all night, taking a cab home, then asking the cabdriver to wait while you rushed inside for a shower and a fresh shirt before promptly heading back to the office. The schedule was so crazy that, with the exception of late-evening meals at some of the pricier restaurants in town, there was hardly any time to actually spend the money you were making.

"What this job demands is that you ruin your life," David said. "We come in well-rounded people, and two years later we're single-minded drones who aren't any fun at all." But, he continued, the misery was well worth it for the gold-plated future laid out in front of him. "I'm willing to give it all up, to sacrifice everything, to be an investment banker."

Not everyone could cut it. The attrition rate among analysts was high; there were clearly people who just weren't built for the eat-or-be-eaten culture that had taken hold. Which, of course, only energized those who were. "The sleepless shall inherit the earth" was one catchphrase making the rounds.

From a cultural standpoint, perhaps the most interesting thing about the growing popularity of the analyst programs was that they were attracting people who didn't necessarily know much about Wall Street—and weren't even sure they wanted to work in finance. "Bright kids who don't know what to do become analysts," one young Wall Streeter said. In America in 1984, it was just what you did.

*   *   *

These shifts were, unsurprisingly, increasingly reflected in pop culture. The previous fall, the screenwriter and director Lawrence Kasdan (best known as the writer of two of the original *Star Wars* movies, as well as *Raiders of the Lost Ark*) had penned and directed *The Big Chill*, a comedy-drama about the reunion of a group of University of Michigan students whose '60s idealism has given way to '80s careerism. The film had some parallels to Kasdan's own life—he'd been politically active as a student at Michigan in the late '60s, but as the '70s progressed he noted an increasing apathy and cynicism among his friends. The film ultimately wrestles with the same question Jerry Rubin had been grappling with for a half dozen years: Had a generation sold out, or merely grown up? "I'd hate to think it was all just fashion," one of the movie's characters says of their quasi-revolutionary stances and activities in college.

The film certainly captured the attention of real-life Boomers, ultimately earning more than $50 million at the box office (as well as an Oscar nomination for Best Picture). Part of the appeal was the movie's soundtrack of '60s hits, which struck a nostalgic chord among those in their thirties while also inspiring agencies on Madison Avenue to pepper commercials with similarly beloved '60s songs—another tool for capturing the attention of Yuppies with disposable income.

While *The Big Chill* looked backward, in September 1984, a novel appeared that captured some of the excess of the new age. *Bright Lights, Big City* was Jay McInerney's semi-autobiographical tale about a young fact-checker at a *New Yorker*–like magazine who traverses the drug-fueled New York club scene, surrounded by other young professionals with plenty of money but little moral compass. While ultimately the book is about the character's quest to make sense of his own life, it captured the feel and attitude of what New York was becoming.

The book was also interesting from a publishing standpoint. *Bright*

Lights, Big City was published as part of Random House's Vintage Contemporary series—a paperback collection that mixed literary classics with novels from up-and-coming young writers. McInerney had initially been unsure about having his novel published only in paperback—it was a serious book, and it should be in hardcover, he thought—but he was ultimately persuaded that the lower price point on a paperback would make it more appealing to Baby Boomers, who were its most likely audience. The strategy worked. Within three weeks, *Bright Lights, Big City* had sold ten thousand copies—impressive for a first novel from an unknown writer—mostly in big cities around the country. In New York, bookstores couldn't keep it in stock.

The novel never used the word that was on everyone's lips in the fall of 1984, but McInerney would later remember the first time he heard it. It was a year earlier, and he was having breakfast at a restaurant not far from where he lived in the East Village when he spotted a young couple waiting to be seated. He would, he said, have characterized them as "preppies"—they were wearing chinos and oxford shirts—but the guy sitting next to McInerney at the counter, an artist he knew from the neighborhood, used a different phrase for the couple. "Fucking Yuppies," he muttered under his breath.

If the zeitgeist shift was impacting the substance of movies, TV, books, and music, it was influencing, perhaps even more, their style. At a moment when brand names were becoming important, when social status mattered more than ever, when money and success were beginning to trump all, the appearance of things had a new significance. MTV had debuted in the late summer of 1981, first getting traction—due to distribution issues in the cable TV industry—only in smaller markets around the country. But by the summer of 1984, thanks to an impactful ad campaign and a reluctant decision by network execs to begin airing videos by Michael Jackson (whose R & B–influenced pop had previously been considered "outside the format" by MTV), the all-video music channel was becoming a certified cultural phenomenon. What was revolutionary about it, of course, was the way it placed visuals on the same level as—or even above—the music itself. Jackson was already a generational artist, but his gifts as a dancer and his creativity in making videos had elevated him (and now MTV) to unprecedented heights.

Even more instructive was Madonna, whose first album MTV had helped make a hit in the summer of 1983. She was a marginally talented singer and dancer, but she had ambition, knew how to use her sexuality to gain attention, and was a master of the visual form. In the fall of 1984, she released her second album, *Like a Virgin*, whose title track instantly went into heavy rotation on MTV and became her first number one single on the Billboard charts. It was followed by a second single from the album, "Material Girl." One of the song's cowriters was Peter Brown, a Chicago native who'd had a handful of disco hits and shared a manager with Madonna, Freddy DeMann. One night in 1984, Brown was invited out to dinner with DeMann, Madonna, and Madonna's producer Jellybean Benitez, and afterward the group went to a Michael Jackson concert at Madison Square Garden, followed by a postconcert party at Jackson's suite in the Helmsley Palace hotel. A few days later DeMann and his business partner asked Brown to write a song for Madonna.

Brown said yes and spent a week trying to come up with something, without much luck. But one day while he was in his car, he had a burst of inspiration—the music, the chorus, even some of the lyrics just seemed to pour out of him all at once. He kept singing the song to himself as he drove so he wouldn't forget it, and finally captured what he'd written when he got home. His songwriting partner, Robert Rans, finished the lyrics, and a demo for "Material Girl" was sent off to Madonna.

Whether the song's lyrics—a celebration of money and wealth, including lines like "the boy with cold hard cash is always Mister Right"—were meant to be taken literally or sardonically was never quite clear, but as with *The Official Preppy Handbook* and *The Yuppie Handbook*, it probably didn't matter. Listeners heard what they wanted to hear, and the record rose all the way to number two. Madonna's video for the song, inspired by Marilyn Monroe's performance of "Diamonds Are a Girl's Best Friend" in *Gentlemen Prefer Blondes*, played the whole thing as satire—at the conclusion of the video, Madonna's character ends up with a wealthy guy who pretends to be penniless and dazzles her with flowers instead of diamonds. But the singer didn't deny the appeal of a guy with cold hard cash. As she'd tell an interviewer a couple of years later, "You are attracted to people who are ambitious ... like in the song 'Material Girl.' You are attracted to men who have material things because that's what pays the rent and buys you furs. That's the security. That lasts longer than emotions." And that, to be sure, was the wealth-and-self spirit of 1984.

CHAPTER 16

Morning

Headed into the general election in the fall of 1984, Ronald Reagan had pulled off a remarkable political turnaround. In the winter of 1983, Reagan's approval rating among Americans had bottomed out at 35 percent. Eighteen months later, the number of people who said they approved of the job Reagan was doing had risen by nearly 20 points—and it was steadily climbing.

It was hard to imagine Reagan in a stronger position. Not every promise he'd made had been kept—the federal budget was far from balanced, with a deficit of $175 million, and in 1982 and 1983 Congress had undone some of Reagan's tax cuts to keep the deficit from being even larger. But Reagan had arguably delivered on the two big things he pledged to do. America appeared stronger on the world stage, with the embarrassment of the Iranian hostage crisis behind the country and a new, more aggressive stance against the Soviet Union. Meanwhile, the big-picture economic numbers were strong, with GDP growth on track to exceed 7 percent in 1984, its best performance since 1951. For all the criticism he had received, Reagan could argue that Reaganomics had worked.

Walter Mondale understood the mammoth challenge he was facing.

Not only was Reagan popular, but Mondale had been bruised by the long Democratic primary battle. Gary Hart's charge that Mondale and his policies were tied to the past would be difficult for Mondale to shake. To give their campaign a jolt, the Mondale camp had very publicly invited several potential vice-presidential candidates who were not white men to Mondale's home in Minnesota: San Francisco mayor Dianne Feinstein, Los Angeles mayor Tom Bradley, and San Antonio mayor Henry Cisneros. Finally, a few days before the party convention in San Francisco, Mondale announced he had selected Geraldine Ferraro, a third-term member of Congress from New York and a rising star in the party. The choice of the first woman to run on a major party ticket did what the Mondale team had hoped: generated an avalanche of press attention and buzz.

In his acceptance speech at the Moscone Center in San Francisco in mid-July, Mondale emphasized the broad array of constituencies the Democratic Party hoped to represent, including much-chattered-about young professionals. "Just look at us here tonight," he said from the podium. "Black and white, Asian and Hispanic, Native and immigrant, young and old, urban and rural, male and female—from Yuppie to lunch pail, from sea to shining sea. We're all here tonight in this convention speaking for America. And when we in this hall speak for America, it is America speaking."

Mondale went on to say that the party was not the same one that had been trounced by Reagan in 1980. Calling his point of view a "new realism," he said Democrats believed in a strong defense; they knew government had to be well managed; and they understood that a healthy, growing private sector was the key to prosperity. But none of those positions meant that Ronald Reagan should have a second term. On the contrary, Mondale argued, Reagan's policies had overwhelmingly benefited the well-off at the expense of the working class.

"To big companies that send our jobs overseas, my message is: We need those jobs here at home. And our country won't help your business— unless your business helps our country."

What's more, Mondale continued, Reagan's apparent success was an illusion, nowhere more so than with the economy. Those exploding budget deficits Reagan had created? The next president—whether it was Mondale or Reagan—would have no choice but to reduce them.

"Whoever is inaugurated in January, the American people will have to pay Mr. Reagan's bills. The budget will be squeezed. Taxes will go up. And anyone who says they won't is not telling the truth to the American people.

"I mean business," Mondale declared. "By the end of my first term, I will reduce the Reagan budget deficit by two-thirds. Let's tell the truth. It must be done, it must be done. Mr. Reagan will raise taxes, and so will I. He won't tell you. I just did."

Mondale's bold approach appeared to give his campaign a boost. In polls conducted right after the convention, Mondale shot up nine points. He was still behind by at least eight points, but the surge suggested he might mount a credible challenge to Reagan. But the convention bump was short-lived. Shortly afterward, the media began raising questions about the finances and connections of Ferraro's husband, John Zaccaro. Meanwhile, the US performance at the Summer Olympics spurred a wave of patriotic pride—much to Reagan's benefit.

At the Republican convention in Dallas, which began a week after the Olympics ended, Reagan and party loyalists reveled in all the success and good feelings. In his speech accepting the Republican nomination for a second term, Reagan criticized Democrats for past failures, saying Americans had lost hope on their watch. Under his leadership, the economy was performing well, America's defense was stronger, and optimism was on the rise. He reiterated a signature line that had helped him win the White House four years earlier:

"In 1980 we asked the people of America, 'Are you better off than you were four years ago?' Well, the people answered then by choosing us to bring about a change. We have every reason now, four years later, to ask that same question again, for we have made a change.

"The American people joined us and helped us," he continued. "Let us ask for their help again to renew the mandate of 1980, to move us further forward on the road we presently travel, the road of common sense, of people in control of their own destiny; the road leading to prosperity and economic expansion in a world at peace."

*   *   *

Heading into the fall, one of the questions on politicos' minds was which way Gary Hart's most-high-profile supporters—Yuppies—would go in the election. On one hand, there was a case to be made that the Yuppies would, and should, support Mondale. When it came to social issues—abortion, civil rights, gay rights, the role of women in society and the workplace—many young professionals retained their idealism and liberal values from the '60s. Mondale was far more aligned with them on those topics, and a crucial part of Reagan's base was the religious right, who stood in direct opposition to many of those ideals.

But the Reagan camp was intent on attracting as much Baby Boomer support as possible, despite Reagan, at age seventy-three, being the oldest president in history. And they believed pop culture was one way to do it.

In late August, conservative columnist and close Reagan ally George Will attended a Bruce Springsteen concert at the Capital Centre just outside DC, a guest of Springsteen's drummer, Max Weinberg, and Weinberg's wife, Rebecca. Will was hardly an old man—only forty-three—but in the glowing column he wrote about his experience, he painted himself as someone from a far earlier generation. He'd worn his signature bow tie and double-breasted blazer to the show. He wasn't sure if what he was smelling was marijuana smoke. He'd put cotton balls in his ears to dull the noise.

But he came away beyond impressed with the musician, his band, and their fans. "Springsteen, a product of industrial New Jersey, is called the 'blue-collar troubadour,'" Will wrote. "But if this is the class struggle, its anthem—its '*Internationale*'—is the song that provides the title for his 18-month worldwide tour: 'Born in the U.S.A.'

217

"I have not got a clue about Springsteen's politics, if any," he went on, "but flags get waved at his concerts while he sings about hard times. He is no whiner, and the recitation of closed factories and other problems always seems punctuated by a grand, cheerful affirmation: 'Born in the U.S.A.!'"

It was, of course, an interpretation of the song that was 180 degrees divergent from what Springsteen had intended, though Will wasn't completely wrong about what he saw: Audiences *did* cheer along with "Born in the U.S.A." Was it in strong, united defiance of the country's economic policies? Was it in solidarity with those who were suffering? Or was it simply a mass misreading—aided by a little too much beer and a little too much weed—of what Springsteen was talking about?

Will concluded his column by marveling at Springsteen's work ethic (the show had lasted four hours).

"If all Americans—in labor and management, who make steel or cars or shoes or textiles—made their products with as much energy and confidence as Springsteen and his merry band make music, there would be no need for Congress to be thinking about protectionism," he said. "In an age of lackadaisical effort and slipshod products, anyone who does anything—anything legal—conspicuously well and with zest is a national asset. Springsteen's tour is hard, honest work and evidence of the astonishing vitality of America's regions and generations."

If Will's column showed a misunderstanding of both Springsteen's music and the forces driving America's economy—the seventy thousand GE workers who'd lost their jobs would certainly have taken issue with the idea that they were all lazy incompetents—it didn't deter the Reagan campaign from trying to leverage Springsteen's popularity.

In mid-September, six days after Will's column appeared in the *Washington Post* and other newspapers around the country, Reagan traveled to the small, rural community of Hammonton, New Jersey, for a campaign rally, where the president's speechwriters spiced up his normal stump speech with a local reference designed to generate some applause.

"America's future," Reagan told the audience, "rests in a thousand dreams inside your hearts. It rests in the message of hope in the songs of a man so many young Americans admire—New Jersey's own, Bruce Springsteen. And helping you make those dreams come true is what this job of mine is all about."

Hearing that Reagan had referenced him on the campaign trail, Springsteen, who was about to play two shows in Pittsburgh, was frustrated. While his music was increasingly influenced by politics, he'd never been partisan. But two nights after Reagan's speech, while doing a show in a city where the main industry, steel, had been decimated, Springsteen paused between songs to talk to the crowd.

"The president was mentioning my name in his speech the other day, and I got to wondering what his favorite album of mine must've been," Springsteen told the crowd wryly. "I don't think it was the *Nebraska* album. I don't think he's been listening to this one." From there, the E Street Band kicked into "Johnny 99," a fierce *Nebraska* song about a laid-off autoworker who can't find a new job, gets drunk, shoots a night clerk, and is sentenced to ninety-nine years in prison (and then asks the judge to execute him instead).

The following night, playing another show in Pittsburgh, Springsteen went even further. "There's something really dangerous happening to us out there now. We're slowly getting split up into two different Americas," the singer said. "Things are being taken away from the people that need them and given to the people that don't. There's a promise getting broken. In the beginning the idea was we all live here a little bit like a family where the strong can help the weak ones, the rich can help the poor ones. You know, the American dream.

"I don't think it was that everybody was going to make a billion dollars, but that everybody was going to have an opportunity and a chance to live a life with some decency and some dignity. I know you've got to be feeling the pinch here where the rivers meet." With that, he launched into "The River," that song about lost hope that had been inspired by his own sister.

The rhetorical run-in with Reagan had an impact on Springsteen.

As his tour wore on, he continued to speak out politically, and he began making donations to food banks in cities where he played. But if his goal was to stop members of his own generation from supporting Reagan, he was less than successful.

As the presidential campaign progressed, it became clearer and clearer that many of the Baby Boomers who'd been so excited by Gary Hart's fresh vision were ready to vote for Ronald Reagan. In a poll of voters between the ages of eighteen and thirty-four who made more than $25,000 per year, 70 percent held a positive view of the president—seventeen points higher than Reagan's standing among all age-groups—and Reagan held a twenty-four-point lead in a head-to-head matchup with Mondale.

For some young professionals, their support was based on Reagan's manner and leadership style. The country was stronger, they told pollsters, and Reagan deserved credit for making that happen. Equally important was Reagan's handling of the economy. Educated young professionals had done better than most over the last four years, and seven in ten of them believed Reagan was more likely than Mondale to keep making them better off financially.

One day in October, graduates of an East Coast prep school gathered at an alumni function in Chicago. One of the attendees at the function—which was filled, according to a reporter, with people wearing blue blazers and red pindot ties while they sipped wine and nibbled on cubes of cheese—was a twenty-six-year-old corporate financial adviser, who, despite disagreeing with Reagan on several issues, made clear he was voting for him nonetheless. "He has reestablished the image of the United States domestically and overseas," he said. "In 1981, I was in France, and they thought Reagan was a joke. I was just back there, and the change was incredible. He's a President who is regarded abroad. Mondale just doesn't project an image of authority." The young man also agreed with Reagan's cutting of social programs that helped lower-income Americans. "It's time for people," he said, "to pull for themselves."

Other young professionals at the party focused even more directly on economic issues. "The economy has improved quite a bit," a twenty-five-year-old filmmaker shared, "and Mondale just hasn't advanced the issue."

"As incredible as it may seem to our elders, the young see the Democratic Party as an agent of their destruction, not salvation," twenty-nine-year-old Brett Duval Fromson wrote in a guest opinion piece in the *New York Times* in early October. He quoted a young career woman in New York, who told him: "The way I see it, I don't care what [politicians] did for others in the past. I want to know what they will do for me in the future."

Fromson continued: "Yuppies have no faith that the Government will come to the rescue in an economic pinch. We also accepted Reagan's trade-off—prosperity in the long run in return for a short recession in the early 1980s. Why? More of us assumed we would make it on our own even during a recession—and didn't give much thought to those who didn't."

Of course, Fromson concluded, just because they were supporting Reagan now didn't mean they were on board forever. "We will wait to see if President Reagan and his party can deliver the lasting prosperity they have promised. Yuppies, if we do anything at all, respect those who deliver the goods. How else are we going to afford our Ferragamo pumps, Brooks Brothers suits, country houses, European cars and California chardonnays?"

* * *

On TV and the campaign trail, the candidates continued to press their cases. Mondale portrayed Reagan's defense escalation as reckless, while on the economy he pressed for fairness, criticizing the president for tax cuts that had saved the most affluent Americans tens of thousands of dollars each. "I refused to make your family pay more so that millionaires can pay less," Mondale said. Reagan's campaign was summed up by two commercials, created by adman Hal Rainey, that would become iconic. In one called "The Bear," making the case for Reagan's strong stance against the Soviet Union, a grizzly bear roamed through the woods while an announcer—Rainey—said: "There is a bear in the woods. For some people, the bear is easy to see. Others don't see it at all. Some people say the bear is tame. Others say it's vicious and dangerous. Since no one can really be sure who's right, isn't it smart to be as strong as the bear?"

The other ad, "Morning in America," harkened back to the quote from Psalms that Reagan had used a year earlier, and it captured the sense of optimism and renewal that the president hoped to project. It all but declared the restoration of the American Century, the dominance that Americans had been pining after for at least a decade.

"It's morning again in America," a voice (Rainey's) said as the screen showed an array of images of ordinary Americans. "Today more men and women will go to work than ever before in our country's history. With interest rates at about half the record highs of 1980, nearly 2,000 families today will buy new homes, more than at any time in the past four years. This afternoon 6,500 young men and women will be married, and with inflation at less than half of what it was just four years ago, they can look forward with confidence to the future. It's morning again in America, and under the leadership of President Reagan, our country is prouder and stronger and better. Why would we ever want to return to where we were less than four short years ago?"

On Election Day, the president soared, ultimately winning forty-nine states and topping Mondale by seventeen million votes. It was the second-largest landslide victory in American history. To the extent the election had been a referendum on economic policy—Reaganomics vs. the ideas and policies of the New Deal—the American people had made their voices abundantly clear.

*   *   *

Six weeks after Election Day, in its final issue of 1984, *Newsweek*'s cover story summed up the mood of the moment. The magazine proclaimed it not the year of Ronald Reagan, nor the year of America's economic comeback, nor the year of America's Olympic dominance. It was, instead, "The Year of the Yuppie."

"It is on the move again," *Newsweek* wrote, "that restless vanguard of the baby boom generation, continually reinventing itself as it conquers the undefended decades of the 20th century. In unruly ranks assembled, its members marched through the '60s, then dispersed into a million solitary joggers, riding the crest of their own alpha waves, and now there they go again, barely looking up from the massive gray columns of the *Wall Street Journal* as they speed toward the airport, advancing on the '80s in the back seat of a limousine."

The piece, written with a certain degree of snark, offered a wide-ranging overview of the Yuppie phenomenon, from Yuppies' focus on status and their obsession with food to their insistence on high-quality stuff, along the way quoting various Yuppies about their lives, lifestyles, and values. It spotlighted networker-in-chief Jerry Rubin, who said that Yuppies were challenging ossified corporate structures in the same way they'd once challenged college administrators and the traditions of academia.

But perhaps the most telling point made by the piece was this one: For all the attention Yuppies had gotten, for all the political and economic and cultural power they had, they represented just a small slice of the Baby Boom generation, which was, overall, struggling.

Gary Lawrence, one of the pollsters for the 1984 Reagan campaign, pointed out, "The more accurate statistical profile of the baby-boom generation goes like this—married couple living in an apartment in the suburbs, with 1½ kids and 1½ cars. He has a job as a sales rep, or in middle management; she works, too."

As various other sources and statistics would show, at a time when the public was paying attention to young urban professionals, the true story of the Baby Boom generation was not about achievement or success or boutiques or renovated brownstones or fitness classes or choosing from among a hundred types of cheeses. It was about downward mobility.

Between 1979 and 1983, median income for families in the twenty-five to thirty-four age bracket actually fell 14 percent. And compared with their parents at the same age, two-thirds of Baby Boomers were actually worse off economically. In the 1950s, a family making the median income in America at the time could afford a house, kids, TV, and vacation on one income. Now, young families were struggling to afford any of that on two incomes. For those in the bottom third economically, where people of color were overrepresented, homeownership wasn't even on the radar.

The notion of a restored America that Ronald Reagan had campaigned on so vigorously and that so many people had supported was, in many respects, an illusion. The country's storied postwar dominance had come after defeating totalitarianism in two hemispheres, then building an economy that lifted everyone. This new American moment? It had come after the invasion of a small Caribbean island and the creation of an economy that was working only for those at the top. But they were the ones who held the power, and more than ever that's what mattered.

PART IV

1985–86

The Debate

Even as the unofficial Year of the Yuppie came to an end, Yuppie domination of the culture—or at least people looking to cash in on Yuppieness—continued. In February 1985, at the annual American Toy Fair in New York, Mattel unveiled an all-new version of America's most iconic doll, Barbie, completely made over for the success-driven '80s. Where once Barbie sported a swimsuit and sunglasses, Yuppified Barbie now looked like she was ready for one of Jerry Rubin's networking events, with a briefcase, credit cards, business cards, and a suit designed by Oscar de la Renta. Across the country, in California, a young entrepreneur who favored BMWs and Club Med vacations was securing a limited trademark on the word "Yuppie," with hopes of producing a line of Yuppie-branded products. In Fort Lauderdale, a group organized the first-ever Yuppie Convention and Trade Show, with thirty vendors hawking everything from Tofutti (a tofu-based frozen dessert) to yachts.

Others latched on to Yuppieness with a mixture of celebration and irony. In San Francisco that winter, five hundred young professionals showed up for the inaugural Yuppie Cotillion, a black-tie event featuring live music, white wine, pâté, and raspberry sorbet. A portion of the ticket price went to charity—not helping the homeless or feeding the poor but funding a proposal to build a downtown baseball stadium in San Francisco. "We are achievers," one of the organizers deadpanned, "but we are civic-minded." In Chicago, an opportunistic young businessman rolled out a print called *The Last Yupper*—a spot-on send-up of da Vinci's *Last Supper*, with Yuppies standing in for the apostles and a bevy of Yuppie stuff (Brie, sushi, Trivial Pursuit) laid out on the table. Seated at the center of the painting was a serene, Christlike figure in a three-piece suit, tallying the check with a pocket calculator. And in Nashville, the mayor and his team were busy planning Yuppie Day, a celebration that would feature food, drink, and plenty of games, including competitions to see who had the most foreign car keys on his key chain and which American Express cardholder had the highest credit limit.

As the snarky tone of the *Newsweek* cover story had suggested, a backlash to—if not outright disdain for—Yuppieness was developing. From the time of Roz Chast's *New Yorker* cartoon in early 1983, outsiders looking at the ambitious young professional class had done so with a wink and a smirk, but now something was changing. Yuppie jokes began to make the rounds. *How many Yuppies does it take to screw in a light bulb? Two. One to call the electrician, the other to open the Beaujolais.* Young professionals began working hard to distance themselves from the label, including several of the people featured in *Newsweek*'s Yuppie story, who claimed their quotes, and occasionally life stories, were taken out of context by the magazine. (Years later, a woman featured in the *Newsweek* piece would call it one of the most painful experiences of her life.) Still others complained that as a class, young professionals were being caricatured in the media and misunderstood. "In terms of the lifestyle, I am a total Yuppie," a young New Yorker said. "I have an Akita—a Japanese dog known as the Yuppie Puppy. I drive a Saab Turbo. I live in a co-op in New York. I'm pregnant, which is totally Yup. But underneath all this stuff is a person who has very basic values, who loves her husband, is excited about having a child, is involved in women's causes and gives a lot of money to different charities. Just to label me a Yuppie is yucky."

The label had, in fact, become yucky. In the space of just a few years, the term had morphed from a simple descriptor to a cultural archetype to, now, a pejorative. Little wonder that some companies, which the previous year had rushed to embrace Yuppieness in their advertising, were backing away. In 1984, Grape-Nuts had aired a campaign oozing with Yuppie smugness: "There's no question Grape-Nuts is right for you," a young man said into the camera. "The question is, are you right for Grape-Nuts?" A year later, the cereal had toned things down with a new tagline: "You know when you have it good." Even more dramatic was the shift made by that icon of Yuppieness, the American Express card. In a new campaign, Amex took its Yuppie image head-on, saluting "those who know there's more to life than a VCR, a food processor and a new pair of running shoes." Meanwhile, as part of the campaign, the company announced it was searching for young people who combined successful careers with volunteerism. Their reward? A thousand-dollar bequest to their favorite charity from Amex—and, of course, a luxury vacation.

In one respect, the retreat was predictable—it was the backlash portion of the trend cycle, which occurred whenever something or someone was hyped excessively in the media. And yet, this particular recoiling seemed to spring from something deeper—an examination of the values that Yuppieness represented. And ironically, the best place to see those values held up to the light and argued about was in a series of debates between Jerry Rubin and Abbie Hoffman.

*   *   *

By the winter of 1984, Jerry and Mimi Rubin's splashy networking events at Studio 54 had run their course, and the couple decided to spend three weeks at a resort in Mexico while they figured out their next steps. When they arrived at JFK Airport in New York for their flight south, sitting there at the gate were none other than Abbie and his girlfriend, Josie, also headed for a vacation in Mexico. The pairs hadn't seen each other for a couple of years, ever since Jerry and Mimi turned

Abbie down when he asked to use their database of influential names. But the moment they laid eyes on one another, any acrimony fell away. There were hugs, and just like that the hard feelings were forgotten. The couples ended up sitting next to each other on the plane and spent much time together in Mexico over the next several weeks. Abbie even tried to teach Jerry to swim.

If Jerry had changed—multiple times—since the '60s, so, too, in a different way, had Abbie. After emerging from his time underground in 1980 and serving a prison sentence on drug charges, he remained a committed left-wing activist. But there were no overt calls for revolution, as there had been in the '60s, and no more stunts designed purely to make fun of the establishment. His activism was more serious now, zeroed in on protecting the environment and opposing US involvement in Central America.

That summer, Abbie covered a Woodstock fifteenth-anniversary concert for *Esquire* magazine and wore a T-shirt that read "Yippie sí, Yuppie no." Jerry saw a photo of Abbie wearing the shirt and had a brainstorm: a series of debates between the two old friends, with Abbie standing up for the ideals and practices of the '60s while Jerry advocated for his new approach, capitalism. They got an agent, Don Epstein, interested, and following an appearance on Phil Donahue's TV show, "The Yippie vs. Yuppie" tour began playing at colleges across America and Canada.

In some respects, there was some pathos connected to what they were doing. Two men who had been countercultural titans in the '60s were now middle-aged and cashing in on both their fame and a pop-culture trend. (Their speaking fee, split among themselves and their agent, was typically $4,000 per engagement, plus expenses.) It felt a little like an aging rock band reuniting just for a payday and some attention. And yet, the debates that ensued over the course of the next year were not only entertaining but substantive, with two bright men speaking passionately about the direction of the country, their generation, and each other. And while early on the encounters had some warmth to them, two longtime friends teasing each other while they engaged in a spirited disagreement, as the months passed, the barbs got a little sharper, the tone a little meaner. By the end, the warmth they shared was replaced by a sense of genuine distaste.

*   *   *

Typical was a Friday evening in early March 1985, a month and a half into Ronald Reagan's second term, when the duo was invited to appear at Red Deer College in Alberta, Canada. The format for the evening loosely followed classic debate structure: a fifteen-minute opening statement by each speaker, followed by ten-minute rebuttals, followed by questions from the audience.

After they took the stage, Jerry kicked things off. Dressed in a dark blue suit and red tie, with two bottles of Perrier perched near his podium, he began with a clever, if somewhat self-aggrandizing, set piece he'd created that mimicked American Express's popular "Do you know me?" commercials.

"You may remember me from the 1960s," he began. "I led thousands of young people into the streets, and presidents fighting wars quivered at the sound of my name. I was known—and not wanted—in many states and countries, including Canada. I was the subject of hundreds of thousands of arguments around the dinner table between parents and their children. And then in the '70s, I took off my beard and no one recognized me anymore. So now I never leave home without my American Express card."

He pulled out a green Amex card, and the crowd broke into laughter and applauded.

"Now you *do* know, don't you, that's a joke?" Jerry said, smiling.

From there, he launched into his major point: "I have a message tonight that may be new to some of you," he said. "It's that the people that were active in the 1960s and went through internal changes in the 1970s, in the 1980s are in the process of taking over America.... And to those people who say that, because we've put on a tie or changed our dress a little bit, we've sold out, I say that's absurd. We're taking over."

The strategy of this generation, he continued, was to transform America—and Canada—through entrepreneurial capitalism. Yes, in the '60s they were against capitalism and big business, but they'd all learned that the alternative to capitalism doesn't really allow much freedom, and so he and others in his generation were in the process of transforming capitalism from big business to entrepreneurship. "One of the differences between the two debaters tonight is that I'm going to tell you who's going to change society over the next few years and decades," he said. "And that is the Baby Boom generation, those seventy-five million Americans born after World War II who did so many positive things in the '60s.

"We realize that the tactics of the '60s are no longer appropriate for the '80s. And we made an even more important realization, and that is: We're the majority in the United States. We will control the election in 1988. Why define ourselves as protesters, as outsiders, as rebels protesting the policies of the people in power—when we can *become* the people in power?"

The key to doing that, Jerry continued, was business; more specifically, it was the tens of thousands of new businesses being launched each year.

"And who is starting the businesses? It's the young urban professionals, the Yuppies, the Baby Boom generation that challenged the government in the '60s, changed themselves in the '70s, and in the 1980s are transforming the economic system from an industrial country to an information country.... America is becoming the information capital of the world, and it's being done by the young urban professionals."

The election in the fall, he said, had been disappointing. Ronald Reagan was an old-fashioned imperialist, while Walter Mondale represented the 1930s and the old idea of big government.

"Had the Democratic Party nominated Gary Hart...you would have seen a very close election," said Jerry, an enthusiastic Hart supporter. Then he made a prediction: "In 1988, a Yuppie-oriented, a Baby Boom–oriented candidate, will be elected president of the United States. And this candidate will have a social base made up of those same people that were active and were part of the '60s constituency that Abbie Hoffman and I represented.

"I respect Abbie Hoffman as an activist, but it saddens me that he has isolated himself from the very generation that he was active with in the 1960s."

That generation, Jerry said, now wanted to be successful, and there was nothing wrong with that.

"You can be wealthy and still care about changing the world. As a matter of fact, it's okay to be successful. We were against success in the '60s. We're *for* success in the '80s. The only difference is now we're going to combine success with a social conscience.... You can become successful and still want to eliminate poverty, successful and still want to eliminate nuclear war.

"In the '60s, they fought," he said, talking about Boomers as he finished up. "In the '80s and '90s, they'll implement what they fought for."

*　　　*　　　*

When Jerry's opening statement was over, the crowd applauded politely, then turned its attention to Abbie. Bearded, wearing a plaid shirt, jeans, and a newsboy cap, he looked out from the podium.

"I'm not here to resurrect the politics of sex, drugs, rock and roll, freak clothes, and long hair," he said in his thick Massachusetts accent. "That was a fad, and that fad is over. But I am interested in continuing a politics built around activism on issues like social justice, poverty, environmental abuse, control of nuclear arms, and especially against US intervention in Central America.

"I'm doing these debates to attack the mythology that all of us who were politically active in that era eventually became disillusioned, self-centered, and consumed only with the accumulation of wealth.... Not all of us who were active rush to embrace that materialistic lifestyle with the gusto of my debating opponent."

Abbie was disappointed, he said, in the generation that had come after his.

"The activism of today is being carried on by activists of my generation. It's not a question of what happened to our Woodstock Nation. It's a question of where is the Woodstock Nation of this generation?... The campuses have become hotbeds of social rest. About as exciting as hospital food or watching television bowling."

The crowd laughed and applauded, and Abbie started talking more about Jerry and what he stood for. "There's a world out there, and it's a world with a lot of problems," he continued. "It's not the rosy [scenario] that Jerry Rubin sees when he jogs through life on Manhattan's Upper East Side. His world has become very narrow—as narrow as his tie. It's twenty blocks of high-rise buildings, armies of uniformed doormen. It's the Hamptons in the summer. It's the life advertised in the slick magazines. Listen carefully to what he says: These young urban professionals, these so-called Yuppies, are gonna run the world from the top down, and war and poverty and environmental abuse and all the nasty things that we don't like are all going to disappear because they wish it to. And after the Yuppies become rich, they're just gonna give away their money because they're naturally generous and benevolent. But it's all gonna happen down the road. Don't ask me now, I'm too busy. I'm busy now getting my hunk of the pie. And it's a big hunk at that."

Abbie shifted to the broader economic picture in the United States.

"Obviously some people are doing better. They're doing better than they were two or three years ago. But they're not doing better than a generation ago," he said. "There's a bigger gap between rich and poor than there was a generation ago. A bigger gap in the earning capacities of Blacks and whites. Women are still making half as much money as men for the same amount of work. We have twice the unemployment now that we had in the '60s, and what's worse, people have become accustomed to it.

"Even the Yuppies themselves are a myth. I mean, how many people out of the whole seventy-five million Baby Boomers that Jerry names— he equates the two. How many people can achieve the lifestyles of young urban professionals with the Porsches, the Rolexes, et cetera, et cetera?

It's always gonna be a small minority. The Baby Boom generation as a whole cannot afford to buy the homes that its parents are living in today, and that's a fact. Entrepreneurs? I'm not against entrepreneurship. I love the idea. I love the people that invented Trivial Pursuit and all the new forms of entrepreneurship that are going on . . . Apple computer. But the concept of entrepreneurship does not address the needs of those who are less fortunate. You can't say to a Black woman living in Harlem with ten kids and no education, 'Go out and invent Apple computer.' You can't say it to a farmer whose family has been in business for a century and the government just pulled the rug out from under him. You can't say it to an unemployed steelworker. That is no solution to the problem.

"I'm not afraid of big government. I am concerned about the quality of life the government provides, and not just for its most fortunate citizens, but for its least fortunate. Ronald Reagan and George Bush will spout the same Horatio Alger stories about striking it big, and that's what Jerry Rubin does. And that's why I compare them, ultimately. The Yuppie attitude lacks basic compassion for those that can't get in on the Big Deal."

The crowd applauded loudly.

*   *   *

When it came time for the rebuttals, Jerry focused mostly on what was practical. You couldn't get rid of poverty, he said, without jobs, and jobs were created by entrepreneurs. He also said that people were innately interested in being successful.

"I assume in this room there might be a few people that intend, perhaps, to be entrepreneurs," he said. "There might be a few people that intend to go into business. There might be a few people, heaven forbid, who want to make money. Anyone in this room want to make money? Or maybe I'm in a room where no one wants to make money?" There was a decent amount of applause. "Okay, since some of you want to make money, the question is, does that then make you one of 'them'? Or can you make money, become successful, even become rich, and then still have a social conscience? The young urban professionals are the agency that's going to change North America in the next years."

In his rebuttal, Abbie zeroed in on Jerry's—Yuppies'—definition of success. "When he says success, does it not mean the accumulation of wealth? Or is it an artist painting a painting for self-expression? No. Is it someone helping disadvantaged kids? No. Success comes with a dollar sign. It's very narrowly defined."

After an hour of back-and-forth between the debaters, the audience got its chance to ask questions; it was clear that most of them were on Abbie's side, at least philosophically. Some of the questions even seemed designed to embarrass Jerry.

"I would like to ask you what you will earn tonight, and where you intend to spend your money?" one person said.

Abbie replied that his share of their speaking fee was about $1,300. "Where will it go? I support myself; I support two other activists. The organizations I work for, I charge a dollar a year. About 35 percent of my income goes to the things I'm involved with. I don't have stocks, bonds, I don't have medical insurance, I don't have a lot of things of material value.... I'm trying to strike that proper balance between my personal needs, my family's needs, and my responsibility as a citizen of the community and the world."

When it was Jerry's turn, he said he was making the same fee as Abbie. But, he added, he didn't like it when Abbie proudly announced he didn't have things of material value. "There's nothing wrong with having things of material value. I'm not a particularly materialistic person, but I like having good things, and I don't think there's any contradiction between having good things and also wanting to be idealistic and wanting to change the country."

Another attendee asked Jerry, point-blank, how much money he was worth. After explaining that it was complicated because he owned a couple of businesses, Jerry eventually said, "I am not a rich man. I have a positive cash flow. I probably have a...$40,000 net worth." But that, he said, was because it wasn't until 1980 that he'd gone into business. Before that he'd had Abbie's philosophy on making money.

After more than two hours, the evening finally came to a close. "That's the end," Abbie said into the microphone. "Thanks for bringing us to Red Deer. If you're interested in going to Nicaragua, come see me. If you're interested in making a million dollars, go see Jerry."

The crowd laughed one last time.

*　　*　　*

In a way, it was hard not to feel sorry for Jerry Rubin. Abbie's gibes were often more personal and cutting than Jerry's. Abbie's lines got more applause.

"It was painful for him to always be booed," Mimi would later say, adding that it was one of the reasons that, after a year or so, Jerry stopped doing the debates. Of course, that decision only added to the acrimony between the two men. As Mimi noted, Abbie really needed the money.

CHAPTER 18

Raiders

Two weeks after the Yippie vs. Yuppie debate in Alberta, Mike Milken also found himself standing onstage. This one was a world away, at the lavish Century Plaza hotel in Los Angeles, and Milken was looking out at an audience of fifteen hundred guests. For many of them, he was the center of the universe.

The occasion was the closing-night dinner of the annual high-yield bond conference Milken hosted for Drexel's best clients, a gathering that included financiers he had helped make rich through his junk bond revolution; professional money managers representing various pension funds, insurance companies, mutual funds, and their ilk; and the entrepreneurs who led small- and medium-sized companies hoping to raise capital. The first conference Milken had put together, in 1979, had been attended by only about sixty people, but as Milken's success and power had grown, so, too, had this annual event, which was now spread out over four days and could feel equal parts pep rally and bacchanal (it had been nicknamed "the Predators' Ball"). Black limos chauffeured attendees all over Beverly Hills. Lavish dinners were held at some of LA's finest restaurants. Cozy gatherings were put together that included well-compensated escorts. One Drexel partner would recall camping out each night in the Polo Lounge, inside the Beverly Hills Hotel, drinking Cristal 'til dawn and the start of another day of official conference programming. (It began at 6:00 a.m. The conference ran on Milken time.)

And there was entertainment. At the closing dinner, Milken and the crowd stood back and watched a slick video that celebrated Drexel and included a new version of the theme song from the previous summer's big movie, *Ghostbusters*. "When you need money," the revamped lyrics said, "call Drexel!" When it was over, Milken introduced the headline act for the evening. The previous year it had been Frank Sinatra; tonight, it was Diana Ross—who was said to have waived her normal performance fee in exchange for a stake in one of Milken's investment partnerships.

For all the frivolity, there was also serious business being done. Over the course of the week, the up-and-coming companies, all Drexel clients, would pitch themselves to the investors. The investors, if they were persuaded, would then buy up millions in Drexel-originated junk bonds, giving the young companies the capital they craved, the investors the high returns they needed, and Drexel the lavish transaction fees that were driving the firm's revenues higher and higher. "Whatever the conference cost us, in the millions, we made it up in the first hour because deals were being done," a Drexel banker said. And nowhere would that be truer than at the 1985 conference.

The fast-track mindset that so many young professionals had been espousing since the late 1970s—buttressed by the adoption of Reaganomics in Washington, DC, and the notion of shareholder primacy—now predominated in corporate America and on Wall Street. But what had begun as an effort to restore the American Dream and reinvigorate American capitalism, then evolved into a narrow focus on financial success, now seemed to have become something else: a rapaciousness.

By the beginning of 1985, the corporate merger boom that had begun in earnest at the dawn of the Reagan administration, and that had been kicked into an even higher gear with William Simon's eye-popping LBO windfall in 1983, had reached a new level. In 1984, there had been more than two thousand corporate mergers worth nearly $125 billion. And there were no signs that things were slowing down.

At the center of all the activity was Milken. He and his colleagues were the face of this new, high-flying, money-driven era. While Drexel continued to back small outsiders, as it had for a decade, it was increasingly doing business with Fortune 500 clients, which were using Milken's junk bonds to help finance their large mergers. His reputation and influence could be seen not just at the Predators' Ball, but in the waiting area outside his office in Beverly Hills, which was sometimes filled with people waiting to see him at five thirty on Sunday mornings.

Despite his power and the vast sums he was making, Milken only seemed to want more. But his drive was less about the money itself than the impact he could make. His belief that the management of many large American corporations was inept—and that shareholders were thus being deprived of value—had only deepened, and he saw junk bonds as a way to correct that. Drexel's bonds were being used as part of the financing of large mergers, as well as in so-called "friendly" leveraged buyout attempts, in which the buyer and the seller were willing participants. But Milken's goal was to use them as the main financing tool in *hostile* corporate takeovers—in which an outside investor, against the wishes of management and the board, attempted to seize control of a corporation by acquiring the majority of its shares. That was how change could be forced; that was how stockholders could be rewarded; that was how corporate America could be saved from itself.

Milken began working with his longtime stable of investors—men who always attended the Predators' Ball—to find exactly the right takeover target. Among the investors was T. Boone Pickens. In many regards Pickens was a real-life J. R. Ewing, a colorful Texan who'd done well in the oil business over the previous several decades. But beginning in the early 1980s, Pickens, who chaired a company called Mesa Oil, had shifted his attention from searching for oil to searching for oil companies he could acquire. And from the time he first met Milken, during a get-together at the Helmsley Palace in New York, he was persuaded Milken could help him. "He showed up, had a goofy toupee on, which disarmed me," Pickens said. "I thought, 'Who in the hell is this guy?' He talked very authoritatively, like: 'Sit down and listen.' He came in very handy for us. He doesn't hold back. If he knows anything, he'll sure as hell share it with you."

Pickens first drew significant attention in the fall of 1983, when he started buying shares of one of America's largest and most successful energy companies, Gulf Oil. With financing raised largely through Milken's junk bonds, Pickens—whose company, Mesa, was *sixty times* smaller than Gulf—had begun purchasing the larger company's stock at $41 per share. He kept amassing the stock, and by March 1984 his purchases had driven Gulf's share price all the way up to $80. Convinced that Pickens would destroy Gulf if he acquired control, the company's board of directors decided the only way it could defend itself against a takeover was by selling Gulf to its biggest competitor, Chevron. Pickens didn't get the ultimate prize, control of Gulf, but in exchange for giving up his fight he secured a premium buyout of his shares from Gulf. Total profit for him and his partners: $760 million.

They weren't the only winners. Pickens fashioned himself as the champion of the "little-guy" investor, and by driving up the stock price and forcing the merger with Chevron, he noted that they, too, had benefited. Also scoring a windfall were arbitrageurs—stock speculators who'd begun buying Gulf stock when it became clear Pickens was attempting a takeover. Their windfall: $300 million. They were so thankful that in the summer of 1984, fifty of them got together to honor Pickens with a dinner at the Regency Hotel in Manhattan. New York City mayor Ed Koch was also an attendee that evening, and he gave Pickens a crystal replica of the city's symbol, the apple, in recognition of what Pickens had done for New York: The deal had ultimately generated $50 million in fees for New York–based bankers and lawyers.

In fact, everyone at the top of the ideas and information economy seemed to make out beautifully in Pickens's raid on Gulf Oil. The people who didn't? The twenty thousand oil company workers that Chevron laid off after the merger.

* * *

In the months that followed, Pickens and other Milken clients continued looking for companies that were appealing takeover targets. Dealmaker Saul Steinberg made a hostile run at Disney, and while he didn't acquire it, he walked away with tens of millions in profit. The same was true of arbitrageur Carl Icahn and his failed, but lucrative, raid on Phillips Petroleum.

Finally, in the spring of 1985, around the time of that year's Predators' Ball, a Milken-backed client actually succeeded in a hostile takeover. Triangle Industries, a relatively small vending machine outfit run by an entrepreneur named Nelson Peltz, acquired National Can, a company that was nearly ten times larger. Peltz pulled off the deal thanks to $535 million in junk bond financing arranged by Milken. That represented 90 percent of the money needed to complete the deal, debt that was secured not by Peltz's personal assets but by the company itself. Fiscally speaking, it was like your average Joe neighbor buying the local millionaire's mansion with a few thousand dollars down and the rest charged to a credit card—the millionaire's credit card.

The deal, not surprisingly, drew enormous attention, and at a moment when mergers and takeovers were getting larger than ever, people wondered: If a relative nobody like Nelson Peltz could walk in and simply take over a major corporation, was any company truly safe from corporate raiders? As if to emphasize that the answer was no, Milken clients, all just a fraction of the size of their targets, mounted no fewer than five hostile takeover attempts in the next month. Lorimar went after Multimedia. Financier Sir James Goldsmith went after Crown Zellerbach Corporation. Steve Wynn's Golden Nugget went after Hilton. Farley Industries went after Northwest Industries.

It was a frenzy, and it only grew with another Milken-backed raid that summer: an attempt by investor Ron Perelman to take over international cosmetics company Revlon. The fight for the company took several months—there were lawsuits, and various charges hurled back and forth between the parties—but by the fall Perelman had won out, acquiring Revlon for $900 million, $750 million of which Milken had arranged for him to borrow through junk bonds.

For the companies being acquired in such deals—and for much of the business establishment—what was happening was head-spinning. Michel Bergerac, the ousted, French-born CEO of Revlon, was hardly a sympathetic figure by normal standards. In many regards, he epitomized the sort of self-satisfied corporate executive that Milken resented, with an opulent Paris office and a company-owned 727 that Bergerac used when he wanted to go on safari in Africa. But he had an emotional investment in Revlon; he had helped build it. Ron Perelman, in contrast, saw the company as an asset to be acquired—something he would need to break apart and sell off in parts to pay down the enormous debt he incurred buying it. Perelman quickly unloaded Revlon's health businesses, its best-performing units. As for the cosmetics division that was at the center of Revlon? Perelman made cuts to its operating expenses but didn't show a great deal of interest in actually running the company. As one Drexel executive would say, "Ronnie's a deal person. He wants to do deals."

Perhaps even more head-spinning were the astronomical amounts of money being thrown around as the corporate raids proliferated—and who was pocketing that money. Frank Considine, the ousted CEO of National Can, had worked at the company for more than twenty years, but after Peltz and Milken's hostile takeover, he found himself on the outside looking in. More than anything, it was the magic-trick nature of what had happened that Considine seemed unable to get past.

"I don't believe in being greedy," he said. "It's just that when you look and see everyone making so much, and you know that you and your people are the ones who built the company, and instead here is Drexel making all this money." Then again, he seemed resigned to the fact that this was the new reality, this was the age we were in. As he put it, "you can't spend your time looking back."

*   *   *

The avalanche of deals, the money Milken and his partners at Drexel were making, the way they were setting the agenda for what was happening on Wall Street—all of it pushed Drexel to even greater heights. By the summer of 1985, the press was paying close attention to the firm, which Milken hated. He refused to grant interviews, which only added to his mystique and power.

Of course, the truth was that while Drexel had turbocharged the M&A activity, it hadn't created it, and it was hardly the only Wall Street firm involved. If 1984 had been the Year of the Yuppie, then 1985 was the Year of the Merger.

By the end of the year, there would be twenty-four mergers worth $1 billion or more. After losing out in his pursuit of Phillips Petroleum, Carl Icahn successfully took over legendary airline TWA. Wall Street firm KKR acquired Beatrice, the mammoth food processing company. R. J. Reynolds bought Nabisco. Philip Morris took over General Foods. Capital Cities bought ABC.

In many cases, Wall Street's investment firms were both the instigators and the beneficiaries of the deals. So much had changed since the 1970s. Back then, the firms had largely been passive players, simply taking orders from their corporate clients. Now, investment bankers were boldly making suggestions to corporations on which other companies could be acquired. And with an obvious motivation: The fees the firms collected for facilitating deals were becoming astronomical. Before 1980, only a handful of people on the Street were making more than $500,000 per year. Now, bankers as young as thirty were making that much, and more high-powered players were earning well into the millions. More and more, too, it was a young man's game. Once there had been an apprenticeship system, with younger Wall Streeters willing to observe and learn from longtime vets. No longer. Brash young bankers were making their own rules.

To critics of what was happening—and this included several members of Congress, who opened hearings on corporate takeovers—the raft of megadeals was problematic in several ways. For starters, many of the acquisitions seemed to serve no strategic purpose—there was no sense that two complementary companies were being brought together to create one more effective whole. On the contrary: In many deals, the precise goal of taking over a company was to break it apart, either to "unleash its value," as the saying now went, or, more practically, to pay down the massive debt that was incurred in buying the company in the first place. All the debt that was being created was another problem; American companies were more leveraged than they'd ever been, and the high debt service often meant that jobs needed to be eliminated or long-term investments forgone.

Finally, there was the impact that threatened takeovers had on the entire corporate ecosystem. CEOs at publicly traded companies suddenly lived in fear that a weak quarter would lower their stock price and make them a takeover target; many execs began preemptively slashing costs in order to boost profits and keep their stock prices high.

To advocates of what was happening, the extreme belt-tightening was exactly the point. The deals, and the threats of deals, were making corporate America writ large leaner and more efficient. The problem? One person's efficiency was another person's lost job. By the end of the decade, Lane Kirkland, head of the AFL-CIO, would estimate that ninety thousand union jobs were eliminated thanks to all the mergers and acquisitions. And that didn't count the nonunion jobs that were lost, or the workers who'd kept their jobs but been forced to accept reduced wages.

The big winners in all this? In addition to the corporate raiders like Peltz and Icahn, as well as all the Wall Street firms that were seeing profits soar, it was the people and institutions that held stock. While the number of Americans invested in the market was growing, it was still just 20 percent of the country—most of whom were already on the more affluent end of the wealth spectrum. But now the well-off were becoming even more well-off. After being relatively flat in 1984, the stock market climbed 27 percent in 1985, reaching a brand-new high. The driving force wasn't greater productivity in the economy overall. According to a report from Goldman Sachs, 70 percent of the rise was simply due to all the merger activity driving up stock prices.

*   *   *

At General Electric, the unprecedented bonanza of deals taking place in corporate America was making Jack Welch feel anxious and envious. The job cuts and unloading of entire divisions that had characterized his first few years as CEO—and given him the nickname Neutron Jack—had left GE with plenty of cash to spend, and Welch was eager to join the dealmaking party. As he confided to an audience at Harvard Business School in the fall of 1985, "I don't think I've moved fast enough." Which was, no doubt, news to the mass of GE employees whose jobs Welch had already eliminated. By that point, it was more than one hundred thousand.

Welch's vision remained the same: to transform GE from a company mostly focused on traditional manufacturing to something more modern, one that led in technology and services. He believed, in particular, in the profit potential of GE's financial services division, and he'd begun making acquisitions there to turbocharge its growth. The biggest move was the purchase, for just over $1 billion, of Employers Reinsurance Corporation, whose main business was insuring liabilities on insurance policies other companies had written.

Still, with massive deals being done all over Wall Street, Welch was anxious for something even bigger and more dramatic. His opportunity finally came in November 1985. One evening, he got together for cocktails with the investment banker Felix Rohatyn and Thornton Bradshaw, CEO of RCA, the storied electronics and broadcasting company whose assets included NBC. Months earlier, the Reagan administration had quietly lifted a consent decree that had been in place for half a century that prevented GE from owning any stake in RCA (which it had cofounded back in 1919 and been forced to divest for antitrust reasons). Now Bradshaw was interested in making a deal.

At RCA, the crown jewel had become, to the astonishment of many, NBC. The urban-focused "quality" strategy that Grant Tinker had put in place at the network a few years earlier had paid off handsomely. The true difference maker had been *The Cosby Show*, a sitcom about an upscale Black couple—Buppies, some had called them—and their kids that had become the most popular show on television since debuting in 1984. Thanks to its performance and the overall strength of Thursday nights, NBC was now number one in both ratings and profits, with operating income of more than $300 million per year. The problem facing RCA? Many of its other divisions were not doing as well—NBC accounted for half of the parent company's profits—and Bradshaw believed RCA was itself vulnerable to a hostile takeover. Welch and Bradshaw met for a second time in early December, and a week later came together at a press conference for a dramatic announcement: GE would acquire RCA for $6.5 billion. It would be the largest non-oil-company deal in the history of American business.

The merger seemed a natural. One of the country's most iconic corporations, RCA had a rich legacy in radio and television, with a robust color TV factory in Bloomington, Indiana; a highly regarded innovation lab in Princeton; and, of course, NBC. Putting GE and RCA together would create a formidable US company to compete against the Japanese electronics firms that were taking increasing market share. What's more, from Bradshaw's standpoint, being acquired by a giant like GE would prevent RCA from being targeted and taken over by a raider whose only goal was to break the company apart for a fast profit. "We did not want to see the company broken up willy nilly," he said.

At the press conference announcing the deal, Jack Welch said all the right things. He was excited about what the combined entity could accomplish. He was committed to the newly expanded consumer electronics division, which would continue to manufacture televisions in Indiana. Privately, though, Welch made clear his real interest in the deal had been in acquiring NBC. That was the part of RCA that best fit his vision of what he wanted GE to become: not an old-line manufacturing company, but a modern firm.

Investors loved the deal. After languishing for much of the year, GE's stock shot up on news of the announcement and continued rising. If Welch's primary goal was to keep GE shareholders happy—and it was—then he had succeeded. As for his commitment to the expanded consumer electronics division? It was short-lived. Within a couple of years, Welch shut down the TV manufacturing plant in Indiana and shipped the jobs overseas.

CHAPTER 19

New Elite

In 1980, when he announced to the world that he was now a capitalist, Jerry Rubin had written that, just as rebellion had dominated the '60s and the search for self had characterized the '70s, "money and financial interest will capture the passion of the '80s." Nearly half a dozen years later, he had been proved 100 percent correct. The public at large might have had its fill of Yuppies, but in many respects that didn't matter. In the world that was being created, the people with power were the people with education and money. They were a minority, but so what? More and more they set the rules.

In the summer of 1985, Jerry and Mimi Rubin had found a new home for their networking events—the Palladium, the onetime theater and concert hall that had been newly transformed into a nightclub by Steve Rubell and Ian Schrager, the creators of the original Studio 54 (who were reemerging into the public eye after their prison stints). Designed by world-renowned architect Arata Isozaki, the club's new interior was far more spectacular than Studio 54 had been and quickly became the buzz of New York—and the Rubins' networking nights hit new levels of success, with thousands of people every week showing up, paying the cover charge, and handing over their business cards to be added to Jerry and Mimi's massive Rolodex (which now totaled a reported sixty-seven thousand names). "I don't like to use the word, but every Yuppie in New York comes," Jerry said. The couple had created, in essence, the largest private club in New York.

The promise of sex remained part of the appeal of the evenings, but so, too, was the fact that networking was now standard practice for any ambitious, self-respecting young professional. Local chambers of commerce from across the country were routinely reaching out to Rubin, asking for his advice on how they, too, could host networking events in their cities. It was an extraordinary change. Five years earlier, Rubin's idea for professional networking had been exotic. Now it was mainstream.

Indeed, a bold, self-conscious quest for success displayed itself everywhere, in ways both subtle and overt. Even young New Yorkers committed to making it could be heard complaining that the only things anyone wanted to talk about anymore were real estate, money, and careers. "This is a city built around work," one of them told a journalist. "Your whole identity is tied to that." The vibe—and the messaging behind it—were hard to escape, even if you wanted to.

But the success ethic wasn't just soft and psychological; it had hard, real-life implications, too. In New York and its immediate suburbs, the median price of a single-family home—condo, co-op, detached house—had gone up an astonishing 78 percent between 1982 and 1985. One of the driving factors had been what real estate agents were calling "the Yuppie Syndrome," the preponderance of two-income professional couples who were suddenly buying homes. In Manhattan, prices had gotten so steep that not only were working-class families driven out, so were the artists and creative types who in the '70s had helped give once-struggling neighborhoods like the Upper West Side and SoHo a sense of cool. Now, at least some members of the artistic class who'd lived through the changes were increasingly bitter: The Upper West Side had been ruined by the upscaling of Columbus Avenue, they griped, while SoHo died the day Dean & DeLuca opened in the late '70s. As one furniture maker who'd left New York's fast-changing Lower East Side said with a sigh, "When David's Cookies appeared, I knew it was time to get out."

*   *   *

As money became increasingly important, there was, just below the surface for many in the professional class, a gnawing anxiety. In part it was the exhausting pace the fast track required; two-income couples in particular complained that there weren't enough hours in the day for all the things that needed to be done, let alone to maintain a healthy relationship. A sense of precariousness pervaded everything. In the 1950s and 1960s, America's booming economy had benefited all classes across the board—people with money and people with smaller incomes. The Reaganomics-driven economy of the 1980s, in contrast, rewarded those at the top. The demarcation between winners and losers had rarely been so stark, and you didn't want to make a misstep that would leave you on the wrong side of that line.

One place that anxiety was increasingly revealing itself was in the raising of kids. From the mid-'60s to the late '70s, the number of births in America had trended downward, thanks to birth control, women's growing financial independence, and the delaying of marriage—especially among more educated people. But beginning in 1979, as the biological clocks of older Baby Boomers ticked more loudly, the number trended up again, causing a mini–baby boom. In 1985, 3.76 million babies were born in America, the most in twenty years.

For many educated, upwardly mobile new parents, raising kids was yet another task to be mastered—another way to demonstrate the professionalism and devotion to achievement that were the hallmarks of nearly every other part of their lives.

One area of focus was all the stuff associated with baby raising, from cribs and high chairs to outfits and toys. In the past, most of it had been fairly utilitarian, but across the country, retailers—particularly in higher-end stores and boutiques—would not let professional parents settle for utilitarian when so much more was possible.

"We look for natural fibers, top design, and excellent wearability in our clothing," one children's boutique in the Bay Area said in its catalog. "Our toy selections must stimulate creativity and present extended play value. The books we choose must be fun or educational or both and be bias-free. As always, we guarantee all our products to be the best in their area."

Perhaps nothing represented the rise of the upscale baby market as much as the booming success of the Aprica stroller. Aprica Kassai was a Japanese company founded in 1947 by a young entrepreneur named Kenzo Kassai; after working with troubled youth immediately after the war, Kassai became passionate about manufacturing high-quality products for children. When his first attempt at a stroller bombed, he turned to a group of Japanese pediatricians for help. What kind of stroller, he asked them, would be best for an infant's physical development? The doctors worked on the project for seven years, and their recommendations—which included better support for a baby's hips than in a typical stroller—became the foundation of the company. Kassai then turned to Isabelle Hebey, a French designer who would later work on the Concorde jet, to create the stroller's actual design.

Kassai's stylish, doctor-approved stroller became a hit in Japan, and in 1980 he set his sights on America. The problem? He wanted to sell the Aprica stroller for $200 or more, four times the cost of any other high-end stroller and ten times the cost of an economy model. But Kassai was convinced that a subset of American parents would pay a serious premium for a premium product, and in the quality-obsessed, label-mad 1980s, he was absolutely right. Within a couple of years baby specialty stores were selling fifty thousand Apricas a year, and by 1985 the number was two hundred thousand.

Ensuring a child's physical development was only one part of the parenting equation. Well aware that their own path to the professional class had started with a good education, a segment of parents doubled down on their children's intellectual development from the moment they emerged from the womb. There were flash cards and educational toys and music pumped into nurseries, along with lessons for everything you could imagine. The goal of all of it was to help the child reach their potential, but if it also gave the kid an edge over all the other kids, that wasn't so bad, was it?

When it came to getting an edge, the real battlefield was becoming school itself, and the equation was simple: The better the school your child got into, the better the chances were of that child getting ahead in life. Between 1980 and 1984, the number of kids attending private school across the US grew by four hundred thousand, while the number of kids attending public school dropped by 1.3 million.

"The issue of getting your child into a good private school was really difficult," Kathy Kehoe, who raised two children on New York's Upper East Side, later recalled. "There was a lot of competition because the Baby Boom was having babies. You wanted your child to go to the best possible nursery school, then the best possible kindergarten. Conversation revolved around it. And of course you were thinking about college already: If your child didn't go to a good school, she won't get into a good college."

In New York, the battle to get into one of a dozen or so of the most prestigious private schools was so fierce that four-year-olds were being tutored for entrance exams and kids were being dragged to six, seven, even eight interviews. The fight for spots became so fierce that in 1984, it was harder to get into pre-K at prestigious Horace Mann than it was to get into Harvard.

The stress and competition only grew alongside the kids. Anxious to go to an elite college, high school students were doing four or five hours a night of homework on top of a backbreaking level of extracurriculars to show how well-rounded they were. There were increasing reports of cheating and burnout and mental health crises.

The thing was, from a results standpoint, none of the thinking that drove the behavior was necessarily incorrect. The better the school you went to, and the better you did at that school, the better your odds were of getting into an elite college. In 1984, 773 kids graduated from New York's ten best-known private schools; all but two went to college, and a large number landed at elite colleges. Between 1982 and 1984, a full 40 percent of graduates of Manhattan's prestigious Dalton School ended up at Ivy League schools, mostly Harvard, Yale, and Brown. And yes, getting into one of those schools really did matter. Ivy League graduates made up a third of the students at Yale Law School and half the students at Cornell's medical school. At Salomon Brothers, a third of the hard-charging analyst class of 1984 had come from Harvard, Stanford, or Penn. The pre-K to Ivy League to guaranteed wealth pipeline was real.

*   *   *

Despite the warm reception Abbie Hoffman might have received among some college students, the focus on money and success was also increasingly visible on college campuses themselves. The shift that had taken place in a decade and a half was palpable. While there remained students at many colleges who were speaking out about US involvement in Central America or the evils of apartheid in South Africa, the majority of the generation was leaning right politically. In 1984, voters between the ages of eighteen and twenty-four were behind only senior citizens in their support of Ronald Reagan, with 61 percent of young voters choosing him over Mondale. (And surveys suggested college students preferred Reagan at an even higher rate than the age-group overall.)

In many respects, the change was understandable, perhaps inevitable. The students now were part of a different generation—by 1985, half of those on campus were technically members of what would become known as Generation X. More importantly, they'd been shaped by vastly different experiences. While college kids in the late '60s and early '70s had come of age at a time when America seemed infinitely prosperous, college kids now had grown up in a country awash in economic anxiety. While students in the '60s opposed a war they saw as a dark example of American power and imperialism, the current generation had mostly known an America that was weak, one whose economy was upended by the politics of the Middle East. Finally, there were the ideas and ideals they'd been exposed to. Most Baby Boomers were raised at the high point of liberalism; current students had become culturally aware when conservativism and capitalism and love of the free market were on the rise.

In the fall of 1985, a young man named Jeff Zajkowski entered his junior year at the University of Pennsylvania. He'd grown up in Sheboygan, Wisconsin, a middle-class city of fifty thousand people where his dad ran a one-man pharmacy. Sheboygan had a long history of manufacturing, and most of the kids in his high school class didn't go to college, but Zajkowski was on a different track. He was interested in business—he literally read Milton Friedman's *Free to Choose* in sixth grade, a real-life Alex P. Keaton—and when he got to Penn, he majored in finance. On campus, he was certainly aware of some of the more liberal causes other students might be advocating for, but issues like Central America didn't resonate much.

Such practicality was common. Cristina Schoene, a sophomore at Rollins College in Florida, was majoring in economics and intent on being a financial success, in large part because she watched the ups and downs her mother, who worked in real estate, went through. "She's gone from being very poor to being very well off to struggling," Schoene told a journalist. "I see what she goes through when she can't sleep at night because she can't pay the bills. I want to make a lot of money—that's why I'm working so hard."

In 1966, researchers at UCLA had begun doing an expansive annual survey of college kids, including asking about their values. In the late 1960s, "developing a meaningful philosophy of life" was the top value, with 80 percent of all college freshmen saying it was essential or very important. "Being very well off financially" lagged far behind, ranking fifth or sixth, with just 45 percent of freshmen deeming it to be very important or essential. By 1985 those two values had basically swapped places. Being well off financially was the number one value, with some 70 percent of kids deeming it essential or very important. Meanwhile, having a meaningful philosophy of life had fallen to sixth, with just 43 percent saying it was important.

Perhaps no one saw the change more clearly than *Official Preppy Handbook* author Lisa Birnbach. In 1984, she'd released a second book, titled *Lisa Birnbach's College Book*, which, in her irreverent way, gave the inside scoop on hundreds of schools across the country. While researching the book and promoting it afterward, Birnbach spent a lot of time on campuses. By the mid-1980s, less than a decade after she herself had graduated from Brown, she was startled at what a shift had taken place.

"When I graduated from Brown in 1978," she recalled, "I didn't know anyone who went to business school. But everything had changed. I would ask students, who are your role models? And they'd say 'Blake Carrington.' And I'd say, 'Excuse me? You know Blake Carrington is not a real person, right?' But they loved the money. They loved the stuff. It was a 180-degree difference."

CHAPTER 20

Yupscale

The house was breathtaking. It sat on the side of a hill in Strawberry, California, in Marin County, just north of San Francisco. With striking pitched roofs and massive bay windows, the multimillion-dollar mansion looked out over a serene marina below. Meanwhile, its owner, Richard Thalheimer, had surrounded himself with the trappings of luxury. On the basement level was a wine cellar whose collection topped those of many leading restaurants. In the garage sat a two-seater 1962 Mercedes sports coupe (among various vehicles). At an airport not far away was the plane Thalheimer purchased after becoming interested in flying a few years earlier: a six-seat Piper Malibu worth a half million dollars.

Eight years after he'd taken out an ad in *Runner's World* magazine to sell a digital watch via mail order, Richard Thalheimer was a wealthy man. The Sharper Image was now generating sales of nearly $100 million per year, thanks to a catalog that was sent out to millions of people in just the right zip codes and more than two dozen retail stores in upscale city neighborhoods and malls across the country. His formula for success hadn't changed much from the earliest days: He sold toys for grown-ups—gadgets and other products one could certainly live with-out, but that if you had the money, you'd joyfully buy anyway. A safari hat equipped with a solar-powered fan ($59). An electronic bathroom scale that said "Have a nice day" ($99). A samurai sword set ($295). A home robot that served drinks ($495).

And Thalheimer still stirred with ideas and ambition. A couple of years earlier, tapping into the spirit of entrepreneurship that was coming into vogue, he'd produced a daylong seminar in San Francisco called Thinking Big, featuring presentations by successful entrepreneurs like Bill McGowan from MCI, Stanley Marcus from Neiman Marcus, and Sherry Lansing from Paramount Pictures. "For people too important to attend, a seminar too important to miss," the event's tagline read. Now, Thalheimer was expanding Sharper Image to Japan and preparing the company for a public stock offering later in the year.

Roughly a decade after Boomers had begun colonizing certain city neighborhoods in search of self-fulfillment and cosmopolitanism and a version of adulthood that looked nothing like that of their parents, their attitude about consumption—their embrace of an exclusive type of materialism—was now unabashedly mainstream. In 1983, when Alice Kahn had written for the *East Bay Express* about the fictional Yuppies named Dirk and Bree and their obsession with just the right brands and just the right material goods, it was obviously caricature. Only a few years later, it sounded like real life.

"You couldn't help but notice that the materialism got really crazy, really out of control," Lisa Birnbach remembered. "Instead of people saying, 'Oh, my car's in the shop,' Yuppies would say, 'Oh, my Mercedes is in the shop.' Instead of, 'I'd like a vodka on the rocks,' it was, 'I'd like a Stoli on the rocks.' Or, 'I can't read what time my Rolex says.' Every-thing had to reflect money."

And everywhere companies were trying to cash in. The luxury car market might have been relatively narrow—there were only about a million people in the country willing and able to spend $20,000 or more on a car—but it was getting an increasing amount of attention from carmakers. Honda was preparing the debut of its high-end Acura brand; Toyota was readying new offshoot Lexus; Nissan was preparing Infiniti. From the carmakers' point of view, the calculus wasn't complicated: Luxury cars had a far higher profit margin—around 20 percent—and the overall luxury car market was growing two and a half times as fast as the car market in general.

An arms race of luxury—a race to the top—was taking hold everywhere. Giorgio Armani was readying plans for a rollout of lush retail stores around the world. Already established on the retail level were Ralph Lauren and Polo, whose stand-alone stores now numbered three dozen. The goal of the stores was both increased exposure and, just as important, an even deeper, more immersive expression of what buying Polo said about you as a person. "You don't come in and buy a shirt," a Polo executive said. "You come in and buy a lifestyle."

There seemed to be no end to how much you could sell if what you were selling was status. One of the great marketing success stories of recent years was Grey Poupon, which, following the lead of Häagen-Dazs, had figured out the trick of bringing a "gourmet" product to the masses. The brand, which claimed to have pioneered Dijon mustard all the way back in eighteenth-century France, had started being sold in the US in the mid-1970s, without much success. Its price point was twice that of mass-appeal mustards like French's, and it was mostly available only in gourmet food stores. But in 1981 company execs had noticed an increase in the number of food magazine recipes requiring mustard, and they began strategizing for how they might capitalize on it. The solution? To use Grey Poupon's high price not as a detriment, but as its most appealing feature. That year the company test-marketed two TV commercials in Seattle that positioned Grey Poupon as "one of life's finer pleasures." In the first spot, one chauffeur-driven Rolls-Royce pulled up alongside another. The window rolled down and a head popped up: "Excuse me, have you got any Grey Poupon?" The second ad was similar, only using yachts instead of Rolls-Royces.

The results of the test were astonishing: Sales in Seattle shot up 100 percent. The company did a second test in New England—and again saw a robust increase in sales. By 1984, Grey Poupon and its new owner, Del Monte, were so confident in their strategy that they began spending $5 million a year on TV spots—what French's and Gulden's, the two market leaders, were spending combined. Sales of Dijon mustard grew rapidly even as the overall mustard market remained flat, and Grey Poupon began pulling in a bigger and bigger share of the $185 million mustard market. "We're not selling mustard," a company executive said. "We're selling an affordable taste of the good life." In a country more and more obsessed with status, the same strategy seemed to work whether you were selling cars, shirts, or condiments.

Or, as it turned out, coffee. In 1983, Howard Schultz, then the marketing director of the small Seattle-based coffee company Starbucks, made a trip to Italy. While he was there, he became obsessed with espresso, and he was convinced that increasingly sophisticated American palates would be as well if they were exposed to it. He made a pitch to the owners of Starbucks—a trio of partners who'd started the company in 1971, inspired by the success Peet's Coffee was having in Berkeley's Gourmet Ghetto—to start selling espresso drinks in their stores, but they passed. Schultz was so confident in his idea that he opted to go off on his own, opening a string of shops called Il Giornale. In 1986, the owners of Starbucks reached out to Schultz: They were going to focus on the coffee bean side of their business—they'd actually purchased Peet's Coffee—and planned to sell off their cafés. Was Schultz interested in acquiring them? He said yes and rebranded his Il Giornale shops as Starbucks. By 1987 Schultz opened the first Starbucks outside of Seattle, in Chicago and Vancouver, and two years later the chain had forty-six stores. By 1992, when the company went public, it had more than $270 million in revenue.

In many ways it was an extraordinary innovation perfectly in step with the moment and the Yuppie focus on having the best: taking the ultimate commodity, coffee, and transforming it into a higher-end luxury item.

*   *   *

What was happening was turning retailing upside down. For decades, no store had dominated the landscape the way Sears had. It was a company whose growth had, in many ways, mirrored the transformation of the United States in the twentieth century, as it morphed from a mail-order company that brought merchandise to a rural America into a brick-and-mortar retailer that was omnipresent first in cities, then in the suburbs. It was where the middle-class shopped, buying everything from appliances and hardware to clothes and home furnishings, and it was where many in the middle class worked—at its peak, the company employed 350,000 people. Its dominance was so vast that in 1973, at the height of its power, it opened the 110-story Sears Tower in Chicago, the tallest building in the world.

But thirteen years later, Sears was struggling. Retail sales had dropped for six consecutive quarters, and the only thing propping up its profits was its financial services offerings (Allstate Insurance, Dean Witter investing, Coldwell Banker Real Estate). The crux of the issue was that its eight hundred stores were getting squeezed from two sides. On the upscale side, brand-conscious consumers considered Sears pedestrian, opting instead for stores and products that had more cachet. On the other end of the economic scale, middle- and working-class Americans had essentially seen their incomes decline for a decade, as inflation and flat wages had eroded living standards. It had created an opening for discount stores like Walmart, whose low prices spurred its massive expansion in the '70s and the first half of the '80s.

And yet, what was happening when it came to consumption was not quite as simple as a two-tiered system, with high-end brands and stores for one group, discount brands and stores for another, and mid-market retailers like Sears suffering.

The economist Juliet B. Schor would observe a fascinating phenomenon that began in the mid-1980s—a significant shift in how Americans decided which products they wanted. In the '50s and '60s, at the height of the postwar boom, the middle class had mostly looked to other members of the middle class for cues about what to buy or aspire to. It was the sociological underpinning of keeping up with the Joneses. But by the '80s, thanks to more media and more attention on all the money being made and spent at the top end, people had begun looking outside their own class for cues about consumption.

"The comparisons we make are no longer restricted to those in our own general earnings category, or even those one rung up the ladder," Schor wrote. Instead, people were more likely to be making comparisons with people whose incomes were three, four, or five times their own. The result: an upscaling of spending even among the middle and lower classes, what Schor dubbed "the new consumerism."

As a practical matter, the new consumerism meant that a person making $20,000 per year would look at a product owned by someone making $100,000 per year and decide that it was what they needed, too. A BMW. A Cuisinart. Granite countertops. The problem was, they couldn't afford it. Which didn't necessarily mean they didn't buy it anyway. In 1984, consumer debt in the US—everything from mortgages and car loans to credit cards—increased by 21 percent. In 1985, it grew another 18 percent.

"A great many baby boomers are really faced with downward mobility at a time when the dream is upward mobility," a market researcher observed. "The American reality is they will not live as well as their parents did. But you're looking at a group of people who haven't faced that reality. And they're still seeking that big house and a BMW."

For banks and other companies in the credit card business, this swelling materialism created opportunity and profit that were hard to ignore. One company that saw it was Sears. In 1985, it introduced the Discover Card. If it could no longer get people to shop in its stores, at least it could loan them the money to shop somewhere else.

*   *   *

Perhaps the most eye-opening, on-the-nose example of the new attitude about money was the debut in 1984 of the syndicated show *Lifestyles of the Rich and Famous*. Created by Al Masini, who'd previously launched the hits *Entertainment Tonight*, *Solid Gold*, and *Star Search*, the show—an unrestrained celebration of the extravagant lifestyles of entertainers, entrepreneurs, athletes, moguls, and royalty—had been an instant hit. Not only were the ratings strong, but it had become, thanks in large part to its British-born host, Robin Leach, a onetime newspaper reporter, a cultural touchstone.

On the surface were glitz and glamour, but as Leach would say in 1985, he believed beneath that there was a deeper message that was crucial to the show's success. "We look for heroic, rags-to-riches stories," he said. "We're subtly carrying out the legend of the American Dream, and I feel very strongly about this in America. It was true in my case, and it was true in lots of people's cases. You do not have to be born with a silver spoon in your mouth to make it in this country. . . . So within all that sugar of what *Lifestyles* is all about, there is a little pill in there and that little pill says: 'You must keep this. You must maintain what we have in this country. There is everything right about free enterprise. There is everything right about capitalism.'"

It was, without question, an idea of the American Dream different from the one Bruce Springsteen had once talked about from the concert stage, but for millions it was, in fact, the ideal. Leach certainly got no argument from one of the people profiled in the show's fourth season: Richard Thalheimer. With cameras rolling, Thalheimer showed off his house in Marin County and his classic Mercedes and his $500,000 plane, not to mention many of the Sharper Image products that had created his lifestyle.

"I came to San Francisco originally because I wanted to be where I thought things were happening," he said. "I was a young person, I wanted to make a fortune, and I loved toys." It was the only formula he needed to achieve the American Dream.

CHAPTER 21

Hollow

In upstate New York, the "meatball" sign that sat atop GE's building number 27 still shone brightly in the Schenectady night sky. But by the fall of 1986—a century after Thomas Edison first opened shop in what had been a small backwater town—General Electric's presence there was no longer so large, and the feelings that people in the community had for GE had dimmed considerably.

In 1980, the year before Jack Welch became chairman and CEO, GE had employed twenty-four thousand people in Schenectady. By 1985, the number had fallen to fifteen thousand. And the company had announced more cuts were coming in the next year or two: It was moving its gas turbine operations to nonunion South Carolina, and it was closing a large motor manufacturing plant, with those jobs sent to Mexico and Canada.

The company remained Schenectady's largest employer, but the impact of the losses on the city was palpable, especially given that every GE job was said to create two or three others in the region. Mayor Karen Johnson had come to dread Fridays, the day a GE rep would give her a heads-up that more cuts were coming. Meanwhile, the city government she oversaw was struggling with declining tax revenues; in order to reduce its own property taxes, GE had begun demolishing the plants it had closed. So much for "Neutron Jack," the man who wiped out only people, not buildings.

As for the GE employees who'd seen their jobs moved or eliminated, their fates varied. Some were close enough to retirement that they were able to rely on the generous pensions GE had always provided, while others were able to find work at one of a handful of smaller manufacturing companies in the area. But countless would see their lives change for the worse. As a union rep put it, "Too many of these people are going to end up as security guards or hamburger cooks."

Despite what was happening in Schenectady, not to mention other cities and towns where GE had also cut jobs, Jack Welch was more committed than ever to the track the company was on. Five years into his tenure, he'd completely remade the corporation he'd inherited—gutting middle management, insisting that individual business units within GE become more entrepreneurial, and fostering a more competitive, even cutthroat culture. By now Welch had instituted a method of personnel management he'd become famous for called "the vitality curve," which required every manager at GE to place team members into one of three tiers: the top 20 percent, who should be promoted; the middle 70 percent, who should be told what they had to do to improve; and the bottom 10 percent, who should be told their future was elsewhere and ultimately fired. But the vitality curve was just one example of the new culture. Under Welch's predecessor, Reg Jones, GE had been lauded for its commitment to the communities in which it operated, but Welch wanted none of it. Under Jones, management development forms had included a page where employees were supposed to list the community projects they were involved with; under Welch, it was replaced by a page in which the employee was asked to rate their passion for business.

Over the course of five years Welch had radically overhauled the industries the company was involved in, selling off more than 190 industrial units while acquiring 70 companies, mostly in technology and services. When Welch became CEO, half of GE's revenue came from what the company considered core manufacturing. By the middle of 1986, it had fallen to 30 percent. Enamored of the huge profits now being made on Wall Street, in the spring of 1986 Welch had led GE's acquisition of financial house Kidder Peabody for $600 million.

As for the metric that had been Welch's north star, shareholder value, there was no denying his success. Profit margins had increased significantly, and GE's stock had climbed from $30 per share in 1980 to more than $80 per share—an all-time high—in 1986. What had been considered a "GDP company"—a corporation that would generally not grow more quickly than America's overall economy—was now outpacing the average of the Standard & Poors 500, the leading index of large companies.

There were, to be sure, critics, both inside and outside the organization, whose complaint was less that Welch had remade GE than how he had done it. If Welch cared about any of the criticisms, he didn't show it. Then again, why should he? GE was now the third-most-valuable company in the world, and Welch's shareholder-focused, ruthlessly efficient approach to running a company was now the norm in corporate America.

*   *   *

In 1980, when Ronald Reagan had campaigned in Youngstown and other cities where blue-collar workers were losing their jobs, he promised that his policies would get everyone back to work and restore American prosperity. Five years later, there was more wealth in America, but not much had trickled down to the people Reagan was talking to. In the six years between 1979 and 1985, the country had lost nearly two million of the manufacturing jobs that had once helped it build the largest, most influential middle class in history. In the steel industry alone, jobs had been reduced by 30 percent. In Youngstown, the city's population was 105,000—down from 140,000 in 1970. And steel was only one of the industries in the US where workers were facing cuts. Cars. Heavy equipment. Electronics. Computer chips. All of them had seen jobs disappear or sent overseas.

What had emerged was a new business archetype—what *Business Week* magazine dubbed "the hollow corporation." In their pursuit of more robust bottom lines, American companies were rapidly moving manufacturing jobs overseas, transforming themselves, in essence, into marketing and distribution companies for products that were made elsewhere. "Companies long identified with making goods of all sorts now often only produce the package and the label," the magazine wrote in early 1986. Such an approach—in essence, the hollowing out of the American corporation—might benefit individual companies, but in the aggregate it would curtail American productivity, hinder innovation, and undermine the living standards of a large number of Americans.

The evidence and examples were abundant. Heavy equipment manufacturer Caterpillar had erased the red ink from its bottom line by quadrupling the number of component parts it purchased from overseas companies after 1982. Computer company Honeywell was increasingly reliant on components and entire products made in Asia and Europe. The American auto industry was making more and more cars outside the US, and even those still assembled domestically contained a rising percentage of foreign-made parts. All of the microwaves that GE sold—and nearly all of the consumer electronics—were manufactured in Asia. Start-up computer company Apple relied on manufacturing in Singapore.

In some cases, American companies had ceased thinking of themselves as manufacturers at all. At fast-rising athletic company Nike, which passed $1 billion in sales in 1985, only one hundred of the company's thirty-five hundred jobs had anything to do with actually producing its final products; that work was done by other companies. Nike saw itself—and it wasn't alone in this—as an R & D and marketing company, not a producer of goods.

It was true that the shrinking manufacturing sector in the US had not led to a reduction in jobs overall. Since 1980, the economy had added more than nine million jobs—the fastest increase since the Bureau of

Labor Statistics had started keeping track in 1919. The problem? The vast majority of those jobs were in the service sector, which traditionally paid less, sometimes significantly less, than manufacturing jobs did. Yes, some of the service industry positions were for well-educated engineers or doctors or corporate consultants, but for every high-paid McKinsey partner, there were many more people working in fast food or the equivalent. About 60 percent of the new jobs were in what was called "miscellaneous services," a catchall term that included everything from temporary office workers to hotel clerks to health-care technicians. The average job in the sector paid just over $13,000—not far above the poverty line for a family of four. Another 30 percent of the new jobs were in retail, where the average wage was about $9,000 per year—*under* the poverty line.

The growth of those low-wage jobs was one reason that, even as young professionals in places like New York and Boston and San Francisco and DC built lucrative careers, and corporate raiders like T. Boone Pickens made tens of millions of dollars, the average hourly wage in America had actually *decreased* over the previous decade. The supply-side economy had produced winners—but it had created even more losers.

For workers who were displaced, the challenges were manifest, starting with the anxiety of how to support themselves and their families. There was also the feeling that, no matter what skills they had or contributions they'd made, they'd essentially been reduced to a number.

One day Mary Kuykendall, who worked in GE's communications department for decades, was in a Schenectady bar called Scarlatta's when she met a GE assembler who'd just returned from Mexico. The company had sent him there to train the workers who were going to replace him, and when he got back, his severance check was waiting for him. As if that wasn't tough enough, the assembler realized that, because the new workers didn't have any skills, it was going to take four of them to do what he did. Collectively, they'd still make less than he earned.

Meanwhile, a whole class of employees at GE were benefiting at the lower-level workers' expense. In his quest to hire only the best executives to help him run the company, Jack Welch had brought in a slew of young MBAs—what some people referred to, in contrast to blue- and white-collar workers, as "gold-collars." The market for such highly trained professionals was robust, but Welch was willing to give them lucrative stock options to join GE. In 1981, payouts from executive stock options were $6 million. By 1985, they'd risen to $52 million.

All of it was in keeping with what had been happening for a half dozen years in the country. In 1985, the US Census would collect data showing that the share of income going to the top 20 percent of American families had risen to 43.5 percent—the highest it had been since the data were first collected in 1947. Conversely, the income share of the bottom 60 percent of the population was 32.4 percent—the lowest recorded number ever.

As Harvard economist Lester Thurow would write when he saw the numbers, summing up the impact of the fast-track economy, "the rich are getting richer, the poor are increasing in number, and the middle class has trouble holding its own."

PART V

1987

CHAPTER 22

The End of Free Sex

So much had changed since 1980, when Jerry Rubin had first announced he was reinventing himself as a capitalist. The country had embraced a new economic philosophy and new economic policies. The educated Baby Boomers that Rubin had long represented and championed had moved to the center of the culture.

And yet Rubin, forty-eight years old now, still longed for a transformational payday of his own. As far back as 1983, he'd boasted that his networking business would become one of the most important companies of the decade—and three years later, Rubin still held on to that notion. The events that he and Mimi had hosted at the Palladium had been a success, and Jerry dreamed of taking the idea national, not by advising local chambers of commerce on how they might organize their own networking events, but by creating a chain of what he called "networking restaurants."

To fund his idea, Rubin needed capital, and so, in mid-1986, he turned his attention back to Wall Street. In a prospectus for an initial public stock offering in Network America, Inc., Rubin detailed his vision: a chain of branded restaurants in cities across the country designed to facilitate networking and business deals, with the first one to launch in New York City. He was hoping to raise $3 million. To add some sizzle to the offering, Rubin put together an official advisory board that included two of his celebrity friends, Liza Minnelli and Oleg Cassini.

Unfortunately, a man who prided himself on knowing where the culture was going even before it got there had, for maybe the first time ever, gotten the timing wrong.

*   *   *

In many respects, the reckoning was inevitable. By 1986, the booming economy of 1984 and 1985 had cooled, but the atmosphere on Wall Street had only intensified. Where there had been fast-track aggressiveness, there was now flat-out recklessness, with big deals being done seemingly every day and previously unheard-of fees being generated. By the end of the year, there would be more than thirty-three hundred corporate mergers in America worth more than $175 billion—more than five times the number that had taken place just a few years earlier. It was only a matter of time before people began looking for an edge, trying to get information on what companies might be in play, then using the knowledge to buy a stock before merger talks bid the price up.

"It was like free sex," the head of one Wall Street investment bank told the *New York Times*. "You definitely saw the abuses growing but you also saw the absence of people getting caught, so the atmosphere grew relaxed. There really was a deterioration in people's caution, and there were so many deals being done that people must have figured there was plenty of cover for what they were doing."

The first real sign that someone was paying attention had come in the spring of 1986, when authorities brought charges against one of Michael Milken's colleagues at Drexel Burnham Lambert, Dennis Levine, alleging that he'd made more than $12 million in the market over the previous few years by illegally trading on inside information. Levine, thirty-three, seemed like a character out of a movie—he was a middle-class kid from Queens who methodically worked his way into the world of finance, then started using tips he got from a network of people to make big profits on stocks. By the time the feds caught up with him, he and his family were living a lavish life on the Upper East Side, with millions tucked away in a Caribbean bank account.

A few weeks after charges were brought against Levine, another insider trading scandal emerged, this one involving a group of young bankers and lawyers who were quickly dubbed by the tabloids as "the Yuppie Five." They were even smaller fish than Levine—none of them made more than $55,000 from the information they traded on—but it was *who* they were that stood out. They'd gone to elite schools like Wharton and the University of Chicago; four of them worked out at the same gym; one of them had an answering machine message that played the theme from *Chariots of Fire*. It was as if they'd emerged from the pages of *The Yuppie Handbook*.

The big splash came in the fall, when authorities announced they were investigating one of the most powerful arbitrageurs on Wall Street, Ivan Boesky. According to officials, Boesky—a Drexel client whom the feds had been tipped off to by Levine—had netted at least $50 million in profits over the previous few years by playing the market using insider information. As part of a plea deal announced in November 1986, Boesky agreed to plead guilty to two counts of insider trading and pay a civil fine of $100 million.

It was the money that captured people's attention, as well as the greed and excess that Boesky himself seemed to embody. His nickname in financial circles was "Piggy," owing to his proclivity for leaving nothing on the table, and he was said to be worth at least $200 million. In addition to a lavish Manhattan apartment, he had a two-hundred-acre estate in Westchester County that boasted guards at the front gate and works by Monet and Renoir on the interior walls. Boesky had recently gotten a permit from his local township to add a dome to his mansion, hoping to create more of a "Jeffersonian" feel. While giving the commencement address at Cal-Berkeley's business school that spring, Boesky uttered the quote that would ultimately come to define the entire era: "Greed is all right," he told the new graduates. "I want you to know that. I think greed is healthy. You can be greedy and still feel good about yourself." He was greeted by laughter...then cheers.

Of course, what might have been most noteworthy about Ivan Boesky was that he often did business with Michael Milken, who, soon after Boesky's story went public, received a subpoena from the feds.

* * *

The Boesky case flipped a switch in the public consciousness. The eye-rolling at what was happening on Wall Street and griping about fast-track Yuppie values transformed into moral indignation, with columnists and culture watchers denouncing the excess and greed. Writer Ron Rosenbaum took aim directly at the Yuppie investment bankers he said were at the center of all the greed and excess—though he had hope that perhaps things had hit rock bottom: "Maybe I'm giving Yuppies too much credit, but I have a feeling that there are going to be a lot of them so ashamed and revolted by the behavior of their culture heroes that they're going to want to dissociate themselves from the whole disgraced and discredited culture—*but fast.*" To help these now-lost souls, Rosenbaum proposed, tongue in cheek, "Yuppie Re-Education Camps"—places, he said, that would be akin to "Betty Ford clinics for greedheads, detox centers for money-junkies, self-help clinics for sleaze-balls." When they checked in, Rosenbaum said, Yuppies would essentially be deprogrammed, while also learning to live without suspenders. (He recommended Sansabelt double-knit polyester pants.)

In late winter, federal authorities, led by US attorney Rudy Giuliani, arrested seventeen employees of Wall Street firms, charging them with, among other things, dealing cocaine and trading drugs for insider information. The investigation—which the feds had dubbed "Operation Closing Scandal"—had gotten underway four years earlier, when authorities took note of a mink-coat-wearing brunette woman who allegedly had Mob ties and was a regular in investment banking offices, making weekly coke deliveries to five top-level Wall Street executives.

The five brokers—three of whom made more than a million bucks a year—cooperated and ultimately helped the feds set up an undercover operation.

Just weeks before the drug bust, feds had announced another insider trading takedown—a thirty-seven-year-old Harvard Business School graduate named Martin Siegel, who over the years had provided inside information to Ivan Boesky. The two had developed something of a routine: They'd meet in one public place or another and exchange passwords, and then Boesky would hand Siegel a suitcase full of cash, payments that totaled at least $700,000. At the time he pleaded guilty to charges, Siegel was working for Drexel Burnham Lambert, but he was relatively new to the firm. He'd spent most of his career at Kidder Peabody, the investment bank that Jack Welch and GE had purchased just eight months earlier. Within weeks of Siegel's plea deal, two more Kidder Peabody executives were arrested.

*　　　*　　　*

The shift in the culture, not to mention the federal subpoena, could not be ignored by Mike Milken. A decade after being an also-ran, Drexel Burnham Lambert had become Wall Street's most profitable investment banking house, with profits of $1.5 billion. Of that, $250 million belonged to Milken and his team. One of the clients Milken was raising money for was Craig McCaw, a young cable television entrepreneur who had begun quietly buying up many of the cellular communications licenses being auctioned off by the federal government.

Despite the trading scandals, Milken showed no signs of backing down. On the contrary, he was ready to fight. Milken viewed what he'd done with junk bonds as nothing less than a financial revolution, and he was quite cognizant that, whenever there's a revolution, the people who are threatened will push back.

At the annual Predators' Ball in April 1987, Milken stood up in front of the two thousand invitees and tried to offer some context for what was happening with the insider trading scandals. It was all a result, he said, of the fact that he and his junk-bond-backed corporate raiders had put too much pressure on America's CEOs to improve their bottom lines.

"One way to insulate yourself is to deny that change is occurring. You lash out, and who's the easiest person to lash out at?...Wall Street," he said.

"Much of American business has run to the [government] and said, 'Let's change the rules. We don't want competition, we don't want pressure.'" They were, he said, trying to deny the marketplace its rightful judgment on their performances.

The crowd certainly agreed with him. As one observer said afterward, "Corporate America is hoping to indict Mike Milken...so it can go back to sleep for another 30 years."

In the months that followed, Milken—who never did interviews—began talking a little more to the press, including a story with writer Edward Jay Epstein in *Manhattan, inc.* magazine. What junk bonds had done, Milken explained to Epstein, was to democratize finance and business. As for his alliances with raiders like T. Boone Pickens and Carl Icahn and their attacks on big corporations, well, they were simply holding corporate managers accountable to shareholders and rooting out inefficiency.

Ultimately, Epstein concluded, where you stood on Michael Milken probably depended on what your view of a corporation was. Did a corporation exist merely to serve its legal owners, its shareholders? Or did it have obligations beyond that—to employees, suppliers, the community, the nation?

The tens of thousands of people who'd lost their jobs likely had one opinion about that. There was no question that Michael Milken had a different one.

* * *

It had been more than a decade since the Boomer colonization of urban neighborhoods had begun—a half dozen years since Dan Rottenberg had first written about Yuppies in *Chicago* magazine—and their impact was visible in cities around the country, from New York, Boston, and San Francisco to St. Louis, Indianapolis, and Cincinnati. Brownstones and town houses renovated. Warehouses converted. Co-ops built. Upscale shops and trendy eateries opened.

Increasingly, those gentrified neighborhoods existed side by side with neighborhoods where poverty was rising. In New York City, where investment bankers and law partners were pulling in more than a million dollars per year, nearly 40 percent of children now lived in poverty. But that was the harsh reality of a bifurcated economy.

For many in the young professional class, the lure of the city had been identity—of not repeating the seemingly bland lives their parents had embraced. For others, it had been the pull of a good career, of becoming an investment banker or a partner at one of those law firms. For still others, particularly the youngest Baby Boomers now gravitating to cities, it had simply become the expectation, the place where educated young professionals lived.

And yet, even as the influx continued, even as gentrification spread, a reverse trend was happening simultaneously: not-as-young-as-they-used-to-be professionals who'd once devoted themselves to city living picking up and moving to, of all places, the suburbs.

In late 1985, Alice Kahn, who'd been so elemental in defining Yuppie-ness and launching media coverage of Yuppies with her fictional creations of Dirk and Bree, wrote an essay about the state of the phenomenon—and why she believed it was coming to an end. The driving force in the birth of Yuppieness, she said, had been women. "Men had been having it all for years," she wrote. "What was new was that gal in the suit and tie and attache, her bunions bound in Nikes as she commuted home. It was a dream made possible through women's liberation, contraception, and legal abortion."

But now Kahn observed the new baby boom that was in full swing. "What we're really talking about when we talk about the death of the Yuppie," she said, "is the return of the urge to procreate."

The rebound in the birth rate that had started in 1979 was intensifying. There were 3.7 million babies born in America in 1986, and there would be 3.8 million in 1987—the most since 1964, the final year of the Baby Boom. By 1989, the number of new births would top 4.0 million again. Actuarially speaking, it made sense. The most populous part of the Baby Boom generation—the twenty-two million people born between 1956 and 1961—was now approaching or just passing age thirty, and the biological clocks of those professional women who'd waited to have kids were ticking more loudly.

Many young professionals clung to city living even after their first babies arrived. It was the birth of a second child that truly closed the window on the new stage of life that had been created—the responsibility-free, me-focused twenties. It was the second child, too, that so often had young couples spending their Sunday afternoons scurrying to open houses in the suburbs.

The moves were prompted by the realization that the things they'd loved about the city—the restaurants, the museums, the theater, the leisurely weekends spent loitering in bookstores—were no longer relevant when you were pushing a colicky newborn around in a stroller. And while a one-bedroom in the city might seem cozy and chic and sophisticated when it was just the two of you, when there were four of you? It was cramped and crowded.

"When you see the destruction a cooped-up two-year-old can wreak on an apartment, the suburban life begins to look awfully attractive," a thirty-one-year-old attorney named John Kiernan told a reporter writing about the suburban migration. John and his wife, Lisa, owned a two-bedroom co-op on New York's Upper West Side, but when their second child arrived, they sold it and moved to a four-bedroom Tudor in Pelham Manor, just north of the city in Westchester County.

"I was always so committed to the city, but our value system has changed as we've gotten older," said another young mom, Arlene, who'd moved to the Jersey suburb of Montclair with her husband, Rob, and their daughter. "We're not politically more conservative, but socially you do become more conservative. We have these longings to be with other people with kids. We started talking about putting down roots. It has to be the kids that do it to you—it *has* to be." (She wasn't alone in her theory. Another suburban transplant confided that the tipping point for him had been the realization that his daughter's only playmate was the doorman in their building.)

For other Boomers, something even deeper was going on—a questioning of the entire fast-track ethos that had for so long defined their lives. Robert and Rebecca were a couple who appeared to have it all. She worked in finance, he worked in publishing, and together they made more than $90,000 a year—plenty for an apartment on New York's Upper West Side and first-rate childcare for their young daughter. But one day while Rebecca was on the subway, she reached a breaking point—she realized she had no time for her child. No time for her husband. No time for herself. "I was standing on this miserable, crowded, hot train, coming from a job that didn't give me all that much pleasure, to pick up my child, who'd been away from me the whole day, to go home to an apartment so small that my husband and I sleep in the living room on a futon mattress," she said. That night, she told Robert something needed to change. In time they bought a house in a small town ninety minutes from Manhattan, and Rebecca quit her job.

For some, there was a realization that their parents' generation, the one they'd been rebelling against for so long, had perhaps understood something. "I've had to deal with the sense that I was going home again," said a young mom who left New York with her husband and two kids and bought a house fifteen minutes from where she'd grown up. "But I'm realizing maybe my parents knew what they were doing. I used to think it was all about money. That if you had enough, you'd never leave the city. Now if someone handed me a five-bedroom co-op on Central Park West, I'd be hard-pressed to take it."

Of course, in many other ways, the Yuppies' take on the world didn't really change at all. In moving to Montclair, New Jersey, Arlene and Rob had held on to the long-cherished ideal of quality and superiority.

Montclair wasn't a "typical" suburb, explained Rob. "It's integrated, and the people are more urbane than a lot of folks you see in Westchester and Connecticut." Only the best would do.

*   *   *

The arrival of more and more young Boomer families—and the cultural impact of Yuppies in general—was starting to change the suburbs. Outside of cities where the young professional class had thrived, bedroom communities were starting to be reshaped to meet the needs and desires of a new generation. Gyms opened. More-adventurous restaurants appeared. Gourmet food stores sprang up in places that had once known only ShopRites and A&Ps. In 1980 there were four thousand specialty food shops nationwide; by 1988 there were twelve thousand. (This was much to the relief of one displaced city dweller, who said: "Can you imagine buying vegetables in a supermarket?")

The Yuppie sensibility—and the growing level of wealth at the top of the economic pyramid—was showing itself in architecture and home design as well. Some of the educated elite craved old homes with their original features, but others wanted something more customized—and they were willing to pay for it. In large metro areas around the country—and particularly on the coasts—the number of houses being built or sold for $500,000 or even $1 million was skyrocketing. In part, it was simply the market at work, with a growing number of affluent people, the top 10 percenters, bidding up the prices on a finite number of properties. But it was also a sign that money didn't need to be quiet anymore—that a new generation of the affluent, despite their cultural roots in the egalitarianism of the '60s, wanted to live, in many respects, like the old-money tycoons of the early twentieth century.

Homes were not only getting larger; they were sporting the "quality" features that had drawn Back to the City devotees to run-down Victorians and brownstones in the 1970s—high ceilings, mahogany staircases, marble floors. Those were, of course, accompanied by no shortage of more-modern luxuries—Jacuzzis, granite countertops, sprawling entertainment centers—that also screamed quality. And there was no shortage of examples of purely over-the-top extravagances, from the bandstand a Colorado cable entrepreneur had installed in his lavish living room to the swimming pool and waterfall a homeowner in suburban Chicago had installed—in his kitchen.

For the people building the houses, it all meant opportunity. One company capitalizing on it was Toll Brothers, which had been started in the late '60s by Bob and Bruce Toll, two young men who lived in suburban Philadelphia and whose father had also been in the home construction business. By the early '80s the two brothers had expanded into New Jersey and created a strong business building completely customized luxury homes, but they had a couple of revelations that would help them grow even more. The first: The more customized a home was, the less profit they made. The problem wasn't the cost of the amenities; it was the management of the process. And so they'd come up with a solution, creating a menu of expensive amenities—upscale windows, molding, stoves, cabinets—from which customers could choose, then having those products mass-produced at a lower cost. One result of this "semi-custom" approach was that the homes began to have a cookie-cutter look—McMansions, some wag would dub them—but the company's bottom line kept improving.

The other revelation the Toll Brothers had: If they had more capital, they could buy even more property on which to build even more houses. They got connected to Michael Milken and his colleagues at Drexel, who arranged millions of dollars of financing for them, in order to expand. By 1986, with $125 million in revenue, Toll Brothers went public on the New York Stock Exchange, on its way to becoming America's largest builder of luxury homes.

*   *   *

What was perhaps most notable about the Yuppie embrace of suburbia was how culturally and economically self-reinforcing it was. Because they understood the importance of education, young professionals moving to the burbs sought areas with the best school districts. This, in turn, tended to make those districts even better—high-achieving parents were more likely to have high-achieving kids—which only made those neighborhoods more desirable and more expensive, which only narrowed the slice of people who could afford to live there.

The ironic result? A group of people who had often recoiled at how privileged and homogeneous their own suburban upbringings had been now lived in suburbs that were even more privileged and more homogeneous. In the same way that they'd all worn blue jeans and grown their hair long in the '60s and early '70s; in the same way that they'd all lived sophisticated urban lifestyles in the late '70s and early '80s, they now began living suburban lives that were remarkably similar. Mommy and Me music classes when the kids were little. Organized sports when they got a little older. Tutors to make sure they did well in school. Upscale family vacations every Christmas and summer.

No less important was how much such professional-class communities began separating themselves from the rest of America economically. In 1970, 65 percent of families in America lived in middle-income neighborhoods. Over the next several decades it dropped to 42 percent. Meanwhile, the percentage of families living in affluent neighborhoods more than doubled, rising from 7 percent to 15 percent, while the percentage of families in poor neighborhoods spiked from 8 percent to 18 percent.

"There are no more middle buildings," Donald Trump had said in 1980, talking about the divide in the New York real estate market. By the end of the '80s, there was less and less middle anything.

CHAPTER 23

Crash

There were a handful of warnings. Some of them—like the one in the book *The Great Depression of 1990*, which hit the bestseller list in early 1987—were over the top, predicting nothing short of economic catastrophe in the years ahead. Others were more measured, with veteran stock watchers calmly stating that the market was overheated and due for a significant correction.

By the summer of 1987, there was plenty to suggest that the stock market, now five years into its bull run, was indeed overvalued. Since 1982, driven in part by the spike in corporate mergers, the Dow had nearly quadrupled to more than 2700; in 1987 alone, the market had gone up 69 percent. By August, stocks were trading at an average of twenty times their annual earnings per share (for most of the decade it had been less than fifteen). It was a ratio seen only twice before: In 1965, when a relatively modest and brief bear market ensued, and in 1929, when the market crashed and set off the Great Depression.

It was not a complete surprise, then, when ten years and a month after Youngstown, Ohio, had been felled on a day the locals called Black

Monday, another Black Monday arrived—and everything seemed to change, just like that.

*   *   *

What he'd always remember were the two phones, one pressed to each ear. The man holding the phones, the long-bond trader at Goldman Sachs, was fielding call after call after call, taking order after order after order, from clients looking to dump what they owned. "Done," he'd say when an order was completed, then he'd repeat it again for the next trade. "Done." *Done. Done. Done. Done.* Things were moving so fast the trader had to try to keep track of it all in his head.

Watching this was Jeff Zajkowski, the real-life Alex P. Keaton from Sheboygan, Wisconsin, the young man who'd read Milton Friedman in sixth grade. By now, five months after graduating from the University of Pennsylvania, Zajkowski had become an analyst at Goldman, joining the ranks of the ambitious young people who were willing to put in eighty, ninety, a hundred hours a week as they got swallowed up in the world of investment banking. Zajkowski had done well at Penn, and when the time came for a job, he had his pick of offers from Wall Street. He chose Goldman because of the firm's stellar rep and because the work he'd be asked to do sounded interesting. But now, it was hard not to wonder if everything was falling apart.

There wasn't a whole lot for the analysts to do at the moment—this was not the day for deep, in-depth research—and so Zajkowski and four other analysts moseyed up to the equities trading floor, where the real action was happening. There was a kind of intense focus that was palpable, but no panic. That wouldn't necessarily be the case everywhere on Wall Street.

The trouble had begun five days earlier—Wednesday, October 14—when the feds announced that the US had a larger-than-expected trade deficit. The Dow dropped 95 points that day, then two days later plunged another 108 points, the largest single-day point drop in its history. Nearly 10 percent of the market's value had disappeared in just seventy-two hours.

There was hope that the weekend might calm investors, but circumstances only grew worse. That Sunday, the *New York Times* reported that Ronald Reagan's Treasury secretary, James Baker, was threatening to devalue the dollar in an effort to close the trade deficit—a move that would cause turmoil around the globe. The result: Even before the New York Stock Exchange opened on Monday, the nineteenth, markets in Asia had plunged, as had the London market.

In New York, the sell-off began the minute the bell rang at 9:30 a.m. on Monday. Down the Dow went, *down down down*. By 2:00 p.m., it was already off by 295 points, nearly three times its largest single-day point drop—and there were still two hours left of trading. One issue was "programmatic trading," with computers automatically set to sell off certain stocks if they fell below a specified threshold. But much of what was happening was simply investor fear, with people and institutions dumping stocks before things got even worse.

At Shearson, Wall Street vet Wick Simmons had seen plenty of turmoil in the markets before, but never anything like *this*. Simmons had gotten married a week prior—his second time around—but when the trouble started, he told his new wife they were putting the honeymoon on hold. On the afternoon of Black Monday, as he tried to get a handle on what was happening, he called Shearson's over-the-counter trading desk. Nobody answered. They'd all gone to the bar down the street. Simmons got on a call with Shearson branch offices all around the country to try to calm the troops, but he kept hearing the same question: "How low is the market going to go?" *The truth is*, Simmons thought, *I don't have the slightest damn idea.*

The trading, and the losses, only kept growing. In the final hour of the day, the Dow was descending at a rate of 3.5 points per minute, with 1.7 million shares being traded. "Holy shit, I just lost a million," one young trader, staring at a screen, was heard to say. In the men's room of the Chicago Board Options Exchange, another young guy wept quietly.

Outside the stock exchange in New York, more than a thousand people jammed the sidewalk—investment bankers, staffers, passersby, tourists, TV news crews. At least one of the crowd was ready to point fingers.

"It's all over for the Yuppies!" a man screamed. "Down with the MBAs! It's all over. The Reagan Revolution is over!"

Another man appeared, having just left the stock exchange. "He who dies with the most toys wins!" he bellowed.

"How many toys do you have now?" someone asked.

"None," he said.

Over his shoulder, the other man continued, "Down with the MBAs! It's all over for the Yuppies!"

The next day at Goldman, Jeff Zajkowski heard a story that was making the rounds. A firm bigwig had one of those newfangled cellular phones, the kind Mike Milken was backing, installed in his car. Driving home following the worst single day in Wall Street history, he ripped it out and tossed it out the window.

* * *

Overnight, government officials stepped in, hoping to calm the chaos. The stock exchange announced that programmatic trading would be suspended, while the Fed issued a statement saying it stood ready as a source of liquidity. Tuesday was still rough—at one point, the market went down another 200 points—but by the end of the day there was a rally, and the Dow finished up 100 points. The worst of it was over. But the damage was done: More than a trillion dollars in value had been lost.

In the days that followed, the big question was about the health of the overall economy. Was the US headed for a depression, as in 1929? A deep recession, as in 1981? Meanwhile, people were tallying what they'd lost. Individual Wall Street firms were measuring the red ink in the tens of millions of dollars, while across the country individual investors were looking at their own decimated portfolios. A sixty-three-year-old widow told a reporter that she was now destitute—her entire $600,000 portfolio had been wiped out. She said she was looking into food stamps.

Perhaps no one was in greater shock than the young analysts and associates who'd arrived on Wall Street from all those great schools after the summer of 1982. They'd made big salaries and bonuses—and they'd never seen the market go anywhere but up. The weekend after the crash, Stanford business school's Class of '82 got together for its five-year reunion. Microphone in hand, the evening's emcee asked anyone who'd lost $10,000 or more in the previous week to please stand up. About half the crowd rose. A few sat down when the emcee raised the level to $20,000 in losses, and a few more took their seats at $30,000. One young guy was still standing when the emcee asked who'd lost $75,000—although maybe he was just the only honest one in the bunch. Another classmate was overheard to say: "I sat down at $50,000, but I really lost close to $100,000."

*   *   *

The shocks to the system went beyond the MBAs and stock portfolios. In the weeks that followed, luxury Mercedes and BMW dealers, among others, were reporting extremely slow sales—with an occasional remorseful buyer wondering if the dealer might want to buy the car back. In Chicago, First State Pawners, a pawnshop, stayed open late in the wake of the crash, trying to accommodate the line of people hoping to unload their Rolexes and Piaget watches. A twenty-eight-year-old stockbroker in New York put his European vacation on hold indefinitely—and swore he was going to start eating at home more. Yuppies, said Kurt Barnard, publisher of a retail industry newsletter, "have been brutally shaken into the realization that they're not as rich today as they were last week."

For many who worked on Wall Street, bigger challenges now loomed. By the end of the year, more than four thousand people in New York's finance industry would be let go thanks to the crash. Jeff Zajkowski managed to hold on to his job, but plenty of other young analysts on Wall Street weren't so lucky. Six months out of school—and looking for work again.

Around the rest of the country, there didn't seem to be much sympathy for them. In a poll taken three days after the panic, 61 percent of

Americans said they didn't consider the crash to necessarily be a serious concern—and 63 percent said it might actually be helpful since it would force the country to focus on its real economic problems.

Among those disagreeing with the majority was, no doubt, Jerry Rubin. The crash had completely scuttled the IPO he and Mimi were attempting with their networking restaurant company—that dream was now officially dead. Black Monday cost them $300,000.

* * *

So many forces had been building over the previous several years against Yuppies and all they seemed to stand for. The general exasperation at Yuppie behavior and Yuppie media hype. The outrage over the insider trading scandals. The new baby boom and the exodus to the suburbs. Even the politician who'd helped put Yuppies on people's radar, Gary Hart, had taken a fall—ending his second presidential campaign in May 1987 after the media uncovered an affair he was having with a former staffer. The bursting of a stock bubble on top of all that simply felt like the end. Of something.

In offices and bars and gyms in cities around the country, a new wave of Yuppie jokes started to spread.

"What do you call a Yuppie broker?...Hey, waiter!"

"What's the difference between a Yuppie and a pigeon?...A pigeon can still make a deposit on a Porsche."

For professional culture watchers, all of it seemed to signal a shift.

"There was a fad for a while, which was to advertise as if everyone was conspicuously consuming," an ad agency executive told the *Wall Street Journal* in a piece on the abrupt change in the tone of marketing in the wake of the crash. "It was as if people were saying it was okay to be greedy. That now definitely is déclasseé."

In the months ahead, journalists wrote what amounted to obituaries for the Yuppie. After a decade of putting its faith wholeheartedly in free enterprise and free markets, of focusing on achievement and success and money and materialism, the country was ready to slow down again, to get back to normal. Just as the stock market crash of 1929 had ended one hyper-capitalistic era and launched something new, the crash of 1987 would do the same.

"It was bound to happen," *Yuppie Handbook* coauthor Marilee Hartley said when asked about the changing ethos in America after Black Monday. "The Yuppie phase was just a phase."

CHAPTER 24

Revolutionaries

On Wall Street, it took fewer than twenty months for the Dow to return to the record level it had reached before the crash—and from there it went on a ten-year bull run. By 2020, it was worth six times what it had been worth in 1987.

Coverage of Yuppies in the media did fade in the wake of Black Monday, as did use of the word "Yuppie," but it was clear within a few years that no new era had commenced; no new ethos had taken hold. On the contrary, in its push to revive itself, in its zeal to recapture the dominance and prosperity of the postwar era, in elevating self-interest over any sense of the common good, the country had created a new economic and social order that wouldn't easily be undone.

At the heart of it was the money-and-success culture that had propelled Wall Street and politics and corporate America and a certain segment of the Baby Boom generation. In the '80s, the country had been divided—unapologetically—into winners and losers, and that split only continued to be reinforced. The notion of shareholder primacy that Milton Friedman had championed was officially endorsed by the Business Roundtable, a collection of America's most powerful and prominent

CEOs, in 1997, though by that point the philosophy was already standard operating procedure. The Business Roundtable would repeal that stance two decades later—a company had an obligation to all its stakeholders, including employees, it said—but there was little evidence that the pronouncement changed anyone's behavior. Stock price, and quarter-to-quarter earnings, drove most decisions. A robust bottom line justified almost everything. In corporate America, profits increased nearly 1,000 percent between 1990 and 2020.

Meanwhile, the narrative that Ronald Reagan had popularized and ridden to the White House—that government was at the root of most problems, and that many Americans were lazy freeloaders—only seemed to intensify as well. After getting crushed in the presidential election of 1984, Democrats nominated a technocrat, Michael Dukakis, in 1988, but he was painted as just another liberal and lost to George H. W. Bush, Reagan's vice president and an actual Preppy. Democrats finally read the public mood in 1992 and nominated Bill Clinton, not only a centrist but a Yale- and Oxford-educated Baby Boomer—the Yuppie president that Jerry Rubin had long predicted was coming. After getting elected, Clinton tried to pass national health insurance, but he was bludgeoned for it politically and tacked right. He championed NAFTA, which made it easier to ship manufacturing jobs to Mexico; signed welfare reform; and proclaimed that "the era of big government is over." Clinton was easily reelected in 1996.

As for the well-educated Baby Boomers—Yuppies—who had come to the fore in the first half of the '80s: Their prominence and clout in the country only increased. Their basic political philosophy—liberal on social issues, conservative on economic ones—dominated for decades, with support for gay marriage and abortion rights growing at the same time that taxes continued to be cut and globalization increased. In the meantime, their lifestyle obsessions—food, fitness, designer brands—became even more mainstream. Increasingly, they—a well-off professional class—lived among themselves. In 2012, a researcher identified several hundred "super zip codes," some within cities, most just outside of them, which attracted an extraordinary number of well-educated, affluent families. Still, their lives seemed plagued by an anxiety that it could all go away just like that, or that their kids wouldn't live equally well. Those kids applied to elite colleges in record numbers.

The rest of America's general distaste for Yuppies evolved into an impatience with what became known as "the elites," and in many respects it was understandable. The decline of US manufacturing intensified, and the number of lower-wage service jobs increased by thirty million between 1998 and 2020. By 2016, families at the top of the economic pyramid controlled 79 percent of all wealth in America, up from 60 percent in the 1980s. The percentage of wealth owned by the middle class dropped from 32 percent to 17 percent.

In time, the resentment of those at the top metastasized into something darker. In 2016, Donald Trump somehow persuaded many working-class Americans that he was on their side, although in office his only significant legislative accomplishment was a tax cut for wealthy Americans that was several times larger than the one Ronald Reagan passed. Despite attempting a coup following his loss in the 2020 election, Trump still maintained the support of many people in the working class. A good number of them believed he spoke for them, and they said they appreciated his apparent loyalty—something they hadn't felt in many years.

*   *   *

In 1988, Mike Milken was indicted on ninety-eight charges of insider trading, and he ultimately pleaded guilty to three counts. He served two years in prison, paid a fine of $600 million, and was barred from working in the securities industry for the rest of his life. Milken maintained any violations he committed were mere technicalities no one had ever been prosecuted for before, and that his only real crime was challenging the ossified ways of the business establishment. In any event, the financing mechanism he popularized, high-yield bonds, is now commonplace, and within business and finance circles Milken is widely regarded as an innovative hero. In 2020, he was pardoned by Donald Trump.

Jack Welch continued to grow GE's stock price and market value, and in 2000 *Fortune* magazine named him "Manager of the Century." When he retired the following year, he received a severance payment of $417 million. By the time he passed away in 2020, however, Welch's reputation had declined. He himself called shareholder primacy "the dumbest idea in the world." GE, meanwhile, fell upon hard times under Welch's handpicked successor, and in 2020 it was delisted from the Dow Jones Industrial Average.

As for Jerry Rubin: In 1988, he and Mimi had their first child, followed by a second one two years later. Hoping for a quieter place in which to raise kids, they bought a home in suburban Connecticut, but their marriage was troubled. In the early '90s, they divorced.

By that point Jerry had latched on to a new trend: He saw a growing interest in health among Baby Boomers who were hitting middle age, and he got involved in the nutrition supplement business, ultimately moving to California. He was said to be very successful. In 1994, he was struck by a car as he crossed Wilshire Boulevard in Los Angeles, and he died shortly afterward. He was fifty-six years old.

Once upon a time, Rubin had dreamed of being part of something large—a fundamental remaking of middle-class, hopelessly middlebrow America. He laid out a utopian vision of what he wanted the country to be at the end of *Do It!*, his 1970 manifesto:

At community meetings all over the land, Bob Dylan will replace The National Anthem.
   There will be no more jails, courts or police.
   The White House will become a crash pad for anybody without a place to stay in Washington. The world will become one big commune with free food and housing, everything shared.
   All watches and clocks will be destroyed.

Barbers will go to rehabilitation camps where they will grow their hair long.

There will be no such crime as "stealing" because everything will be free.

The Pentagon will be replaced by an LSD experimental farm.

There will be no more schools or churches because the entire world will become one church and school.

People will farm in the morning, make music in the afternoon and fuck wherever and whenever they want to.

That vision had never come to pass, because it was silly and juvenile, and Rubin had moved on from it. The great irony was that he, and so many others, had somehow managed to become part of a revolution nonetheless.

Acknowledgments

In 1984, when *Newsweek* proclaimed it the "Year of the Yuppie," I was twenty years old and a junior in college. I certainly didn't have enough money in my pocket to be a Yuppie, but I was paying attention to what was going on, and I was fascinated by it. All these years later the experience of having lived through that period—and understanding where the country has ended up four decades down the road—is what made me want to write this book.

In terms of telling this story, I'm deeply indebted to the hundreds of newspaper, magazine, and television reporters whose work in the 1970s and 1980s laid out a path for me to follow and provided many of the details in this narrative. I'm also grateful to the book authors and scholars who went deep on the subjects I tackle in this book, from Baby Boomers and Wall Street to General Electric, the politics of the Reagan era, and the changing shape of the US economy. And my sincere thanks to the dozens of people who agreed to talk with me and share their memories and observations of what was happening in the late '70s and early '80s. Not all of them are quoted or referred to in the text, but their input was crucial. I've done my best in the notes section to cite the main sources I used in putting this story together.

This book wouldn't exist without two of humankind's greatest creations: coffee and libraries. My thanks to the baristas at Green Engine Coffee in Haverford and the Story in Ardmore, two of my favorite coffee shops, as well as the staffs at Haverford College, the Ludington Library, and the Free Library of Philadelphia, where I spent many hours researching, thinking, and writing. The book also wouldn't exist without the support of many friends, including Christy Lejeune, Chris Vogel, and Larry Holmes, who were always interested in and enthusiastic about what I was up to. My special thanks to Bob Huber and Ashley Primis, who each provided smart insights and much-needed pep talks during a period when I wasn't quite sure what I'd gotten myself into.

My agents, Larry Weisman and Sascha Alper, have provided wonderful input and fantastic representation throughout this process, and I'm grateful to them. I'm also deeply appreciative of the team at Grand Central, including editorial assistant Ian Dorset, copy editor Deborah Wiseman, and my terrific editor, Colin Dickerman, who somehow manages to see the big picture and the small details. You're a total pro.

Finally, enormous love and thanks to my daughters, Hannah and Sarah, for their support and making me so proud, and to my wife, Kate, whose patience, intelligence, beauty, questions, jokes, texts, and photos of small animals make every day better. I'm a lucky guy.

Notes

Introduction

vii. **It arrived just after Christmas in 1984:** *Newsweek*, December 31, 1984.

Chapter 1

3. **with the inflation rate at home:** U.S. Bureau of Labor Statistics, bls.gov.
3. **In an attention-grabbing op-ed:** Jerry Rubin, "Guess Who's Coming to Wall Street?," *New York Times*, July 30, 1980.
4. **A few months later, to publicize a massive anti-war rally:** Pat Thomas, *Did It! From Yippie to Yuppie: Jerry Rubin, an American Revolutionary* (New York: Simon & Schuster, 2017).
5. **For the first time in his adult life:** Mimi Leonard Fleischman, interviewed by author, November 2021.
6. **In early 1980, the conservative economist Milton Friedman:** Rick Pearlstein, *Reaganland: America's Right Turn 1976–1980* (New York: Simon & Schuster, 2020).
7. **The *Times*, for instance, was so besieged:** *New York Times*, August 16, 1980.
8. **"If you would talk to her about fame":** Thomas, *Did It!*
8. **One day in 1978:** "Jerry Rubin's Change of Cause: From Antiwar to 'Me,'" *New York Times*, November 11, 1978.
9. **America had transformed itself:** David Halberstam, *The Reckoning* (New York: William Morrow, 1986).
10. **Rubin mockingly called the charges:** Jerry Rubin, *Do It! Scenarios of the Revolution* (New York: Simon & Schuster, 1970).
10. **In the wake of the trial:** Jerry Rubin, *Growing (Up) at Thirty-Seven* (New York: M. Evans, 1976).

11. **In his journal:** Thomas, *Did It!*
12. **In the 1960s, family income in America grew by an average of $6,000:** "The Work Revolution," *Newsweek*, January 17, 1983.
13. **The belief that the country was headed in the wrong direction:** "The Baby Boomers Come of Age," *Newsweek*, March 31, 1981.
14. **Sociologists would credit it:** Landon Y. Jones, *Great Expectations: America and the Baby Boom Generation* (New York: Coward, McCann & Geoghegan, 1980).
14. **the "Pepsi Generation":** "Allan M. Pottasch, 79, Dies; Creator of the 'Pepsi Generation,'" *New York Times*, August 2, 2007.
15. **"Never have the young been so assertive":** "Man of the Year: The Inheritor," *Time*, January 6, 1967.
15. **Indeed, 90 percent of American soldiers:** Jones, *Great Expectations*.
15. **"All of my college years were totally about the war":** Jim Kunen, interviewed by author, November 2021.
17. **Daniel Yankelovich, the well-respected researcher:** Daniel Yankelovich, *New Rules: Searching for Self-Fulfillment in a World Turned Upside Down* (New York: Random House, 1981).
17. **"A lot of us had these misspent youths":** "Live On, Yuppie Scum," *Philadelphia*, December 2003.
18. **In 1960, forty-five hundred students:** "Students Are Bullish on the MBA," *New York Times*, April 30, 1978.
18. **In 1977, a California real estate broker:** Robert Ringer, *Looking Out for #1: How to Get from Where You Are Now to Where You Want to Be* (robertringer.com, 2019).
18. **Six weeks after the election:** "Jerry Rubin to Direct Development at Muir," *New York Times*, January 15, 1981.

Chapter 2

20. **a new restaurant was opening:** "The Rise of Steven Poses," *Philadelphia Inquirer*, November 11, 1984.
21. **Poses, a soft-spoken, humble guy:** Steve Poses, interviewed by author, April 2022.
22. **As one observer put it:** *Inquirer*, November 11, 1984.
22. **In just twenty years:** "The Rise of the Suburbs," *The American Yawp* (Stanford, CA: Stanford University Press), americanyawp.com.
23. **Robin Palley set down roots:** Robin Palley, interviewed by author, January 2022.
25. **By the late '70s:** "Wicker Park Sees Land Values Soar in Neighborhood Turnaround," *Chicago Tribune*, April 1977; "Back to the City," *Philadelphia Inquirer*, July 31, 1977; "And the Shift from Suburbia Gains," November 23, 1977.
25. **In 1977:** *Young Professionals and City Neighborhoods*, Parkman Center for Urban Affairs, August 1977.
26. **On Capitol Hill in Washington:** "Rejecting the Suburban Ideal," *Washington Post*, January 5, 1978.

27. **One place you could see it:** "West Side Story: From Gang Fights to Class Wars," *New York*, June 5, 1978.

27. **West had grown up in New England:** Betsy West, interviewed by author, January 2022.

28. **Quinlan wasn't a Boomer:** Robert Quinlan, interviewed by author, February 2022.

28. **By 1980, the number of people:** "The New Class," *New York*, May 13, 1985.

29. **"Who wants to live in a building":** *New York*, June 5, 1978; "The Future of New York: A Tale of Two Cities," *New York*, July 23, 1979.

29. **titled *The World Cities*:** Peter Hall, *The World Cities* (New York: McGraw Hill, 1966).

30. **In January 1979:** "The New Elite and an Urban Renaissance," *New York Times Magazine*, January 14, 1979.

32. **Rottenberg's story:** "About That Urban Renaissance…," *Chicago*, May 1980.

32. **Rottenberg would always insist:** Dan Rottenberg, interviewed by author, January 2020.

Chapter 3

34. **One summer morning in the 1950s:** John Whitehead, video interview in "Remembering Wall Street, 1950–1980: The Bonnie and Richard Reiss Wall Street Oral History Archive," New-York Historical Society, nyhistory.org.

34. **Simmons—known as Wick:** Hardwick Simmons, interviewed by author, March 2022.

35. **More than 150 investment firms:** "Ten Survivors of the Wall Street Crash," *New York*, January 27, 1975.

36. **Felix Rohatyn was turning:** Judith Ramsey Ehrlich and Barry J. Rehfeld, *The New Crowd* (New York: Little, Brown, 1989).

36. **he was already something of a legend:** Connie Bruck, *The Predators' Ball* (New York: Simon & Schuster, 1988).

37. **Once, the story went:** James B. Stewart, *Den of Thieves* (New York: Simon & Schuster, 1991).

37. **Milken was born in 1946:** Bruck, *Predators' Ball*.

39. **an academic named W. Braddock Hickman:** Stewart, *Den of Thieves*.

41. **"Mike was on a mission":** "Renegades of Junk: The Rise and Fall of the Drexel Empire," Bloomberg.com, April 1, 2015.

Chapter 4

44. **Or like Dennis Greenwood:** *Newsweek*, March 31, 1981.

44. **the average salary:** *Newsweek*, March 31, 1981.

44. **William Zinsser, the writer and editor:** Mary Alice Kellogg, *Fast Track: The Super Achievers and How They Made It Early to Success, Status and Power* (New York: McGraw Hill, 1978).

45. **"This generation was in many ways educated for success":** Kellogg, *Fast Track*.

45. **a term that had originated in the railroad industry:** William Safire, "Perils of the Fast Track Vetting," On Language, *New York Times Magazine*, November 2, 1980.
46. **In 1960, only about 30 percent:** *Newsweek*, January 17, 1983.
46. **She'd been raised in Tucson, Arizona:** Mary Alice Kellogg, interviewed by author, February 2022.
47. **In 1960, the average woman:** "Comparing Millennials with Gen Xers," Pew Research, pewresearch.org.
47. **"It was very important for me":** *Newsweek*, March 31, 1981.
48. **Jane Fonda broke her foot:** Jane Fonda, *My Life So Far* (New York: Random House, 2005).
49. **Fonda and Cazden began:** Fonda, *My Life So Far*.
51. **the Gallup Organization noted:** "An Intimidating New Class: The Physical Elite," *New York*, May 29, 1978.
51. **In April 1980:** "25 Years Ago, Subways and Buses Stopped Running," *New York Times*, April 4, 2005.
52. **A telling indicator:** "The Good Gray Times: It Ain't What It Used to Be," *New York*, July 18, 1977.
53. **Julia Child helped to popularize:** David Kamp, *The United States of Arugula* (New York: Crown, 2007).
54. **In 1976, Gustave Leven:** "The Ad Campaign That Convinced Americans to Pay for Water," priceonomics.com, June 10, 2016.
55. **In 1971, a retired American electrical engineer:** "C. G. Sontheimer, Cuisinart Backer, Dies at 83," *New York Times*, March 26, 1998.
55. **the ice cream was made in New Jersey:** "Ice Cream Chic at Häagen-Dazs," *Fortune*, March 9, 1981.
56. **In 1977, Bob Quinlan:** Quinlan, interview.
57. **At Sutton Place:** "Getting Fancy Food up to the Competitive Level," *New York Times*, October 5, 1986.
58. **In a highly mobile society:** Daniel Boorstin, "Welcome to the Consumption Community," in *The Decline of Radicalism: Reflections on America Today* (New York: Random House, 1969).
59. **"the point of owning Henckels cutlery":** "Going Through Your Bookstore May Give You a Case of the Yumpies," *Hattiesburg American*, March 25, 1984.
59. **the journalist Andrew Tobias:** Andrew Tobias, "Getting By on $100,000 a Year," in *Getting By on $100,000 a Year (and Other Sad Tales)* (New York: Simon & Schuster, 1980).

Chapter 5

61. **Five years after buying:** "A 60s Liberal Comes to Uncertain Grips with Choices in the Real World," *Courier Post*, November 25, 1979.
63. **Carter's approval rating:** "Carter's Approval Rating Takes Big Drop," Associated Press, November 1, 1979.

64. **During a prime-time speaking spot:** Ted Kennedy, Address to Democratic National Convention, August 12, 1980; John F. Kennedy Presidential Library and Museum, Boston, jfklibrary.org.
65. **The series had been created:** "'Dallas' at 40: The Inside Story Behind the Show That Changed Texas Forever," *Texas Monthly*, March 2018.
66. **Romanian president Nicolae Ceauşescu:** "'Dallas' at 40," *Texas Monthly*, March 2018.
67. **"There are no more middle buildings":** "Trumping the Town," *New York*, November 17, 1980.
67. **In the summer of 1980:** "Getting In," *New York*, June 30, 1980.
68. **In the spring of 1980:** Lisa Birnbach, interviewed by author, April 2022.
69. **"It is the inalienable right":** Lisa Birnbach, ed., *The Official Preppy Handbook* (New York: Workman Publishing, 1980).
71. **Jerry's growing obsession:** "Jerry Rubin," *Washington Post Magazine*, October 18, 1981.
71. **his newly single self:** Fleischman, interview.
72. **In June 1981:** "Jerry Rubin's Last Chance Saloon," *New York*, June 8, 1981.

Chapter 6

78. **For the people of Youngstown:** "Steelyard Blues," *Mother Jones*, April 1978.
78. **Balluck told his wife:** "The Heartbreak of Ohio's Steel Valley," *Washington Post*, October 26, 1980.
80. **An activist priest:** *Washington Post*, October 26, 1980.
80. **With an abandoned steel mill:** "Reagan in Youngstown," *Ripon Forum*, October–November 2006.
81. **When he campaigned for president:** "The Welfare Queen," *Slate*, December 19, 2013; Josh Levin, *The Queen: The Forgotten Life Behind an American Myth* (New York: Little, Brown, 2019).
83. **His aversion to big government and taxes:** Lou Cannon, *President Reagan: The Role of a Lifetime* (New York: Simon & Schuster, 1991).
83. **The most prominent among them:** Rick Pearlstein, *Reaganland: America's Right Turn 1976–1980* (New York: Simon & Schuster, 2020).
84. **Also gaining Reagan's attention:** Pearlstein, *Reaganland*.
85. **In early February 1981:** "Address to the Nation on the Economy," February 5, 1981, Ronald Reagan Presidential Library and Museum, reaganlibrary.gov.
87. **Despite skeptics:** Cannon, *President Reagan*.
88. **the budget made significant cuts:** Sheldon Danziger and Robert Haveman, "The Reagan Administration's Budget Cuts: Their Impact on the Poor," *IRP Focus*, Winter 1981–82.
89. **while a family earning the median income:** "The Rich Get Richer," *New York*, September 7, 1981.
89. **As Stockman would tell journalist William Greider:** "The Education of David Stockman," *The Atlantic*, December 1981.

90. **"They are in violation of the law":** "Text of Reagan Talk on Strike," *New York Times*, August 4, 1981.

90. **more than six in ten Americans:** "In Showdown with the Air Traffic Controllers, Public Sided with Reagan," Pew Research Center, pewresearch.org.

91. **During the previous year's campaign:** "Robert E. Poli, Leader of Pivotal Strike by Air Traffic Controllers, Is Dead at 78," *New York Times*, September 21, 2014.

Chapter 7

92. **it came in the form of angry:** "Paul Volcker, Who Waged War on Inflation, Is Dead at 92," *New York Times*, December 9, 2019; "Wood 2x4 Mailed to Mr. Paul Volcker, Chairman, Board of Governors," circa 1980, Fraser, fraser.stlouisfed.org.

93. **He'd first appreciated it:** Paul Volcker, "Federal Reserve Board Oral History Project: Interview with Paul A. Volcker," February 25, 2008, federalreserve.gov.

93. **the Fed needed to do something bold:** "The Great Inflation," Federal Reserve History, federalreservehistory.org.

94. **In October 1979:** "Volcker's Announcement of Anti-Inflation Measures," Federal Reserve History, federalreserve.org.

95. **NBC broadcast a documentary:** *If Japan Can... Why Can't We?*, 1980 NBC Special Report, Deming Institute, deming.org.

95. **In 1970, Friedman had written:** "A Friedman Doctrine—the Social Responsibility of a Corporation Is to Increase Its Profits," *New York Times Magazine*, September 13, 1970.

97. **Michael Jensen and William Meckling agreed with Friedman:** Michael Jensen and William Meckling, "Theory of the Firm: Managerial Behavior, Agency Costs, and Ownership Structure," *Journal of Financial Economics*, October 1976.

97. **It was a provocative theory:** David Gelles, *The Man Who Broke Capitalism: How Jack Welch Gutted the Heartland and Crushed the Soul of Corporate America—and How to Undo His Legacy* (New York: Simon & Schuster, 2022).

97. **the most aggressive and brash:** "Jack Welch: GE's Live Wire," *Newsweek*, December 23, 1985; "Can Jack Welch Reinvent GE?," *Business Week*, June 30, 1986.

98. **it wasn't only size that gave GE its reputation:** Thomas F. O'Boyle, *At Any Cost: Jack Welch, General Electric, and the Pursuit of Profit* (New York: Vintage Books, 1999).

98. **"When [my dad] got a job with General Electric":** "When General Electric Left Schenectady, So Did a Way of Life," *Guardian*, November 6, 2016.

99. **Nowhere was that clearer than in Schenectady:** William B. Patrick, *Metrofix: The Combative Comeback of a Company Town* (Schenectady, NY: Downtown Publishing, 2021); "World War II at 75: General Electric's Key Contributions," *Daily Gazette*, July 27, 2020.

100. **"National productivity has been declining":** O'Boyle, *At Any Cost*.

101. **Welch and his friends had frequently played baseball and basketball:** *Business Week*, June 30, 1986.

101. **"Take a look around you":** O'Boyle, *At Any Cost.*
101. **In early December 1981:** Jack Welch with John A. Byrne, *Jack: Straight from the Gut* (New York: Warner Business Books, 2001).

Chapter 8

104. **Kehoe had grown up on New York's Upper East Side:** Kathy Kehoe, interviewed by author, November 2022.
105. **the biggest economic shift since the Industrial Revolution:** "Info City," *New York*, February 9, 1981.
106. **"the archetypal post-industrial city":** "San Francisco Boutiquing Spawns Ghettos for Yuppies," *Los Angeles Times*, April 5, 1985.
106. **One of the most symbolic shifts:** Brian J. Godfrey, "Inner-City Revitalization and Cultural Succession: The Evolution of San Francisco's Haight-Ashbury District," in *Yearbook of the Association of Pacific Coast Geographers*, 1984.
107. **"I just can't be part of the sameness again":** "The Ghost of Hell's Kitchen," *New York*, April 12, 1982.
108. **the stretch of Columbus Avenue:** "New York's New Left Bank," *New York*, August 30, 1982.
108. **"Taste and scholarship are in evidence everywhere":** "College Town," *San Francisco Examiner*, December 4, 1980.
108. **One young professional who lived in Boston's Back Bay:** "A City's Changing Faces," *Boston Globe*, June 11, 1981.
109. **Milton Levine, proprietor of a junk shop:** "A New Chelsea Morning," *New York*, May 31, 1982.
110. **By the early months of 1982:** Fonda, *My Life So Far.*
110. **Karl became a waterbed salesman:** "From Fonda and Hart to Flops and Hot Water," *New York Times*, February 7, 1988.
111. **New fitness clubs were continuing to open:** "Let's Get Physical," *Boston*, May 1982.
112. **He'd grown up in Arkansas:** Richard Thalheimer, interviewed by author, November 2021.
113. **Thalheimer had transformed Sharper Image:** "The Cost of His Toys," *San Francisco Examiner*, March 23, 1983; "Toys for the Executive Pushes Sharper Image Sales to $33 Million," *Miami News*, July 21, 1982.
114. **"It was a time when people were aspirational":** Thalheimer, interview.
115. **"America's first wardrobe engineer":** "Behind the Bestsellers: John T. Molloy," *New York Times*, March 12, 1978.
115. **In 1975:** John T. Molloy, *Dress for Success* (New York: Warner Books, 1975); *The Woman's Dress for Success Book* (New York: Warner Books, 1978).
116. **The business, which had more than two dozen stores around the country:** "Brooks Brothers Key to Allied Deal with Garfinckel," *New York Times*, September 3, 1981.

117. **BMW, in particular:** "In the Driver's Seat: BMW," *Daily Item*, January 20, 1985; "Max Hoffman Made Imports Less Foreign to Americans," *New York Times*, March 18, 2007.

117. **One evening in 1981:** Marissa Piesman, interviewed by author, November 2021.

118. **"They are the biggest single factor":** "Going After the Mightiest Market," *Time*, September 14, 1981; "Madison Avenue Chases the Baby Boom," *New York Times Magazine*, May 31, 1981.

119. **In 1981, *Rolling Stone*:** "Rolling Stone Tones Up," *New York*, January 26, 1981.

119. **Magazine publisher Condé Nast:** "Can Vanity Fair Live Again?" *New York*, April 26, 1982.

120. **In turning to Tinker:** "Grant Tinker's First Six Months at the Helm of NBC," *New York Times*, February 11, 1982; "The Grant Tinker Show," *New York*, November 29, 1982.

120. **The premise for *Family Ties*:** "'Family Ties' Creator Gary David Goldberg Dies at 68," *Hollywood Reporter*, June 23, 2013.

121. **Where he wanted to win:** *New York*, November 29, 1982.

121. ***Hill Street Blues* became the first:** "They Live to Buy," *Newsweek*, December 31, 1984.

Chapter 9

122. **the Reagan team thought long and hard about their strategy:** "Trying to 'Stay the Course': President Reagan's Rhetoric During the 1982 Election," *Presidential Studies Quarterly*, Winter 1984.

124. **Reagan's approval:** "Ronald Reagan Public Approval" (Gallup Data), The American Presidency Project, UC Santa Barbara, presidency.ucsb.edu.

124. **the decision was made:** *Presidential Studies Quarterly*, Winter 1984.

125. **Speaking from the Oval Office:** "Address to the Nation on the Economy," October 13, 1982, Ronald Reagan Presidential Library and Museum, reaganlibrary.gov.

126. **By August 1982:** "Youngstown, Ohio Remained the Nation's Highest Unemployment Area," UPI, November 16, 1982.

127. **Ecumenical Coalition of the Mahoning Valley:** *Mother Jones*, April 1978; *Washington Post*, October 26, 1980.

127. **By the end of 1982:** "Booms, Busts and the Birth of a Rust Bowl," *Time*, December 27, 1982.

128. **Chicago...was in the midst of a twenty-year economic downturn:** "The Social Fallout of the Economic Crisis," *Chicago Tribune*, May 13, 1981.

129. **Academics looking at the cuts:** Danziger and Haveman, "The Reagan Administration's Budget Cuts."

130. **As the explosions went off:** "End of Steel in Youngstown: Blast Furnaces Came Down 35 Years Ago," WKBN27, April 28, 2017, youtube.com.

130. **Nowhere was that clearer than in New York City:** "A Helluva Town—Jobs Are Up, Inflation Is Down," *New York*, May 10, 1982.

131. **"We've found the very wealthy"**: "Meanwhile, a Luxury Boom," *Newsweek*, March 8, 1982; "There's No Recession in the Luxury Market," *U.S. News and World Report*, November 23, 1981.

132. **In the summer of 1982:** "Downward Mobility," *New York*, August 16, 1982.

Chapter 10

135. **Reagan had campaigned at an array of fairs:** *Presidential Studies Quarterly*, Winter 1984.

136. **In great contrast to Jimmy and Rosalynn Carter:** "Social Notes from Reagan's Washington," *New York*, February 15, 1982.

138. **One of the new stars of the social world:** "Educating Susan," *Vanity Fair*, November 1991.

139. **"The '80s were defined by winning and losing":** Stuart Samuels, interviewed by author, January 2022.

140. **The crowds got so large:** Fleischman, interview.

140. **The salons…had become Rubin's prime focus:** "Jerry Rubin's New Venture," *Fortune*, May 2, 1983.

141. **"My company will be one of the most important":** "From Yippie to Yuppie," *Chicago Tribune*, March 23, 1983.

142. **Abbie asked Jerry and Mimi:** Fleischman, interview.

143. **Greene found himself having drinks at a bar:** West, author interview.

143. **"What we stress is business achievement":** *Chicago Tribune*, March 23, 1983.

Chapter 11

148. **Reagan's approval rating had dropped to a new low:** Ronald Reagan Public Approval (Gallup Data).

149. **For Fonda, the success was gratifying:** Fonda, *My Life So Far*.

150. **"It's another embodiment of the American way of getting ahead":** "Toning Up Muscles—and That Edge," *Boston Globe*, January 8, 1985.

151. **In Philadelphia:** *Philadelphia*, December 2003.

151. **She'd grown up in suburban New Jersey:** "The YAP Generation," *Philadelphia Inquirer*, November 25, 1983.

152. **the paper ran a photo of the publisher's girlfriend:** Buzz Teacher, interviewed by author, November 2021.

153. **"I came to Berkeley in the era of Dustin Hoffman's *The Graduate*":** "The Wacky Side of Chicago-Born, Berkeley-Bred Alice Kahn," *Chicago Tribune*, March 28, 1986.

154. **"Instead of a scraggly bunch of old hippies and die-hard lefties":** "The Demise of the Yuppie: The Young Urban Professionals Get Together," Los Angeles Times Syndicate, November 18, 1985.

154. **"Going beyond the usual chitchat":** Alice Kahn, *Multiple Sarcasm* (Berkeley: Ten Speed Press, 1985).

156. **in 1983 Piesman and Hartley were introduced to two fellow New Yorkers**: Piesman, interview.
157. **Cathy Crimmins's book:** Cathy Crimmins, *Y.A.P.: The Official Young Aspiring Professional's Fast-Track Handbook* (Philadelphia: Running Press, 1983).
159. **In the late fall:** *Philadelphia Inquirer*, November 25, 1983.

Chapter 12

160. **what was truly fascinating:** Bloomberg.com, April 1, 2015.
162. **One day, it was said:** Stewart, *Den of Thieves.*
163. **In 1983, nearly half the profits:** "The Traders Take Charge," *Business Week*, February 20, 1984.
164. **"To invest in new products or processes":** Robert Reich, *The Next American Frontier* (New York: Times Books, 1983).
165. **"We were just darn lucky":** "Windfall," *New York*, August 8, 1983.
165. **One night in January 1983:** Welch with Byrne, *Jack: Straight from the Gut.*
167. **In towns and cities around the country:** "Seventy Years of Struggle: A Brief History of UE Bargaining with GE," United Electrical, Radio and Machine Workers of America, ueunion.org.
167. **One example was GE's consumer housewares division:** O'Boyle, *At Any Cost.*
168. **Welch started hosting roundtable conversations:** Welch with Byrne, *Jack: Straight from the Gut.*
169. **"We didn't fire the people":** Welch with Byrne, *Jack: Straight from the Gut.*
169. **In 1981, GE announced:** Gilda Haas and Holly Sklar, *Plant Closures: Myths, Realities and Responses* (Boston: South End Press, 1985).
169. **"They can make a bigger profit":** "It Was a Dark Day in Ontario When the GE Flatiron Plant Closed," *Daily Bulletin*, April 22, 2019.

Chapter 13

171. **in early January 1984:** Marissa Piesman and Marilee Hartley, *The Yuppie Handbook* (New York: Pocket Books, 1984).
172. **"Who are all these upwardly mobile folks":** "Here Come the Yuppies!" *Time*, January 9, 1984.
173. **One of the first was in the *Boston Globe*:** "Good Morning, Hub—What's Yup?," *Boston Globe*, January 10, 1984.
174. **In upstate New York:** "Yurps," *Democrat and Chronicle*, January 9, 1984.
174. **In Memphis:** "When Only a Yup Will Suffice," *Commercial Appeal*, January 15, 1984.
177. **a young political strategist:** Susan Berry Casey, *Hart and Soul: Gary Hart's New Hampshire Odyssey and Beyond* (Concord: NHI Press, 1986).
178. **The Mondale campaign:** William A. Henry III, *Visions of America: How We Saw the 1984 Election* (Atlantic Monthly Press, 1985).

178. **"Yuppies have become the strike force":** "CBS 'Yuppie' Piece Poked Fun at Hart," *Dallas Morning News*, March 28, 1984.
179. **In the *New York Times*:** "Hart Taps a Generation of Young Professionals," *New York Times*, March 18, 1984.
180. **young *upwardly mobile* professional:** "Here Come the Yumpies," *Time*, March 26, 1984.
180. **Richard Darman, a young special assistant:** "Yuppies Favor Hart. But What's a Yuppie?" *Boston Globe*, March 26, 1984.
180. **"This truly is the Year of the Yuppies":** "The Year of the Yuppie," *New York Times*, March 25, 1984.
182. **"Hart's people have christened":** "Hart's New 'Code' Word," *Indianapolis Star*, March 20, 1984.

Chapter 14

185. **Lincoln, Nebraska:** "Yuppies Climb Ladder of Lincoln Success," *Lincoln Star*, September 30, 1984.
186. **Yuppieness was a common topic:** "Happiness Isn't Being a Yuppie, Grads Told," Associated Press, May 28, 1984.
187. **"They don't see any corporation":** "Baby Boomers Push for Power," *Business Week*, July 2, 1984.
189. **A telling example:** "The Fizz Biz," *New York*, January 16, 1984.
190. **Another brand:** "New Michelob Commercials Yup It Up Good," *Californian*, November 7, 1984.
191. **Then there was American Express:** "Credit Card Drives Wooing the Affluent," *New York Times*, March 15, 1984; "Card Times," *New York*, November 15, 1985.
192. **And so began what amounted to Operation Yuppie:** "Detroit's New Goal: Putting Yuppies in the Driver's Seat," *Business Week*, September 3, 1984.
193. **As a sales manager at a BMW dealership:** "1985 Cars Are Made for Yuppies," *Fort Worth Star Telegram*, September 23, 1984.
193. **For decades the Spiegel catalog:** "Doing It by the Book," *New York*, May 14, 1984.
194. **"I just stand on the street corner":** "Toy Stores Catering to the Yuppie Crowd," *Los Angeles Times*, November 12, 1984.
195. **a development called Copley Place:** "Store Wars," *Boston*, February 1984; "In Search of the Boston Yuppie," *Boston Globe*, March 13, 1984.
195. **In Tampa that fall:** "Tampa Mall's Expansion Puts Its Emphasis on the Wealthy," *Tampa Bay Times*, November 29, 1984; "Yuppie Heaven Could Mean the Ouster of the City's Elderly," *Tampa Bay Times*, March 30, 1984.
197. **Speaking out in favor:** *Philadelphia Inquirer*, November 11, 1984.

Chapter 15

198. **On Sunday night:** "LA Olympics Closing Ceremony—Breaking, Popping, Streetdance Highlights 1984," youtube.com.

200. **"Our days of weakness are over"**: "Military of U.S. 'Standing Tall,' Reagan Asserts," *New York Times*, December 13, 1983.
200. **"Vietnam ended"**: Kunen, interview.
201. **On Manhattan's Upper West Side:** *New York*, May 13, 1985.
203. **the pull to live a certain way:** Palley, interview; Kellogg, interview.
203. **there was a growing obsession:** "Restaurant Madness," *New York*, November 26, 1984; "Strike Is a Tall Order for Old Frisco Eateries," *Los Angeles Times*, October 31, 1984; "Blue Collar Spaghetti Has Become Oh-So-Chic Yuppie Pasta Passion," Associated Press, March 11, 1985; "Bildner's, Grocer to Boston's Yuppies," *Boston Globe*, April 30, 1985.
205. **A young woman:** Judy Langer, interviewed by author, August 2021.
206. **a Florida real estate developer:** "Author: Yuppie Is a State of Mind," *Bradenton Herald*, December 9, 1984.
206. **"It's become, 'How much money am I making?'"**: "How Wall Street Created Ivan Boesky," *New York Times*, November 23, 1986.
207. **"Yuppies started to come into the business"**: Simmons, interview.
207. **The cocktail of money and swagger:** "Agents Tell of Drug's Grip on Wall Street," *New York Times*, April 18, 1987.
208. **In the early '70s, several of the large investment firms:** "The Young and the Sleepless," *New York*, June 9, 1986.
211. **The novel never used the word:** "Yuppies in Eden," *New York*, September 22, 2008.
212. **One night in 1984:** Peter Brown, interview, disco-disco.com.

Chapter 16

215. **"Just look at us here tonight"**: "Address Accepting the Presidential Nomination at the Democratic National Convention in San Francisco," July 19, 1984, The American Presidency Project, UC Santa Barbara, presidency.ucsb.edu.
216. **"In 1980 we asked the people of America"**: "Remarks Accepting the Presidential Nomination at the Republican National Convention in Dallas, Texas," August 23, 1984, The American Presidency Project, UC Santa Barbara, presidency.ucsb.edu.
217. **In late August:** "Bruce Springsteen's U.S.A.," *Washington Post*, September 13, 1984.
218. **"America's future"**: Geoffrey Himes, *Bruce Springsteen's Born in the U.S.A.* (London: Bloomsbury Publishing, 2005).
220. **In a poll:** "Younger Voters Tending to Give Reagan Support," *New York Times*, October 16, 1984.
220. **One day in October:** "Wine and Cheese Set Agree: Reagan's Their Man," *Chicago Tribune*, November 1, 1984.
221. **"As incredible as it may seem"**: "Reaganomics' Lure for the Yuppies," *New York Times*, October 2, 1984.
223. **"It is on the move again"**: *Newsweek*, December 31, 1984.

223. **It was about downward mobility:** "Blue Collar Boomers: The Most Frustrated of All," *Business Week*, July 2, 1984; "Forgotten Baby Boomers: The Second Wave Is Falling Behind," *Newsday*, November 3, 1984.

Chapter 17

227. **Yuppie domination of the culture:** "Barbie, Patchers Enter Yuppie Era," *Miami Herald*, February 10, 1985; "Yuppie Festival Draws 500," Associated Press, February 5, 1985; "Stereotyped Image Irks Many Yuppies," UPI, June 29, 1985; "Yuppie Day in Nashville," *Tennessean*, July 4, 1985.
229. **In 1984, Grape-Nuts:** "Retreat of the Yuppies: The Tide Now Turns amid 'Guilt' and 'Denial,'" *New York Times*, June 28, 1985.
229. **When they arrived at JFK Airport:** Fleischman, interview.
231. **Typical was a Friday evening:** "Yippie Versus Yuppie," March 8, 1985, youtube.com.
237. **Abbie really needed the money:** Fleischman, interview.

Chapter 18

238. **Two weeks after:** Bruck, *Predators' Ball*.
239. **"Whatever the conference cost us":** Bloomberg.com, April 1, 2015.
240. **Milken's goal:** Bruck, *Predators' Ball*.
241. **"He showed up":** Bloomberg.com, April 1, 2015.
241. **They were so thankful:** "High Times for T. Boone Pickens," *Time*, March 4, 1985.
242. **twenty thousand oil company workers:** "Thousands of Jobs Lost in Oil Mergers," UPI, March 26, 1985.
242. **Triangle Industries:** Bruck, *Predators' Ball*.
243. **an attempt by investor Ron Perelman:** Bruck, *Predators' Ball*; "The Shy Stripper," *New York*, November 18, 1985.
245. **By the end of the decade:** Leveraged Buyouts and Corporate Debt: Hearing Before the Committee on Finance United States Senate, One Hundred and First Congress, First Session, January 26, 1989.
246. **One evening, he got together for cocktails:** *Newsweek*, December 23, 1985.
247. **"We did not want to see the company broken up willy nilly":** "The G.E.-RCA Merger: Forging a Megadeal," *New York Times*, December 13, 1985.
248. **Within a couple of years:** O'Boyle, *At Any Cost*.

Chapter 19

249. **In the summer of 1985:** Fleischman, interview; "Yuppie Networking Is Still the Rage in New York," *New York Times*, September 28, 1985.
250. **"This is a city built around work":** "Second Thoughts on Having It All," *New York*, July 15, 1985.
251. **"When David's Cookies appeared":** "Exodus," *New York*, November 25, 1985.

251. **One area of focus was all the stuff associated with baby raising:** "What Every Yuppie Baby Needs," *Boston Globe*, April 8, 1985; "Baby Formula," *Manhattan, inc.*, July 1985; "You've Come a Long Way, Baby," *Los Angeles Times*, October 19, 1987.

252. **the booming success of the Aprica stroller:** "Now, Japan's Stroller Invasion," *New York Times*, October 12, 1985.

253. **Between 1980 and 1984:** "U.S. Sees Private School Enrollment Surge in '80s," *New York Times*, December 21, 1984.

253. **"The issue of getting your child":** Kehoe, interview.

253. **the battle to get into one of a dozen or so of the most prestigious private schools:** "Pressure Points," *New York*, March 10, 1986.

254. **voters between the ages of eighteen and twenty-four:** "How Groups Voted in 1984," Roper Center for Public Opinion Research, ropercenter.cornell.edu.

255. **In the fall of 1985:** Jeff Zajkowski, interviewed by author, June 2023.

255. **Cristina Schoene, a sophomore at Rollins College:** "Yuppies in Training?" *Orlando Sentinel*, May 5, 1985.

255. **In 1966, researchers at UCLA:** "The American Freshman: Thirty-Five-Year Trends, 1966–2001," Higher Education Research Institute, Graduate School of Education and Information Studies, University of California, Los Angeles, December 2002.

256. **"When I graduated from Brown":** Birnbach, interview.

Chapter 20

257. **The house was breathtaking:** "Lifestyles of the Rich and Famous Featuring Richard Thalheimer," youtube.com.

258. **he'd produced a daylong seminar:** Thalheimer, interview.

258. **"You couldn't help but notice":** Birnbach, interview.

258. **The luxury car market:** "Upwardly Mobile Automobiles," *Forbes*, November 4, 1985; "U.S. Automakers Court Growing Luxury Car Market," *Detroit Free Press*, February 15, 1987.

259. **One of the great marketing success stories:** "When You're Haute, You're Hot," *New York*, January 27, 1986.

261. **thirteen years later, Sears was struggling:** "Where Sears Has Stumbled," *New York Times*, June 5, 1986.

262. **"The comparisons we make":** Juliet Schor, *The Overspent American: Upscaling, Downshifting and the New Consumer* (New York: Basic Books, 1998).

262. **"A great many baby boomers":** "A Yuppie State of Mind," *Hartford Courant*, December 15, 1985.

263. **"We look for heroic, rags-to-riches stories":** "The Frantic Screaming Voice of the Rich and Famous," *Manhattan, inc.*, January 1986.

Chapter 21

264. **By 1985, the number had fallen to fifteen thousand:** "News of Layoffs Dulls GE Centennial in Schenectady," *New York Times*, November 26, 1986; "Downsizing of GE Workforce Was a Painful Period," *Daily Gazette*, September 24, 2017.
265. **Under Welch's predecessor, Reg Jones:** Mary Kuykendall, *Rebuilding the GE House That Jack Blew Down: 40 Years of Chutzpah and Sick Humor at GE* (CreateSpace, 2015).
266. **By the middle of 1986:** *Business Week*, June 30, 1986.
266. **In the six years between 1979 and 1985:** "Singing the Shutdown Blues," *Time*, June 23, 1986.
267. **"Companies long identified with making goods":** "The Hollow Corporation," *Business Week*, March 3, 1986.
268. **About 60 percent of the new jobs:** "Growth in Jobs Since '80 Is Sharp, but Pay and Quality Are Debated," *New York Times*, June 8, 1986.
268. **One day Mary Kuykendall:** Kuykendall, *Rebuilding the GE House.*
268. **a whole class of employees:** Kuykendall, *Rebuilding the GE House.*
269. **"the rich are getting richer":** "A Surge in Inequality," *Scientific American*, May 1987.

Chapter 22

273. **Rubin...still longed for a transformational payday of his own:** Fleischman, interview; "Rubin's Networking to Sell His Network," *Newsday*, March 20, 1987.
274. **"It was like free sex":** "With Key Executives' Arrest, Wall Street Faces Challenge," *New York Times*, February 15, 1987.
274. **Levine...seemed like a character out of a movie:** "Insiders," *New York*, July 28, 1986.
275. **"the Yuppie Five":** "Wall Street Yuppies," *New York Daily News*, June 1, 1986.
275. **In addition to a lavish Manhattan apartment:** "The Fall of a Wall Street Superstar," *Time*, November 24, 1986; "True Greed," *Newsweek*, December 1, 1986.
276. **Ron Rosenbaum took aim:** "The Wrong Dream," *Manhattan, inc.*, April 1987.
277. **a thirty-seven-year-old Harvard Business School graduate named Martin Siegel:** "A Raid on Wall Street," *Time*, February 23, 1987.
277. **At the annual Predators' Ball in April 1987:** "How Mike Milken Made a Billion Dollars and Changed the Face of American Capitalism," *Manhattan, inc.*, September 1987.
279. **nearly 40 percent of children:** "Children of Poverty: Crisis in New York," *New York Times*, June 8, 1986.
279. **"Men had been having it all for years":** "Where Have All the Yuppies Gone?" Los Angeles Times Syndicate, September 24, 1985.
280. **The moves were prompted:** "A Return to the Suburbs," *Newsweek*, July 21, 1986; "Back to the Suburbs," *New York*, September 1, 1986.

281. **Robert and Rebecca were a couple:** *New York*, July 15, 1985.
282. **In large metro areas:** "What, No Pool in the Foyer?" *Time*, September 21, 1987.
283. **One company capitalizing on it was Toll Brothers:** "Chasing Ground," *New York Times Magazine*, October 16, 2005.
284. **In 1970, 65 percent of families:** "The Rise of Residential Segregation by Income," Pew Research Center, August 1, 2012, pewresearch.org.

Chapter 23

286. **What he'd always remember were the two phones:** Zajkowski, interview.
287. **At Shearson:** Simmons, interview.
287. **"Holy shit, I just lost a million":** "After the Meltdown of '87," *Newsweek*, November 2, 1987.
288. **"It's all over for the Yuppies!":** "After the Crash...," *New York*, November 2, 1987.
289. **The weekend after the crash:** "Yuppies and the Bear," *Courier-Mail*, October 31, 1987.
289. **Yuppies, said Kurt Barnard:** *Newsweek*, November 2, 1987.
290. **Black Monday cost them $300,000:** Fleischman, interview.

Chapter 24

293. **The Business Roundtable:** "Business Roundtable Redefines the Purpose of a Corporation to Promote 'An Economy That Serves All Americans,'" August 19, 2019, businessroundtable.org.
293. **In 2012, a researcher identified several hundred "super zip codes":** "SuperZips and the Rest of America's Zip Codes," American Enterprise Institute, February 13, 2012, aei.org.
294. **The decline of US manufacturing intensified:** "Botched Policy Responses to Globalization Have Decimated Manufacturing Employment with Often Overlooked Costs for Black, Brown, and Other Workers of Color," Economic Policy Institute, January 31, 2022, epi.org.
294. **By 2016, families at the top:** "Trends in Income and Wealth Inequality," Pew Research, January 9, 2020, pewresearch.org.
295. **"the dumbest idea in the world":** "Welch Condemns Share Price Focus," *Financial Times*, March 11, 2009.
295. **He laid out a Utopian vision:** Rubin, *Do It!*

Index

Index

Index

SaferWay, 57
Salomon Brothers, 36, 138, 254
Salvation Army, 126
Samuels, Stuart, 139, 141
San Francisco, 106–7, 112–13, 132, 204, 227–28, 258
San Francisco Examiner, 108
Schoene, Cristina, 255
Schor, Juliet B., 261–62
Schrager, Ian, 140, 249
Schultz, Howard, 260
Screen Actors Guild strike of 1960, 91
Seale, Bobby, 10
Sears, 57, 261–62
Securities and Exchange Commission, 35
security analysts, 208–10, 286, 288–89
Seiko, 113
sexism, 9, 47
shareholder value, 95–97, 100, 163, 292–93, 295
Sharper Image, 113–14, 194, 257–58, 263
Shearson Lehman, 36, 207, 287
Siegel, Martin, 277
Silver Palate, the (Washington, DC), 56–57
Simmons, Hardwick "Wick," 34, 36, 207, 287
Simon, Bob, 178–79
Simon, William, 164–65, 206, 239
Sinatra, Frank, 136, 239
Smith College, 104, 105
Social Security, 82, 88
SoHo (New York City), 29, 56, 106, 250–51
Sontheimer, Carl, 55
Sorensen, Jacki, 50
South Africa, 254
Soviet Union
  invasion of Afghanistan, 12–13
  Moscow Summer Olympics (1980), 3, 13, 199
  Reagan and, 81, 199–200, 214, 221–22
Spiegel, 193–94

Springsteen, Bruce, 183–85, 217–20, 263
Stack, Walt, 113
Stallone, Sylvester, 150, 184
Standard & Poor's, 38
Stanford University, 186, 187, 208, 254, 289
Stanton, Ed, 80, 99, 127
Starbucks, 260
Starr, Kevin, 108
steel industry, 78–81, 126–27, 129–30, 266–67
Steelyard Blues (movie), 35
Steinberg, Saul, 242
Sting, The (movie), 35
Stockman, David, 85, 87–88, 89
stock market crash of 1987, viii, 285–91
Strawberry Statement, The (Kunen), 16, 200
Studio 54 (New York City), 139–40, 142, 143, 153, 229, 249
suburbia, 22–23, 32, 280–84
Supple, Gerald, 35
supply-side economics, 84–85, 87–88, 131, 144, 148, 268
suspenders (braces), 205
Sutherland, Donald, 35
Sutton Place Gourmet (Washington, DC), 57

Tampa, 195–96
Tartikoff, Brandon, 120
taxes (tax policy), 6, 83–89, 123, 125, 131, 135–36, 148, 214, 294
  Economic Recovery Tax Act of 1981, 88–89, 123, 125, 131, 214, 294
Taxi (TV show), 121
Taylor, Linda, 82, 124, 136–37
Teacher, Larry, 153
Ted Bath Worldwide, 190
Texas International, 40
Thalheimer, Richard, 112–14, 194, 257–58, 263
Thalheimer Business Systems, 113

About the Author

Tom McGrath is an award-winning writer and editor. He served as editor in chief of *Philadelphia* magazine, as well as chief content officer of Metro Corp, the parent company of *Philadelphia* and *Boston*. He's written two previous books: *MTV: The Making of a Revolution*, a business and cultural history of the influential cable network; and *Fitness Made Simple*, which he coauthored with fitness celebrity John Basedow. He lives in suburban Philadelphia.